RECONSTRUCTING VIOLENCE

Southern Literary Studies

SCOTT ROMINE, *Series Editor*

RECONSTRUCTING VIOLENCE

The Southern Rape Complex in Film and Literature

DEBORAH E. BARKER

Louisiana State University Press   Baton Rouge

Published by Louisiana State University Press

Manufactured in the United States of America
First printing

DESIGNER: *Mandy McDonald Scallan*
TYPEFACE: *Whitman*
PRINTER AND BINDER: *Maple Press (Digital)*

Library of Congress Cataloging-in-Publication Data
Barker, Deborah Ellen.
Reconstructing violence : the southern rape complex in film and literature / Deborah E. Barker.
pages cm. — (Southern literary studies)
Includes bibliographical references and index.
ISBN 978-0-8071-6062-6 (cloth : alk. paper) — ISBN (pdf) 978-0-8071-6063-3 — ISBN 978-0-8071-6064-0 (epub) — ISBN 978-0-8071-6065-7 (mobi)
1. Violence in motion pictures. 2. Violence in literature. 3. Race relations in motion pictures. 4. Race relations in literature. 5. Power (Social sciences) in motion pictures. 6. Power (Social sciences) in literature. I. Title.
PN1995.9.V5B35 2015
791.43'6552—dc23

2015008665

The paper in this book meets the guidelines for permanence and durability of the Committee on Production Guidelines for Book Longevity of the Council on Library Resources. ♾

I dedicate this book in memory of my mother,
Betty Barker McLeod, 1921–2013,
and my father Joseph Barker, 1919–86.

CONTENTS

ACKNOWLEDGMENTS

I want to thank my friends, families, and colleagues for their support and feedback during the writing of this book. Thanks to Jay Watson for his excellent skills as a reader over the years and as an editor. His advice has been invaluable. Thanks also to the Americanist Reading Group for their insights and suggestions: Leigh Ann Duck, Cristie Ellis, Ann Fisher-Wirth, Kathryn McKee, and Annette Trefzer. Special thanks to Katie for support and discussions of our work over many Big Bad Breakfasts and to Karen Raber and Annette for retail therapy and lots of coffee.

Thanks to the English department and to dean Glen Hopkins and Liberal Arts for summer grants that assisted me in researching and completing the project.

I am grateful to Peter Lurie for his role as editor of *Faulkner and Film* and his very useful advice and thanks also to Ann Abadie at University of Mississippi Press.

A special thanks to my research assistants Scarlett Cunningham, Sara Williams, Amy King, and Troy Smith for all their help with research, proofreading, and citations. Another special thanks to my undergraduate and especially my graduate classes on the South in Film for many lively and productive discussions, which make working in this area so rewarding.

At LSU Press I would like to thank Margaret Lovecraft for her faith in the project and for making this process a pleasure. I could not ask for a better editor.

As always, my greatest appreciation goes to Ivo Kamps for all his love, support, and patience and for reading countless versions of this book as well as listening to countless discussions about the book. I am truly blessed to have a partner with whom I can share my life and work. Thanks to Malcolm for his pep talks and his unflagging confidence in me.

Earlier versions of portions of this book are reprinted here with permission: "Moonshine and Magnolias: *The Story of Temple Drake* and *Birth of a Nation*,"

Faulkner Journal 22.1–2 (Fall 2006), copyright 2007 by the University of Central Florida, reprinted with the permission of the *Faulkner Journal* at the University of Central Florida and reprinted in *Faulkner and Whiteness*, ed. Jay Watson (Jackson: U of Mississippi P, 2011), 107–46, and reprinted here with the permission of the U of Mississippi P; "Demystifying the Modern Mammy in *Requiem for a Nun*," *Faulkner and Film*, ed. Peter Lurie and Ann J. Abadie (Jackson: U of Mississippi P, 2014), reprinted with permission of U of Mississippi P.

RECONSTRUCTING VIOLENCE

Introduction

VIOLENCE IS A KEY element of the spectacle of cinema, and its manifestations are myriad. The type of violence associated with the American South and southern cinema, however, is often racialized and participates in the dominant narrative of what W. J. Cash coined the "southern rape complex."[1] Combining the highly charged mix of racial and gender politics and its impact on American identity, the southern rape complex has shaped our very notion of racial violence—historically, literarily, and cinematically—while tapping into fundamental issues of individual, regional, and national identity formation, all of which are complicit in the larger Western narrative of domination, the coloniality of power.[2] As Linda Williams asserts, it is this "racial melodrama" that defines American culture (44). The typical narrative of the southern rape complex assumes a black male rapist, an innocent white female victim, and a white male vigilante: the innocent white victim is transformed into a symbol of a threatened southern culture, while the black male rapist symbolizes that threat, and the white male is thereby sanctioned by the "code of honor" to seek revenge in the form of lynching.[3] The logic behind the narrative asserts that post-emancipation blacks and whites can only live together "peacefully" if African Americans are controlled through extralegal violence. This violence is justified on the basis that it is the only way to protect the purity of the white race, as white domination requires the "certainty" of white lineage.

The image of the threatening black male at the heart of the southern rape complex, despite its association with the South, is not limited geographically to the South or temporally to the past, as recent historical and cultural events confirm: from the sensational TV spectacle of the trial of O. J. Simpson to the "birther" movement's refusal to believe that President Barack Obama is a United States citizen to the disproportionate number of black men stopped in New York's stop-and-frisk policy to the killing of teenager Trayvon Martin in Sanford, Florida, to the shooting of Michael Brown in Ferguson, Missouri, to the shooting of twelve-year-old Tamir Rice in Cleveland, Ohio, to the shooting of Walter L. Scott in North Charleston, South Carolina (and unfortunately these are only a few of the more highly publicized shootings). Similarly, the link between white purity and white domination, which the complex reinforces, is still essential to white control, as evidenced by a recent television interview of white supremacist Craig Cobb ("Video of White"). Cobb, who was trying to establish an all-white community in North Dakota, agreed to have his DNA analyzed as part of his appearance on a talk show, only to discover that 14 percent of his genetic makeup originated in sub-Saharan Africa. Cobb dismissed the revelation as only "statistical noise," but as Trisha Goddard—the African American host of the show—explained amid the audience's laughter, "Sweetheart, you got a little black in you." Goddard went straight to the heart of white anxiety about racial purity, proving that appearance and family "history" are not proof of one's genetic background. Because the elements of the southern rape complex continue to circulate in contemporary culture, rather than dismissing it as a worn-out, racist cliché of the Jim Crow South, this study examines the protean power behind the iconic images and the dominant narratives associated with the southern rape complex and how they have been assembled and reassembled over time in film and literature, in conjunction with the shifting and contentious racial and sexual politics not only of the South but of the nation as a whole.[4] Only weeks before I was to receive the final page proofs for this book, the nation experienced a devastating reminder that the southern rape complex still motivates and is used in an attempt to justify senseless violence against African Americans. One hundred years after *The Birth of a Nation*, it is tragic, but unfortunately not surprising, that on June 17, 2015, a young white man invoked the southern rape complex—that black men rape white women and that blacks are trying to take over the country—as his reason for gunning down nine African Americans, including women and the elderly, during Bible study at the Emanuel African Methodist Episcopal Church in Charleston, South Carolina.

Cinema, because of its broad dissemination, has arguably had a greater influence in shaping cultural perception of the southern rape complex than its literary and even historical articulations. Part of the effectiveness of the cinema is its ability to draw on powerful images and capitalize on cultural narratives that resonate from one film to another. Films, however, do not simply or passively transmit cultural narratives; they often reinforce but can also amplify, appropriate, and intervene in their presentation. Despite the rise of new forms of media, rather than eclipsing the cultural impact of cinema, new media forms have only made cinema more accessible through DVD sales; YouTube postings of out-of-copyright films; a variety of online film rentals such as Netflix and Amazon.com; and television programming, especially stations dedicated to showing films from the past, such as TMC, or independent films on HBO, IFC, and Showtime as well as pay-per-view access to movies not out on DVD. Films that were once difficult for the average viewer to obtain—silent films, foreign films, and independent films with a limited release—are readily accessible. A whole new generation of viewers has greater access to films and greater control over how and when they watch them. Now more than ever, the various cinematic images of southern violence impact our cultural view of the South. While scenes of rape and lynching are certainly not limited to movies set in the South, in the southern context they carry with them a dramatic resonance associated with southern history and issues of war, Reconstruction, racial conflict, and white domination.[5]

One of the earliest and most influential cinematic depictions, and also the most blatantly propagandistic in its employment of the southern rape complex, is D. W. Griffith's *Birth of a Nation* (1915), based on Thomas Dixon's novel *The Clansman*, the play version *of The Clansman*, and the novel *The Leopard's Spots*.[6] In addition to its role in disseminating the southern rape complex, *The Birth of a Nation* has been cited as the origin of the Hollywood feature film because of its combined use of narrative structure, cinematic techniques, literary source material, its appeal to a middle-class audience, and its use of sensationalism, race, sex, and violence to sell a movie.[7] Because of its prominent place in America's cultural and filmic imagination and its crucial role in articulating and visualizing the complex, *The Birth of a Nation* serves as my model for the cinematic southern rape complex. In addition to the narrative and logic of the cinematic southern rape complex, there are iconic images in *The Birth of a Nation* that continue to resonate in American cinema, including the vulnerable white woman, the initial gaze of the threatening black male and his continued surreptitious surveillance of white women, the bodily contact between the black man and white woman, and finally, the white (robed) vigilantes. There are also significant scene sequences such as the pastoral scenes of the prewar South in which slaves are depicted as happy in their servitude; postwar scenes of black "insolence"; the politicalization and racialization of public spaces as a precursor to the violation of private space; the chase scene in which the belle flees from her attacker; the "trial" and punishment (often in the form of lynching) of the black man; white men's helplessness, blindness, or absence as facilitating the assault on white women; the crosscutting ride to the rescue in which white vigilantes "save the day"; and the final "triumph" of white America over African Americans in an attempt to re-create the racial order of the earlier images of the Old South.

No film subsequent to *The Birth of a Nation* has encompassed all the elements of the southern rape complex, but what we do see is a series of permutations and variations of these basic features, reassemblages that form new filmic, historical, and political configurations. Therefore, although I use *The Birth of a Nation* to establish the early cinematic tropes of the southern rape complex, I am not attempting to codify it as a cinematic genre with a specific set of stylistic features, character types, or a controlling narrative. Instead, I will demonstrate how these tropes are used across genres, in different time periods, in different stylistic modes, and with significant variations in narrative and character. Typical variations of the complex include reversing the race, gender, or class of the victim, the attacker, and/or the rescuer, but other variations include questioning the purity of the belle, presenting the black-coded white male as a sexual threat, and portraying the lawyer or lawman as a heroic, yet inadequate, alternative to the Klansman as rescuer. Each variation shifts the guilt or innocence of the participants in this racial triangle but still questions the vexed relationship between vigilante and legal "justice," who decides what is and is not justice, and who is or is not a citizen.

Rather than presenting a broad survey of films that employ variations of the southern rape complex, which would allow me only to discuss the general outlines of these variations, I have chosen to do a more in-depth analysis of several key films, which, like *The Birth of a Nation*, are filmic adaptations of literature and thus allow for a productive comparison between film and literature to better understand how the films in question employ the southern rape complex. The films chosen are *The Story of Temple Drake* (1933), based on William Faulkner's novel *Sanctuary;* the movie *Sanctuary* (1958), based on William Faulkner's *Requiem for a Nun; Touch of Evil* (1958), based on the pulp novel *Badge of Evil* by Whit Masterton (pseudonym of Robert Wad and H. Bill Miller); *Cape Fear* (1962), based on *The Executioners* by John D. MacDonald; and *To Kill a Mockingbird* (1962), based on Harper Lee's novel of the same name. Uses of the complex are not limited to high or low art, and therefore the literary source material varies from the works of award-winning novelists to pulp fiction. As a result, some of the films and/or directors have received more critical attention than the source materials and/or the authors, and vice versa. Furthermore, I have included films that have as well as those that have not been analyzed extensively in relation to the complex to show its pervasiveness—even in films whose violence is not directly associated with it—but also to demonstrate how the violence in these films reassembles the complex.

Significantly, in films such as Oscar Micheaux's *Within Our Gates* (1920) there have been important filmic rebuttals to the southern rape complex by African American directors and writers that feature the abuse of black women by white men, which is occluded by the basic premises of the complex. But because the southern rape complex originated as a response to a crisis of white southern identity after Reconstruction, I have selected films that play out the white fears and fantasies the complex evokes. Consequently, many of the films I examine do not explicitly address race or lynching, yet they tap into the logic, narrative, and/or iconic images associated with the complex as an expression of white anxiety. Despite the continued importance of race and gender, not limiting the cinematic versions of the complex to the black male aggressor and white female victim enables a greater focus on other aspects of the complex (class, economics, law, whiteness, violence, vagrancy) that are often overshadowed by its sensational use of race and gender.

Although these films are set in different eras, with their own specific issues, they all register the tensions between national and state laws and/or culture in an effort to maintain white middle- and upper-class domination as an unproblematic norm. To this end I have focused on films that correspond to periods of American crisis, the Depression and/or the civil rights movement: *The Story of Temple Drake* was set in and released during the Depression, while *Sanctuary* and *To Kill a Mockingbird* were set during the Depression but released during the civil rights movement, and finally *Cape Fear* and *Touch of Evil* were set in and released during the civil rights movement. These reassemblages draw their power from the emotional intensity and violence inherent in the complex and demonstrate how the narrative, logic, images, and scene sequences of the cinematic southern rape complex are employed in service of continued white apprehension in the face of changing racial dynamics.

The southern rape complex thus captures the problematic nature of the shifting and often contradictory economic, legal, sexual, racial, gender, political, mythic, psychoanalytical, and historical connotations the phenomenon encompasses at one and the same time. There have been excellent cinematic, literary, and historical studies of various aspects of the southern rape complex—focusing on lynching, Reconstruction, economics, politics, miscegenation, interracial rape, the Ku Klux Klan, and the legal system—that have explicitly or implicitly questioned and critiqued Cash's original explanation of the phenomenon.[8] I have retained Cash's term, however, in part because of its cultural legacy but also because it facilitates a focus on the "complex" of ideas, emotions, and events surrounding the cinematic southern rape complex, so as not to be limited to any one aspect of it.

The Birth of a Nation is an appropriate model for the cinematic southern rape complex because, though Cash rejected Dixon's novels as "rabid" (375)—especially *The Clansman,* which Cash notes was made into *The Birth of a Nation*—his description of the southern rape complex is a perfect recapitulation of the ideas and sentiments dramatized in the film. Cash does not condone the racial violence associated with the complex but does believes it is a "genuine" expression of "real fear" and "even terror." He rejects as malicious the "Negro apologists and others bent on damning the South" who conclude that because there was no actual "rape menace" in the South, the rape complex is "therefore a fraud, a hypocritical pretext behind which the South has always cynically and knowingly hidden mere sadism and economic interest" (115). As in *The Birth of a Nation,* Cash blames "Yankees" for stirring up "ignorant Negroes" and thus creating the race hatred among even upper-class southern whites (among whom he claimed it did not exist), which inevitably led to racial violence in the form of both mob and individual attacks on African Americans. While Cash debunks economic motivations, he alludes to unconscious fantasies that are at play in the southern rape complex, the "subconscious purposes" that led the "best men in the South" to condone "a broken head or death" as a "fair punishment for the sassy nigger" and the "real fear" on the part of "neurotic old maids and wives, hysterical young girls," who reacted "in a fashion well enough understood now, but understood by almost nobody then" (119, 115).

Despite the subconscious impetus of the complex, Cash sees as "real," and not merely "symbolic," the connection between southern white women and the (white) South. White female purity is crucial to the justification of white domination based on a claim of white superiority, which requires the "certainty" of white lineage. As Cash explains, "The ultimate content of the Southerner's rape complex," and "explicitly what [is] contained" in the "taboo on the white woman," is "the right of their sons in the legitimate line, through all the generations to come, to be born to the great heritage of white men" (116–17). Tellingly, the "great heritage of white men" needs to be qualified as the "legitimate" line, which suggests a racially mixed illegitimate line and unfettered white male access to African American women. Cash's description of the southern rape complex, though not historically accurate, has played a vital role in defining and perpetuating what historian Diane Miller Sommerville refers to as the "invented tradition" of racial and gender violence imaginatively localized in the South, which still impacts American culture (*Rape and Race* 4).

Critics have called the southern rape complex "obsolete" and "a masculine appropriation of rape and victim for use in a contest for social power" (Patterson 38, 39). Cash's *Mind of the South* (in which he coins the term *southern rape complex*) has also been deemed a "nuisance," a "tear-jerker," and even a "corpse" (O'Brien 179, 180). Yet like *The Birth of a Nation*, *The Mind of the South* remains an integral, if dubious, part of southern cultural history,[9] just as the term *southern rape complex*, even if objected to, refers to a narrative that has had a devastating material and psychical impact. Angela Davis, in her discussion of the "myth of the black rapist," calls it one of "the most formidable artifices invented by racism" and attests to the myth's influence in the United States, citing the statistics that 405 of the 455 men executed for the charge of rape between 1930 and 1967 were African American (172). Confirming Claude Lévi-Strauss's assertion that myths do not form from past experience but are "invented to explain the facts" of the present (492), Joel Williamson observes that *The Mind of the South* "captures its own time superbly even as it sought to capture time past" (*Crucible* 3), just as each variation of the southern rape complex reinvests the complex to explain current racial struggles.

EMERGENCE OF THE COMPLEX

As Sommerville's historical analysis confirms, the southern rape complex did not spring from a deeply held moral conviction about the sanctity of all southern white womanhood. During the antebellum period black male/white female rape cases did not necessarily result in lynchings or even in public outcries, depending on the class of the white woman and her sexual history and whether or not the alleged attacker was a slave or free. Because of the economic value of an adult male slave, slave masters had little interest in killing a slave if the charge pertained to a lower-class white woman. Black men were not only allowed a trial by jury; they were often acquitted in the courts, especially if there were no eyewitnesses.[10] Furthermore, both Frederick Douglass and Ida B. Wells, in their respective work on the history of lynching, asserted that during the Civil War no accusations of rape were made against black men, suggesting that there was no widespread fear of, nor reports of, sexual violence at the hands of black men (Douglass 498–99; Wells 63–64).

Wells estimates that after the war, between 1865 and 1895, over ten thousand lynchings took place, while only three white men were executed for killing an African American (63–64). Yet during Reconstruction the "justifications" for the lynchings of black men and women were not typically based on the sexual threat posed by the black man; instead, the need to keep blacks from revolting was the dominant justification, and even the Ku Klux Klan and Knights of the White Camellia focused on political and economic repression rather than rape (Olds 179–205). That most lynchings did not actually involve the charge of rape—they were frequently retaliations for political organizing and/or economic competition—suggests that on a profound level whites did not actually believe in racial inferiority but, rather, feared blacks' abilities to succeed politically and economically.[11] In *The Leopard's Spots* Dixon himself articulates this position: "If you train the Negroes to be scientific farmers they will become a race of aristocrats, and when five generations removed from the memory of slavery, a war of races will be inevitable, unless the Anglo-Saxon grant this trained and wealthy African equal social rights." Amazingly, Dixon envisions a democratic form of "aristocracy" predicated on education and the accumulation of wealth and not on blood or race, a vision that predicts actual equality but cannot tolerate social equality, which would be "suicide" for the Anglo-Saxon race (188).

Historically, the southern rape complex did not crystallize into the myth of the black male rapist until the late 1880s. Initially, the term *rape of the South* was commonly used by white southerners to refer to the Union army's occupation of the South, the fear of the literal rape of southern women by northern troops, and the figurative rape of the land (especially regarding General Sherman's scorched-earth policies). Subsequently, it was applied to the role of northern "carpetbaggers" in exploiting the economic opportunities occasioned by the defeat of the Confederate States of America (Seidel 47; Cash 116). Each transformation of the "rapist" in "the rape of the South"—from Union soldiers to Republican politicians and businessmen and finally to black men—marks a movement away from the (white) South as a defeated nation and "conquered province" under military control to an image of a white South, cloaked as a restoration of their Aryan birthright, with unbroken ties to a civilization that preceded the founding of America.

The image of the savage black man was, of course, not a new one. In addition to European colonial images of Africans as primitive, closer-to-home white Americans were already familiar with and frightened by the image of the violent and vengeful slave, especially in connection with the Haitian slave revolt, which provided a terrifying example to many white southern planters (Johnson, *Rivers* 31–33). While the violence to whites was the most sensationalized element of the revolt, it had obvious economic as well as political ramifications: the seizure of land and the citizenship of former slaves, two factors that would be crucial during and after Reconstruction in the American South.

Yet against the backdrop of the American Civil War and the defeat of the Confederate South, the propagandistic use of the vengeful slave was problematic. The American Civil War was not a slave rebellion, and because of the existence of black Union soldiers, the myth of the black male rapist potentially ran the risk of equating the raping of white southern women with the victors' taking the spoils of war. For whites to retain control politically and psychologically, the freedman could not be seen as a powerful, victorious opponent or as a rational citizen soldier, and thus the image of the black man as a mindless and dangerous animal was crucial as a justification for those who sought African American subjugation under white rule. Not only was the southern rape complex integrally linked to the lynching of black men, its distorting lens has made socially invisible other forms of interracial sexual violence against black women—as well as intraracial sexual violence and intragender violence—thereby defining rape as black-on-white and heterosexual. The southern rape complex thus deflects attention from the rape of black women and men by white men while assuming that white female purity is a guarantee of white racial superiority.

Historians, sociologists, and psychologists have posited various reasons for the emergence of the rape myth as a political tool in the late 1880s: as a reaction to the federal suppression of the KKK; as white fear of black political equality; as white fear of a rise in the black population as indicated by the 1880 census; as white fear that the New Negro born after slavery was not instilled with the respect for white authority produced through slavery's "civilizing" effect; as white men's guilty projection that black men would seek revenge for the rape and concubinage of black women; and/or as white men's projection and punishment of their sexual desires onto the bodies of black men (Olds 179–205). Given the overdetermined nature of the southern rape complex, there is no single explanation; all of these factors are relevant to the formation and perpetuation of the complex.

The southern rape complex, therefore, simultaneously serves a variety of economic, political, and psychosexual functions. In the context of Western imperialism the southern rape complex is the mechanism by which southern white elites "recolonize" not just former slaves but all blacks, especially those who are economically competitive with whites. White southern men, as Dixon portrays them, are justified in their violent reaction because of the need to protect racial endogamy—that is, to maintain strict legal and social boundaries between whites and blacks. Even as they use the discourse of coloniality to justify white domination, whites, like Dixon, also invert the discourse to link racial intermarriage with the threat of a "Black Empire," thus portraying themselves as the victims of black imperialism. Depicting the black man as a source of fear and destruction also obfuscated the South's dependence on black labor at the same time it sought to control and limit black workers to the status of unskilled agricultural laborers. The post-Reconstruction emergence of the southern rape complex thus constitutes a form of "systemic violence," a devastating by-product of the "smooth functioning" of the everyday activities of politics and the economy for the country as a whole, not just the South (Žižek 2).

CINEMATIC ADAPTATIONS OF THE SOUTHERN RAPE COMPLEX

Early cinematic adaptations, such as *The Birth of a Nation*, tended to use the prestige of literary classics to bolster the acceptability of film and to draw a middle-class audience, as opposed to the early street front nickelodeons with the taint of risqué material and a lower-class audience. Initially, adaptation studies followed suit by prioritizing the status of literature and therefore judged the adaptation based on its ability to translate faithfully the literary work into a filmic medium. Adaptation theory, however, has long moved away from "fidelity criticism."[12] Linda Hutcheon usefully offers a "continuum model," which understands adaptations as "various responses to a prior story . . . as (re)interpretations and (re)creations" (172). The films in question, however, are responding not only to the source material; they are also responding to a "prior story" of the southern rape complex. Hutcheon's conception of adaptation as "a form of repetition without replication" speaks to the unique contribution of each of these filmic reassemblages of the complex (xvi).

Rather than simply confirming the superiority of literature over film or enumerating the changes from literature to film, I want to examine the politics of adaptation and how the specific elements that are omitted, added, or reinterpreted shape our perception of the sexual and racial dynamics of the South. The literary source material therefore provides another significant context for articulating the cinematic rendering of the southern rape complex. I do not, however, treat the literature as merely a backdrop for the films. Putting the novels and the films in conversation with *The Birth of a Nation* and the southern rape complex, as well as in conversation with each other, allows for new readings of the source material. I am also interested in the interactive effect between the film and the novel.

Obviously, the film adaptation cannot influence the writing of its source material, but films can affect our understanding of the novels. This is true in part because many people read the novel only after watching the film (or know of the novel only through the film) but also because of the impact of the films themselves. As I discuss in chapter 6, Gregory Peck's sympathetic performance of Atticus Finch has created one of the best-loved cinema heroes, and for decades it has colored interpretations of the novel as well as the film. Although recent critics, especially lawyers, have been more critical of Atticus, most still assume that the novel paints him as an unproblematic hero and therefore miss the novel's own subtle but insistent critique of Atticus as a lawyer and even as a father. The dynamic between film and literature is even more direct, as I argue in chapter 3, in the case of Faulkner's *Requiem for a Nun*. Structuralist-inspired adaptation studies has examined the interactive effect of film and literature and the general impact of filmic techniques on the works (especially) of Modernist authors, including Faulkner.[13] I argue, however, for a more specific influence of film on writing in the case of Faulkner's *Requiem for a Nun*, which not only is a sequel to Faulkner's *Sanctuary* but also responds to and rewrites key elements of *The Story of Temple Drake* (the Hollywood adaption of *Sanctuary*). Therefore, *Requiem for a Nun* is a sequel to both the earlier novel and its filmic adaptation. The success of the film can even affect how its source material is subsequently marketed. Both *Badge of Evil* and *The Executioners*, for example, were reprinted using the title of the film, not the original novel, and jacket covers of novels are often replaced with an image from the filmic adaptations.

On the level of narrative the films in this study are frequently more conservative than their literary source material and at times reinforce the racist logic of the southern rape complex. Yet when we examine the cinematic features, the reassemblage of these images often unsettles the familiar plot, exposing the contradictions at the heart of the complex itself. As recent adaptation theory has stressed, filmic adaptations are not the unproblematic translation of a narrative from one medium to another. While a comparison of narrative content is a significant feature of filmic adaptations that I will address in this study, as Christine Geraghty argues, it is necessary to go beyond an analysis of content variations to understand the unique contribution of the cinematic depictions (5). We must study these films *as* films and consider the techniques they employ in their appropriations of the complex because in cinema the elements of the southern rape complex are manifest not only in the plots and dialogues of the films but also in the cinematic techniques and images themselves. Or as Stephen Heath explains, "Narrative never exhausts the image" because "narrative can never contain the whole film which permanently exceeds its fictions" ("Film and System," pt. 2, 10). It is precisely through attention to lighting, set design, performance features, sound, cinematography, and editing that we are able to ascertain cinema's impact on the southern rape complex.[14]

Griffith did not invent many of the film innovations he uses in *The Birth of a Nation*—multiple camera angles, moving shots, extensive use of crosscutting, masking shots, tinted frames, location shots, choreographed battle scenes, iris shots—nor, as Robert Jackson points out, was his filmic use of Jim Crow imagery and southern Civil War patriotism unprecedented (27–51). Griffith was, however, the first to combine theses cinematic techniques and cultural images in *The Birth of a Nation* with an action-packed, compelling (to many white audience members) narrative to create something that surpasses the earlier, one- and two-reel industry standards. Griffith tapped into what Gilles Deleuze describes as "the evolution of the cinema, the conquest of its own essence or novelty," which "was to take place through montage, the mobile camera and the emancipation of the viewpoint, which became separate from projection" (*Cinema 1* 3). But as Alice Maurice argues, this transition from the early cinema's "theatre of attractions" (the use of a still camera and spectacle, including minstrelsy) to the narrative of classic cinema (based on continuity editing) was in part facilitated by the cinematic "rhetoric of race."

Early cinema's use of spectacle, sight gags, trick photography, and the play of shadows and light was often predicated on an essentialized belief in racial difference. The "joke" of Thomas Edison's 1903 film *What Happened in the Tunnel*, for example, is that when the train goes through a tunnel, the screen goes black just as a white man tries to kiss a white woman. When they emerge into the light, we see that the white woman has traded places with her black maid, who received the kiss from the startled and chagrined white man.[15] This scene is only "funny" based on the assumption that miscegenation is unnatural, suggesting—contrary to historical evidence—that a white man would never be attracted to a black woman. The same racial rhetoric helped film break out of the still shot, as many of the early chase scenes revolve around or flirt with "race mixing" in various forms: "With the move to longer, multishot narratives, the logic of racial disguise, reversals, and miscegenation continues to meld stasis and motion and to link physical, social, and filmic limits" (Maurice 66). Mirroring white viewers' belief in race as an essential category helped to establish narrative cinema's status as a representation of "real life." Therefore, it is not simply coincidental that *The Birth of a Nation*, with its fixation on miscegenation as the impetus for the elaborate crosscutting chase scenes, helped to usher in the narrative mode of classic cinema.[16]

Griffith so believed in the power of film to depict reality that in 1915, the year *The Birth of a Nation* was released, he famously predicted that someday film would replace books as the source of historical truth: "The time will come, and in less than ten years . . . when the children in the public schools will be taught practically everything by moving pictures. Certainly they will never be obliged to read history again . . . Instead of consulting all the authorities, wading laboriously through a host of books, and ending bewildered, without a clear idea of what exactly did happen and confused at every point by conflicting opinions about what did happen, you will merely seat yourself at a properly adjusted window, in a scientifically prepared room, press the button, and actually see what happened. There will be no opinions expressed. You will merely be present at the making of history" (qtd. in Lang 4). If his prediction is a grandiose view of film as well as a naive view of history, there is also an element of truth in it.[17] Perhaps today more than any other time, more people are likely to know about the Civil War or the antebellum South from films and television rather than from historical accounts. Griffith may not have given his audience "Truth" or "History," in his "blockbuster" *The Birth of a Nation,* but he presented them with what many—including Griffith himself—took to be the "historical truth" of the threat of the black male rapist and its impact on the reconstruction of the South and of the nation. As a result, the film was an important recruiting tool for the resurrection of the second movement Klan in the 1920s.[18]

Despite Griffith's prediction, no cinematic image, regardless of its power, can be understood totally outside of its cultural context, and this is especially true in the case of the cinematic southern rape complex. Just as the southern rape complex creates a synergy between elements of race, gender, and class that goes beyond an analysis of any single feature, so too an analysis of cinematic adaptations of the complex must combine the historical, narrative, and filmic contexts. Therefore, in assessing the contribution of cinematic adaptations, I do not want to be limited to a strictly formal analysis. Placing these films in historical context allows me to analyze how the variations on the complex respond to the changing climate of race and identity in the United States.

As was true during Reconstruction, the vexed issue of federal versus state power continued during the Depression and the civil rights movement. A key symbol of state power was the refusal to accept African Americans as full-fledged citizens, with all the rights and responsibilities citizenship entailed. Although Klan violence decreased during the Depression, racial politics did not. Southern congressmen, in particular, refused to support the National Recovery Act or the Tennessee Valley Authority (despite the fact that both were beneficial to southern states) unless they had assurance that "southern employers could continue to draw without hindrance on the still-enormous supply of inexpensive and vulnerable black labor," thus diminishing the power of national laws to interfere with racial politics. This process was accomplished through an administrative decentralization that ensured state and local discretion, regional differences in wages, and the exclusion of maids and farmworkers (two-thirds of African American southern workers) from key New Deal protections for workers (Katznelson 163).

The southern white reaction to the civil rights movement was even more similar to the reaction to Reconstruction in relation to the increase in violence against African Americans, who were characterized by many whites as threatening "our way of life," a coded reference to white domination. With the resurgence of vigilante violence and the rise of the third movement of the Klan in the 1950s and 1960s, there was often little distinction between the police and the Klan because they were at times one and the same. Hollywood increasingly highlighted the figure of the lawyer—looking to him to adjudicate between a racially biased legal system and the lynch mob. The lawyer, rather than the belle, emerges as the besieged yet "heroic" figure in two films from 1962 starring Gregory Peck, *Cape Fear* and *To Kill a Mockingbird.*[19] While it is tempting to read the reconfiguration of the basic elements of the southern rape complex into a narrative of progressive race relations, that would be far too facile an analysis. Certainly, there is a tendency in these post-*Birth* films to break down or investigate the clichés associated with the complex, but it is also important to consider how these reassemblages reconfigure the status quo of white privilege as well as unsettle it. If in *The Birth of a Nation* the intertitle "Fair Trial" used to describe Gus's lynching is cruelly incongruous, in films that feature an all-white jury and police force, any hope of equality under the law is equally suspect.

THE MOVEMENT-IMAGE AND THE TIME-IMAGE

To move beyond narrative and to elucidate the role of the cinematic in these reconfigurations of the southern rape complex, I find particularly useful the work of Gilles Deleuze in *Cinema 1* and *Cinema 2*, in which he develops the concept of the movement-image and the time-image.[20] For Deleuze the cinematic apparatus has had a profound effect on how we perceive the world in creating a new nonsubjective but individuated "camera consciousness" that is freed from the human eye. Critical to his theory is that cinema does not present a static image to which movement is added; it creates an image that cannot be divorced from its motion: the movement-image. Therefore, the cinematic image requires a new terminology to capture an image in motion, and these cinematic concepts provide a vocabulary and a framework for analyzing the cinematic southern rape complex.[21]

Deleuze's theory of cinema rejects the representational model of film analysis that assumes a transcendental world outside the frame of the screen;

Deleuze also rejects the attempt to understand cinema as a language, as in much of the structural and semiotic approaches to film. Instead, he draws on the work of Henri Bergson to formulate his categories of cinematic images. Bergson's solution to the subject-object split was to understand the world as made up only of images: living images and nonliving images. Unlike nonliving images, living images have the ability to shape their world in a three-part process that proceeds from perception of the world to an affective response to a physical reaction. In applying this framework to cinema, Deleuze categorizes the three components of the movement-image as the perception-image, the affection-image, and the action-image. The perception-image is associated with the framing of the shot and point of view of the camera; the affection-image, which is the interval, pause, or gap between the perception and the action, is associated with the close-up and an affective response; and the action-image is associated with not only the characters' movements within the frame but with camera movement and editing (montage, crosscutting, and shot/reverse shot). In films dominated by the movement-image, this "sensory-motor schema" structures and coordinates the links between the perception-image, affection-image, and action-image based on a chronological, cause-and-effect model.

The movement-image is typified by Hollywood narrative cinema, in which time is presented indirectly through action, suggesting a sequential understanding of causality. Deleuze cites *The Birth of a Nation* as exemplary of the movement-image and acknowledges the foundational importance of the film in American cinema, specifically in creating an American form of montage, action, and close-ups (*Cinema 1* 30–32). Griffith's use of parallel alternative montage is based on an organic "unity in diversity" in which the movement between the binary parts forms a rhythm and relationship, a kind of duel that both threatens the unity of the organic set and then restores it. In *The Birth of a Nation* this threat is associated with race: "It is the nature of the organic set that it should continually be threatened: the accusation raised against the Negroes in *The Birth of a Nation* is that of wanting to shatter the newly-won unity of the United States by using the South's defeat to their own advantage . . . The convergent actions tend towards a single end, reaching the site of the duel to reverse its outcome, to save innocence or reconstitute the compromised unity—like the gallop of the horsemen who come to the rescue of the besieged" (31). Typical of the Hollywood action film, *The Birth of a Nation* constitutes the "large form" of the action-image (SAS). The large form moves from an initial situation, to a reaction or duel, to either a restored situation (SAS) or an altered situation (SAS'). *The Birth of a Nation* contains both types of the large form action-image: in the first section the situation (the harmonious world of white domination through slavery) is shattered by the action of the Civil War (presented primarily as an "honorable" duel between white northern and southern soldiers), but the end of the Civil War does not restore white domination; instead, it brings about a new situation, presented as intolerable to elite whites (SAS'). The second half of the film, set during Reconstruction, presents the intolerable situation, and the duel is primarily between the Klan and black Union troops, the outcome of which then restores the "order" of white domination (S'AS). Analyzing the elements of the movement-images (the perception-image, the affection-image, and the action-image) and the techniques associated with them (e.g., lighting, framing, close-ups, and camera movement) allows for productive comparisons and reassemblages among images, suggesting concepts both inside and outside the confines of the film's narrative.

It is the time-image, however, that shatters the sensory-motor scheme and lets us "see" and respond to cinematic images outside the confines of the narrative logic of cause and effect. The time-image emerged after World War II, when, according to Deleuze, there was a crisis in cinema; Italian neorealism helped to usher in a new form of time that was only loosely constituted through action/plot. The French New Wave, through the use of irrational cuts and noncausal relinkages, broke with the movement-image to emphasize a cinema of the time-image in which time is directly represented purely through sound and visual images that do not lead to action and therefore defy cause-and-effect logic, thus disrupting the sensory-motor schema. In the time-image the gap between perception and action is suspended, and instead of leading to action, thought, or emotion, it leads to unthought, the unbearable, or the impossible.[22]

Two interrelated aspects of the time-image that affect both visual and narrative features of film are the crystal-image and the chronosign. Whereas in the "organic" form of the movement-image, as characterized by *The Birth of a Nation*, reality is established by continuity and causality—"a regime of the localizable relation, actual linkages, legal, causal and logical connection" (*Cinema 2* 126–7)—in the crystal-image these linkages and continuity are severed, and the virtual takes on a life of its own. In the crystal-image the actualized present and virtual past, the real and the imaginary, while distinct, are indistinguishable (as in the famous hall of mirrors scene in Orson Welles's *Lady from Shanghai*): the virtual and the imaginary "chase after each other, exchange their roles and become indiscernible" (127). Space as well as time is detached from the continuity that establishes the organic narrative so that the crystalline narrative forms "as a consequence of disconnected places and de-chronologized moments" (133). In the other aspect of the time-image, the chronosign, nonchronological time impossibly exists in "coexisting sheets of the past" and in "simultaneous peaks of the present" (275). The effect it has on narrative is that—unlike the organic narrative of the movement-image, which operates on the law of cause and effect—narration no longer has a claim to truth. It is not simply a matter of not knowing the truth, as in an ambiguous or inconclusive ending; it is that the film does not lay claim to truth.[23] This is what Deleuze calls "the power of the false," which creates a "falsifying narrative" that "poses inexplicable differences to the present and alternatives which are undecidable between true and false to the past . . . The image must be produced in such a way that the past is not necessarily true, or that the impossible comes from the possible" (131).

Although cinematic images are dominated by either the regime of the movement-image or the time-image, they can move from one to the other or constantly overlap. Predominance of the movement-image in films such as *The Birth of a Nation*, for example, does not preclude the presence of the time-image, which shatters the sensory-motor schema found in narrative films. This feature is of particular importance for my study because in rupturing the film's sensory-motor schema, the time-image also ruptures the narrative of the southern rape complex, the justifying logic of violation, pursuit, and revenge/justice.

Although I draw primarily on the terms from Deleuze's *Cinema 1* and *Cinema 2*, those works are informed by key Deleuzian concepts that helped to shape the rise of affect theory in cinema studies. Eugenie Brinkema, however, accuses Deleuzians of the "sin of generalization," in which terms such as *affect, force,* or *sensation* are undifferentiated and therefore become meaningless abstractions. Brinkema maintains that in attempting to go beyond language and representation to focus on sensation, many Deleuzian readings follow predictable formulas, which result in "only the mild rhetorical force of summary and paraphrase, intoned synonyms, and thematic generalizations," producing "all repetition with no difference" and therefore actually work against Deleuze's basic concept of difference and his focus on the "minor" (xiii). Brinkema, therefore, asserts the need to put affect into textual context because "only reading specific affects as having and being bound up with specific forms gives us the vocabulary for articulating those many differences" (xv). It is in this vein that I use Deleuzian theory and the concept of assemblage to articulate the different variations of the southern rape complex in all their particularities, formal as well as historical and social.[24] Deleuze and Guattari's concept of "assemblage" facilitates my reading of the mutability and complexity of the southern rape complex because an assemblage is open, not fixed, is heterogeneous and nonhierarchical, and creates points of intersection across fields. Rather than assuming a reality outside the text/film of which it is a representation and therefore supposing a division between reality, representation, and the subject, an assemblage creates connections "drawn from each of the orders" and "in its multiplicity, necessarily acts on semiotic flows, material flows, and social flows simultaneously" (Deleuze and Guattari 22–23).

As I will discuss in chapter 1, an example from *The Birth of a Nation*, which illustrates the time-image, is a pivotal scene that depicts the rationale for the formation of the Klan. The famous cross-cutting chase scene—in which Flora (the innocent white belle), Gus (the "renegade" former slave), and Ben (Flora's brother, a former Confederate colonel and Klan member) run through the woods—has been carefully analyzed by critics to try to pin down the movements of the characters based on their association with particular landmarks in the woods in an attempt to connect time to movements. At the beginning and end of the chase the characters' relationships to one another are established, but in the middle of the chase scene it is difficult to tell who is chasing whom or to pin down the location of the characters in relation to one another. The chronological logic of the chase, which establishes victim, perpetrator, and rescuer, is replaced with "disconnected places and de-chronologized moments," and we are left with a series of affection-images of fear and panic on the faces of all the characters as they run wildly through the woods (figs. I.1–3). Thus stripped of its narrative and temporal logic, the infamous chase scene registers not the justification for the lynching of Gus but the hysterical reaction to Reconstruction.[25]

Deleuze's phrase *the power of the false* refers to the time-image, but its more commonsensical meaning is also applicable to the southern rape complex.

FIGS. I .1–3. Looks of fear and panic on Flora, Gus, and Ben during the chase scene. *The Birth of a Nation* (1915).

As Atticus Finch says in *To Kill a Mockingbird*, the southern rape complex is based "on the assumption—the evil assumption—that *all* Negroes lie, that *all* Negroes are basically immoral beings, that *all* Negro men are not to be trusted around our women" (232). Granted, there were actual historical cases of interracial rape involving a black man and white woman; however, the power of the southern rape complex does not come from the reality of these cases but from its arbitrary invocation as a justification for violence against African Americans, a form of what Achille Mbembe calls "necropolitics," which assumes sovereignty through the unauthorized power of life and death. The power of the false elucidates the cinematic destabilization of linear, cause-and-effect narratives that disrupt the southern rape complex, which operates under the power of the false and the not necessarily true past in which someone who rebels from the nation (a traitor by definition) is declared a patriot of that same nation, in which a terrorist organization restores order, in which any and all black men are rapists and can be tortured and killed—by the same patriots who believe in law and order—and in which the rape of a black woman is not a crime.

Drawing on Julia Kristeva's theory of abjection, in chapter 1 I begin with an examination of the basic tropes of the southern rape complex in *The Birth of a Nation* by demonstrating how Griffith and Dixon employ it to reimagine scenes of the abject Confederate body as moments of heroism in the "battle" for Reconstruction. In subsequent chapters the black-coded white man as rapist is a trope that invokes the logic and narrative of the southern rape complex while avoiding the racial controversy surrounding *The Birth of a Nation*, and it features prominently in *The Story of Temple Drake* (chap. 2), *Cape Fear* (chap. 5), and even *To Kill a Mockingbird* (chap. 6).[26] The use of this figure also allows for a more direct depiction of the southern belle as tainted—as culpable for, or even deserving of, the violence against her—a concept that cannot be broached within the logic of the complex, in which all black-white sexual contact is deemed unmitigated rape.[27]

Chapters 2 and 3 examine two filmic adaptations of Faulkner novels (*Sanctuary* and *Requiem for a Nun*), which feature Temple Drake as just such a tainted belle. In *The Story of Temple Drake* the defiled belle does away with the need for the Klan by killing her rapist and then "purges" herself by admitting the truth in open court in order to save an innocent man. The film thus valorizes vigilantism even as it asserts the primacy of law. *The Story of Temple Drake* combines the gritty realism of the gangster movie with the Expressionistic use of chiaroscuro in horror films to create one of the first southern gothic films. Temple Drake appears again in the film *Sanctuary* (1958), which is actually the filmic adaptation of Faulkner's *Requiem for a Nun,* his own sequel to *Sanctuary,* but in addition to the black-coded white man, this film features the incongruous image of the murdering black "mammy," who combines the violence and sexuality of the black rapist with the all-loving mammy figure. Temple rejects the myth of the purity of the belle, crucial to the southern rape complex, but still holds onto the myth of the mammy (as the counterpart to the black rapist) in order to "read" her daughter's death at the hand of Nancy, her black nanny (and Temple's "sister in sin"), as a sacrifice meant to preserve the white family. In the final jail scene, as Nancy awaits execution, a series of alternating close-ups of Temple and Nancy contrast white anxiety with black Christian acceptance, culminating in a close-up that combines Nancy's black hands on Temple's white face. Only in the composite close-up does Temple express tranquillity, which quickly disappears when the black hands are removed. Nancy admonishes Temple to "believe," but the only thing Temple seems to believe in is the myth of the all-loving mammy. While the film is set during and just after the Depression, the use of the protest singer Odetta Holmes to play Nancy allows for an alternative reading of the film's ending that signals a more radical reading of a black woman in jail.

I expand the southern rape complex south of the border in chapter 4 with *Touch of Evil* (1958), Orson Welles's adaptation of the pulp crime novel *Badge of Evil.* Welles brilliantly confounds the basic plot devices of the complex by presenting interracial rape literally, as a staged event. For the black male rapist, however, Welles substitutes the stereotype of the Mexican drug lord and his "greaser" henchmen, demonstrating the portability of the complex to other regions and ethnic groups. If the southern rape complex is meant to create artificial boundaries around whiteness and American citizenship, Welles—whom Deleuze sites as the "first" to isolate a direct time-image and "to make the image go over to the power of the false" (*Cinema 2* 138)—uses this power in *Touch of Evil,* with its many border crossing and ambiguous characters, to undermine any such boundaries and instead create a world where racial and national identity, guilt and innocence, and law and vigilantism are inextricably mixed so that even the most pure are touched by evil.

Lawyers play important supporting roles in many of the films in this study, but Gregory Peck takes center stage as a beleaguered southern lawyer in *Cape*

Fear and *To Kill a Mockingbird* (both released in 1962). Peck portrays the lawyer as heroic yet at the same time inadequate to protect his families or his clients. Both films also employ the black-coded white man as a menace, not only to white women but to the concept of civil rights. In chapter 5 the ex-convict Max Cady, a black-coded white man in *Cape Fear*, represents not just the limits of liberalism but also the systemic violence behind liberal tolerance in a democratic, capitalist country. *Cape Fear*'s contemporary 1960s setting makes the connection to civil rights directly, as Sam Bowden's wife asserts of the black-coded Cady, "A man like that doesn't deserve civil rights." As an ex-convict who used his time in prison to educate himself about the law, Cady embodies whites' fears that education, especially in light of *Brown v. Board of Education*, does not ensure an adoption of middle-class values; instead, it makes the lower classes, white or black, better able to manipulate the system for their own retribution. Through lighting, camera angle, dialogue, and gestures, Cady is visually linked to the predatory black male rapist even as he is distinguished from what Atticus Finch in *To Kill a Mockingbird* refers to as a "humble respectable Negro."

Peck, as Atticus Finch in *To Kill a Mockingbird* (chap. 6), exposes the power of the false in relation to the southern rape complex but not in relation to liberal humanism that preaches equality while tacitly accepting segregation. *To Kill a Mockingbird* is the only film in this study that engages directly with a black-on-white rape (not the black-coded white man), but it is the exception that proves the rule. While the defendant, Tom Robinson, is an innocent "humble" black man, the black-coded white man, Bob Ewell, embodies the negative stereotypes of both the black rapist and the white trash racist. The Depression-era setting of *To Kill a Mockingbird* overlaps not only with the infamous Alabama Scottsboro rape trial but also with the late 1920s anti-Klan movement in Alabama, which villainized the politically powerful second Klan as violent lower-class ruffians, even as it upheld the power of the planter elite and justified the Reconstruction Klan. Boo Radley, as the innocent white avenger who saves Scout from Ewell—the lower-class menace—enacts a nostalgic version of vigilante justice in keeping with the limitations of the anti-Klan movement. Scout's famous "mockingbird" speech, rather than demonstrating the positive aspects of liberal tolerance, exposes its reliance on vigilante violence as well as its reliance on the law (Atticus and Sheriff Tate) to look the other way. Invoking Atticus's famous dictum to reach compromise by trying to walk in another man's shoes, the film uses off-screen space and point of view to put the audience in Boo's shoes, and at the same time it demonstrates Atticus's inability to live up to his own standard of sympathetic understanding.

If many of the films after *The Birth of a Nation* shied away from direct depictions of the Klan, the post–civil rights era returns again to the more overt racism of *The Birth of a Nation*. They do so, however, as a form of condemnation, not valorization, but they employ many of the same variations of the southern rape complex as in earlier films. As with the black-coded white man, the condemnation of the Klan still focuses on poor whites as the locus of racism in the South. To conclude, I examine *A Time to Kill* (1996) as reimagining both *The Birth of a Nation* and *To Kill a Mockingbird*. The film still privileges the story of the white lawyer yet actually films the rape of a young black girl, who is brutally raped by the villainous white trash rapists, from her point of view. The courtroom drama that unfolds centers not around the trial of the white perpetrators but of the African American father who shoots them in cold blood as retaliation for the rape of his daughter. In a disconcerting reassemblage of the southern rape complex, the victorious white lawyer frees a guilty black man by appealing to the all-white jury's racial prejudice and their belief in vigilante justice. *A Time to Kill* exemplifies the way many of the basic cinematic variations of the southern rape complex, as developed in this study, continue to morph after the civil rights movement in response to the changing same of race relations in the United States. Almost one hundred years after *The Birth of a Nation* its cinematic legacy still haunts American cinema, creating a kind of cinematic "rememory," as Toni Morrison described the palpable past of slavery (41). This legacy and its impact on cinematic renditions of the matrices of gender, race, and violence may never go away, which is all the more reason for continued awareness and analysis of its affective power.

CHAPTER 1

Confederate Abjection in D. W. Griffith's Early Civil War Films and Thomas Dixon's *Clansman*

IN ADDITION TO the historical, cultural, and psychological circumstances that gave rise to the southern rape complex and its associated tropes, as outlined in the introduction, in order to articulate *The Birth of a Nation*'s role as a model of the cinematic southern rape complex, it is necessary to examine the "problem" of the abject Confederate body in Griffith's earlier Civil War films, which found its "solution" in *Birth*. While the ramifications and utilizations of the southern rape complex are not limited to the South, a key component of its formulation is the post-Reconstruction rewriting of white southern abjection and loss, such as that found in both Griffith's Civil War films as well as in the source material, Thomas Dixon's *Clansman*. For decades the critical emphasis on Griffith's early Civil War films was on the technical and historical issues of staging the battle scenes as precursors to *The Birth of a Nation*. Apart from the staging, even analyses of the contents of these films focused on them as antecedents to Confederate bravery as depicted in *Birth*. It is only more recently that critics have begun to examine the troubling images of cowardice and shame that emerge in these early films.[1] Susan Courtney has provided the most extensive analysis of the Civil War films in relation to fantasies of miscegenation as they threaten masculinity. Courtney explains that white male agony as presented in the earlier films is transferred to white female suffering in *The Birth of a Nation* (both as a response to the Civil War and at the hands of black men), while the phallic gaze, as "removed, omniscient, seeing but not seen," is associated with white male power, and the "look" is limited to black male desire or white female vulnerability (25). In her broader examination of various forms of cinematic miscegenation (not just black and white), in which white women appear "as tortured spectacles," Courtney compares Griffith's Biograph work as the backstory not only to *Birth* but to the "most classic miscegenation films of the silent era," Cecil B. De Mille's *The Cheat* (1915) and Griffith's *Broken Blossoms* (1919) (19). Clearly, fears of miscegenation pervade a larger national landscape; however—given the significance of the southern rape complex in articulating fears of miscegenation—geography, along with race and gender, is crucial especially because the southern setting continues to be used as a kind of shorthand that evokes fears of miscegenation, even when people of color are not presented as a threatening force. The present study therefore examines specifically how white southern abjection and defeat in the Civil War films is refigured as white southern valor and victory in *The Birth of a Nation* through the apparatus of the southern rape complex.

The southern rape complex serves as the most obvious solution to Confederate abjection offered in *The Clansman* and *The Birth of a Nation*, projecting abjection onto African Americans and then cleansing it through the sacrificial blood of the southern belle and refiguring the defeated Confederate as the victorious Klansman. Yet while both Griffith and Dixon employ the complex and the vigilante violence of the Ku Klux Klan in their efforts to rehabilitate the South, there are significant variations in how they lay the groundwork for the southern Klan "victory." These differences become apparent when we look at how Dixon and Griffith envision Confederate defeat and its negative consequences. In *The Clansman* Dixon mediates both Confederate abjection and its purification through politicized characters, while Griffith, in *The Birth of a Nation*, revises the very scenes of Confederate abjection that appear in his earlier Civil War films. These variations attest to the myriad problems of white postwar Confederate/U.S. identity and citizenship and the ways in which Griffith and Dixon use the drama and hysteria of racialized sexual violence to obfuscate them. Thus, the southern rape complex not only justifies violence in limiting the freedom of African Americans; it also masks white southerners' own problematic relationship to U.S. citizenship.

For Dixon the problem is that while a Confederate victory would create patriots of those who fought for the Confederate States of America (CSA), defeat reduces Confederates to the status of traitors against the U.S. government. In *The Clansman* Dixon presents southerners as abject but does so through the words of Austin Stoneman, a fictional version of Thaddeus Stevens, leader of the Radical Republicans, who is subsequently discredited in order to undercut or even remove the link between southerners and abjection.[2] The vigilantism of the Klan is furthermore presented as revitalizing southern masculinity and reasserting racial domination through the "second civil war" of Reconstruction, which, though it reestablishes white southern domination, does not speak to the all-important question of national patriotism. To tackle this issue, Dixon turns to Abraham Lincoln in an attempt to redefine the fallen Confederates as patriots, and he presents (through Lincoln) a national plan to expunge African Americans through forced colonization.[3] Thus, Dixon's solution does not rest on the Klan alone but uses Lincoln's words (out of context) to cleanse the fallen Confederates. At the same time *The Clansman* envisions a national project to "abjectify" African Americans not only through the act of lynching but through the contradictory call for colonization as a means both to eject African Americans from the nation and to use them as surrogates to colonize Latin America and Africa in the name of the United States of America.

Griffith, on the other hand, in his earlier Civil War films, presents a more devastating depiction of southern defeat, which he conflates with a cowardice that cannot be cleansed but only hidden or masked through the subterfuge of honor.[4] Two 1910 Civil War films in particular expose the abject Confederate body and the artifice of honor.[5] In *The Honor of His Family* the corpse of a Confederate deserter is literally posed on the battlefield to hide the family shame, while in *The House with Closed Shutters* the Confederate deserter is shut away for life, posing as his cross-dressing sister, who died taking his place on the battlefield. In both films the corpse of the fallen Confederate soldier threatens to destroy the family's name and sense of itself as southern and honorable, both of which are cornerstones of social identity. In *The Birth of a Nation,* well before the victorious ride of the Klan (as if to make possible even this problematic concept of southern heroism), Griffith reshoots these earlier scenes of cowardice in an effort to create an image of heroism in the face of defeat; however, to present southern victory, he must turn to the southern rape complex and the KKK.

LINCOLN: THE SOUTH'S BEST FRIEND

The project of *The Clansman* and subsequently *The Birth of a Nation* was to dramatize the revisionist historical accounts of Reconstruction (which depict the Confederates as patriots defending the Constitution and states' rights). Dixon did not invent the historical revision of Reconstruction disseminated by William A. Dunning's influential *Essays on the Civil War and Reconstruction* (1898), but Dixon's books and plays, and later Griffith's movie, helped to popularize "reconstructed Reconstruction" for a mass consumer audience far beyond the reach of any historian.[6] The greatest threat to southern identity in the novel is voiced by Austin Stoneman, whose description of the former Confederates exemplifies Julia Kristeva's theory of abjection. Drawing on anthropological theories of purity and pollution, Kristeva explains that in establishing an independent identity separate from the maternal body, we must begin to differentiate between "me" and "not me." This differentiation extends to bodily waste and fluids (including blood and corpses), which were once me but are now repellant and must be cast off or ritualistically contained. Because it was once me, the abject cannot be easily dismissed as the other; it is neither self nor other, and in this liminal position it has the power to unsettle identity and threaten boundaries.

Stoneman's scorn for the South is peppered with images of waste and pollution. Employing the very language and logic that slaveholders used to justify slavery, Stoneman negatively casts the former Confederates in the role of savages outside the communication of civilized society, thus justifying military control, seizure of lands, and disenfranchisement of white Confederate officers and politicians. Stoneman refers to the "so-called states" that "are now but conquered provinces" as "waste territories" that "are unfit to associate with civilized communities" (43). Stoneman's ultimate response to the South as "conquered soil" is "to blot it from the map" "by the extermination of its landed aristocracy, that their mothers shall not breed another race of traitors" (49, 50). Furthermore, Stoneman's condemnation of the white southerner extends backward in history, and he denounces the Constitution and the American flag as already corrupted by the southern influence of slavery. Dixon thus presents Stoneman as the actual traitor to the Union through his denunciation of the Constitution—a "creation, both in letter and spirit, of the slaveholders of the South," which created "a league with death and a covenant with hell'"—and the flag, which he refers to as "a polluted rag!" (42, 43).[7]

Applying Kristeva's theory of abjection to Stoneman's rhetoric, we see that he casts the white aristocratic southerner—"whose clothes smell of the blood of [his] kindred" and whose heart "has long ago rotted" from the "Satanic Institution of Slavery" that has "tainted the air"—as the abject (50, 53). The postwar Confederate is both American and not-American, part of the foundation of a democratic national identity yet part of an aristocratic slavocracy, a source of contagion and waste that must be cut out and exterminated. The South and slavery, therefore, are the sources of the pollution that threaten the principle of democracy upon which the nation is supposed to be founded. Dixon would no doubt be aware that Stoneman's repeated metaphors tying the South to the image of the rotting corpse would be especially inflammatory to a southern audience.

The unprecedented death toll of the Civil War triggered extreme apprehension about death and burial, while it also renewed interest in the relation of the physical body to the afterlife. Anxiety about burial was particularly acute in the South, given that the bodies of so many Confederate soldiers were unaccounted for.[8] To further add to the insult (from the perspective of the former slaveholders), Stoneman pronounces that only black rule and the equal distribution of property can contain the threat of the treasonous Confederates and purge the nation of the blight of slavery thrust upon the nation by the South (53). Dixon clearly presents these ideas as shocking to the southern reader and Stoneman as vengeful and overzealous, but later in the novel Dixon is also in the position of having to defend the very same ideas in relation to freedmen: the desire to purge them from the country (through colonization). The southern rape complex then becomes that defense, the one crucial difference between white northerners' accounts of the South and white southerners' accounts of African Americans that (in the logic of the novel) justifies the equally vengeful and overzealous retaliation against blacks.

To counter Stoneman's accusations, much of the energy of *The Clansman* (which is not fully conveyed in Griffith's movie) emanates from the rhetorical, not military, battles waged by various characters who try to defend former Confederates as loyal Americans and at the same time to justify their secession from the Union. To defend the South concerning secession, slavery, and the attitudes toward blacks, Dixon employs Lincoln as his spokesman for segregation and African American colonization. Dixon therefore stages the initial debate over the southern states between President Lincoln and Austin Stoneman, establishing the crucial stakes of the argument: the identity of the citizens of the southern states.

Dixon's invocation of President Lincoln as his chief spokesman for the South works on a number of levels. As the victorious defender of the Union, no one is in a better position than Lincoln to pardon and defend the former Confederates without seeming disloyal to the Union. As a fallen martyr, the president has taken on mythic qualities, so that to criticize him would border on sacrilege, but his death also ensures that his views on Reconstruction can only be speculated upon (though his early statements did focus on reuniting the nation). Both sides, therefore, can present his views as theirs, and Lincoln becomes the perfect all-purpose cultural signifier (Foner, *Fiery Trial* xv; Stokes 186–90).[9]

Even before the debate between Stoneman and Lincoln over the status of the South, Dixon positions Lincoln as the embodiment of an indissoluble Union, as both a northerner and as a true southerner. Just as racial status is assumed to be based on visual recognition, so too is geographical origin. When Mrs. Cameron goes to the "great heart" to plead for the life of her only remaining son, she "recognizes" Lincoln as a southerner "by [his] looks, [his] manner of speech, [his] easy, kindly ways, [his] tenderness and humor, [his] firmness in the right as [he] saw it, and above all, the way [he] rose and bowed to a woman in an old, faded black dress, whom [he] knew to be an enemy" (31). Lincoln confirms his southern heritage, explaining that his parents were Virginians and that he was born in Kentucky. Furthermore, at every turn in the debate with Stoneman, Lincoln establishes the mutual interdependence of North and South in all things both before and after the war. Although Lincoln condemns slavery, he asks, "Is not the North equally responsible for slavery?" He also takes responsibility for southern atrocities at the Andersonville prison, maintaining that the death of Union soldiers was the result of the North's refusal to exchange prisoners and their blockade of ports and seizure of medicine and food. History, he maintains, will bear this out, showing "as many deaths on our side as theirs." Lincoln even credits southerners for the actual preservation of the Union: "But for the loyalty of four border Southern states . . . who fought for the Union against their own flesh and blood, we should have lost" (47–48). As champion of the South, Lincoln maintain that the South is and always has been part of the United States and condemns blacks—not Confederates—as the true blight on the nation.

Negating the notion of the South as abject, Lincoln symbolically purifies the "rotted" heart of the South that Stoneman condemns, repatriates Confederate soldiers, and, from the "waste territories" of the South, unifies the nation. Disavowing Stoneman, Lincoln maintains that "we fought no war of conquest" and, therefore, the South cannot be a "'conquered province' for us to spoil" because "a nation cannot make conquest of it own territory." According to Lincoln, the war was one of "self-preservation as an indissoluble Union," and thus the southern states "must be immediately restored to their rights, or we shall betray the blood we have shed" (44). The South, therefore, cannot be abjected because it is and always has been part of the Union: the blood of "my kindred" is a pollutant only if the southern states are not restored. But Lincoln's speech goes on to redeem even the corpses, "the most sickening of wastes" (Kristeva 4), from abjection by magically reanimating them through the "mystic" power of memory.

Rather than reasserting the division between life and death, Lincoln's famous prewar inaugural address of 1861, which Dixon presents as a postwar speech, creates a living connection with the Civil War dead, thereby labeling all the dead, both Union and Confederates, as "patriots." As Kristeva explains, the corpse, when "seen without God and outside of science, is the utmost of abjection"; it is a "border that has encroached upon everything. It is no longer I who expel, 'I' is expelled." While bodily fluids and excrement can be abjected beyond the border of me and not-me, the corpse "is death infecting life. Abject . . . Imaginary uncanniness and real threat, it beckons to us and ends up engulfing us" (3, 4). Regarding his belief in "the honor of Lee and his people" to rejoin the Union, Lincoln declares that memory is the link that will reanimate the corpses in the grave, connecting the living and the dead: "The mystic chords of memory, stretching from every battlefield and patriot grave to every living heart and hearthstone all over this broad land, will yet swell the chorus of the Union, when touched again, as they surely will be, by the better angels of our nature" (53). All the Civil War dead are thus connected by the "chords of memory" to the flesh and blood of living hearts and thereby reunited and cleansed, as Lincoln's prewar plea to the South not to secede—based on a shared military history—becomes the postwar reanimation of the Union and an implicit confirmation of succession as an act of patriotism, not treason. But in "cleansing" the Confederate dead, Lincoln has not gotten rid of the "true" threat of abjection. Ultimately, according to Dixon's Lincoln, it is "the Negro" (not the CSA) who is responsible for "the desolation of ten great states, and rivers of blood" (46), which can only be sanctified through the North-South reunion and the expulsion of African Americans.

Lincoln's assassination, of course, preempted his final decision on Reconstruction; however, taking Lincoln's words out of their historical context, Dixon uses Lincoln's rhetoric against slavery, both before and during the war, to create his own postwar rhetoric of Reconstruction against African Americans. Weaving passages from Lincoln's speeches—especially his references to colonization of freedmen—with his own prose, Dixon lays the groundwork for his narrative justification for colonizing blacks within the country, as he sets them apart from the white population and reimagines them as both American and not-American, as colonial subjects within their own country. Referring to a speech Lincoln made in 1858 during his bid for the Senate—in which he proposed that the former slaves should be colonized—Dixon posits Lincoln as the force behind the postwar desire to "expel" blacks from America because their "assimilation is neither possible nor desirable" (47). Dixon is therefore able to incorporate elements from earlier speeches to demonstrate Lincoln's racial prejudice and his belief that "there is a physical difference between the white and black races which will forever forbid their living together on terms of social and political equality. If such be attempted one must go to the wall" (45). Furthermore, by adding to Lincoln's 1858 condemnation of slavery—"a house divided against itself will not stand. I believe this government cannot endure permanently half slave and half free . . . It will become all one thing, or all the other"—Dixon turns it into a postwar call for colonization: "The Nation cannot now exist half white and half black, any more than it could exist half slave and half free" (47).

It is true that Lincoln sought colonization as a political solution to emancipation—even including money for colonization in the first draft of the Emancipation Proclamation and promoting two attempts at colonization, which were failures. Congress rescinded the monies pledged for voluntary colonization, and Lincoln arranged for the last of the "colonists" to return home. Most historians agree that the Emancipation Proclamation and the use of African American Union troops effectively ended any serious consideration of a large-scale colonization plan and that by war's end colonization had been abandoned.[10] Furthermore, in his earlier support for the plan, Lincoln was consistent in his rejection of the kind of forced emigration that Dixon's Lincoln advocates.[11] Dixon, however, transforms black troops into colonists, substituting rifles for shovels.

Dixon justifies colonization by acknowledging and then undermining Lincoln's progressive stances on African American military service and voting rights. Although Lincoln "suggested to Governor Hahn of Louisiana to consider the policy of admitting [suffrage to] the more intelligent [African Americans] and those who served in the war," Dixon emphasizes that it was *only* a suggestion and one that would be made individually by each state because "the state alone has the power to confer the ballot" (44). Further acknowledging that arming African American troops during the war did not result in calamity, Dixon's Lincoln adds that "no more insane blunder could now be made than any further attempt to use these Negro troops. There can be no such thing as restoring this Union to its basis of fraternal peace with armed negroes, wearing the uniform of this nation, tramping over the South, and rousing the basest passions of the freemen and their former masters." Instead, Dixon's Lincoln maintains that at his request "General Butler, their old commander, is now making plans for their removal" in order "to dig the Panama Canal with these black troops" (45). Regardless of the success of African American troops or the possibility of black suffrage, Dixon's Lincoln maintains that his postwar plan includes colonization of the "negroes," which he "shall continue until it is accomplished" (46).

Dixon's Lincoln's plans for colonization propose an extremely complicated relationship that African Americans are to play with respect to American imperialism: "Within twenty years, we can peacefully colonize the Negro in the tropics, and give him our language, literature, religion, and system of government under conditions in which he can rise to the full measure of manhood. This he can never do here. It was the fear of the black tragedy behind emancipation that led the South into the insanity of secession" (47). Unfit to live with white Americans because of their inherent inferiority, African Americans are now pictured as functioning in the dual role of colonizer and colonist, spreading the very language, literature, religion, and system of government that they supposedly could never attain. The actual plans to send blacks to Haiti demonstrate the same logic. Those in charge of the Haiti scheme treated African Americans as both "native" laborers and as cultural colonizers who could solidify an American stronghold in Central America. Rather than having to rely on actual native workers, the plan was to export U.S. workers who were superior because they spoke English and were used to hard work. African Americans in Haiti would thus serve both as workers and as compradors for white America's imperialist enterprises.[12]

Historically, colonization was never feasible, financially or logistically, not to mention the fact that the agrarian South was still dependent on a large labor force, the majority of whose members were black. Dixon's impassioned call for colonization in 1905 was even less realistic, but rhetorically its import was to cast African Americans, not former Confederates, in the role of both the colonized and the foreigner, to see them as totally different yet familiar.[13] During slavery the me/not-me dichotomy that African Americans disrupted could be contained by their legal status as property, which set them on the side of not-me, not a person. Even though slaves were absolutely essential to the South, were the core of "the way of life" that Dixon argues must be maintained, and many were actually related to whites, the importance of their place in the South could be ignored. After the war the me/not-me became much more threatening to whites now that slavery no longer maintained the legal barriers to kinship, thus paving the way for African Americans to gain full citizenship and legal standing. Colonization offered Dixon a way to reimage that uncanny similarity, turning it into a profitable yet remote "me-over-there-but-not-here" (African Americans as surrogate colonists) while maintaining "me" as white U.S. citizens. At a comfortable distance Dixon can imagine the "full manhood" of the black man. Through the slave trade Americans created an internal colonization of an African diasporic population; post–Civil War white Americans could now export the former slaves (now Americanized) back to Africa and/or Haiti to engage more fully in their own colonialist incursions into Africa and Central and Latin America.

Lincoln's death, in Dixon's version, meant the death of colonization, and the "blood" of the South that Lincoln had symbolically purified was once again in danger of pollution, this time in the form of the "Black Empire," which Dixon associates with disease—the "body of the Black Death"—and poison, the "black broth" that Stoneman is "pressing to their lips" (319). Although Stoneman champions racial equality, Dixon maintains that, even to northern Radical Republicans, African Americans are a source of pollution: "The Negro will never be treated as an equal in the North. We are simply a set of cold-blooded liars on that subject, and always have been. To the Yankee the very physical touch of a Negro is pollution" (324).

COWARDICE AND CROSS-DRESSING

Dixon invokes President Lincoln to cleanse the abject Confederate corpse and to reanimate it as an American patriot as well as to propose African American colonization as a way to rid the nation of the "true" source of abjection. Griffith, on the other hand, who directed ten Civil War films before *Birth*, had difficulty depicting the Confederate soldier as heroic in the face of southern defeat in these early films.[14] Several of them (*The Honor of His Family* [1910], *The House with Closed Shutters* [1910], and *Hearts and Swords* [1911]), rather than elevating the Confederate dead or defeated, highlight their abjection by exposing the masquerade of honor necessary to conceal their cowardice. Unlike Gus in *The Birth of a Nation*, it is not the newly freed slaves who pose the threat to the war or its aftermath in these early Griffith films. In fact, it is often the faithful servant who both during and after the war must carry on to protect the former master's plantation and/or his family, as in *His Trust* (1911) and *His Trust Fulfilled* (1911).[15] Indeed, it is the cowardly southern "aristocrat"—the Confederate officer and the fickle southern belle—who puts the Cause at greatest risk. The aristocratic soldier is threatened with emasculation through cowardice (*The Honor of His Family*) and/or drunkenness (*The House with Closed Shutters*) and is either tempted from his station by the flirtatious belle (*Hearts and Swords*) or in its most extreme form utterly replaced by the cross-dressing belle who must fight in his stead (*The House with Closed Shutters*).[16]

These early Civil War films reveal a great deal of ambiguity about the war, as evidenced by their focus on border states as a liminal space for acting out divided loyalties between North and South, within families and friends divided by the war, and between those fighting the war and those who witnessed it from their homes. The nineteenth-century ideal of the home as a sanctuary from the world and the center of family devotion is in one sense violated in the films because of the proximity of the battlefield to the home: the war literally enters the home. The civilizing aspects of the home still hold true, however, when an enemy soldier enters a home and a kind of truce is made possible by the humanity of the women living there. Although enemy soldiers entering a private home would seem to be the most fearful image of the horrors of war (as it will be dramatized in *The Birth of a Nation*), in Griffith's early films this violation is the setting for mercy and forgiveness and suggests the possibility of reconciliation after the war. In *The Fugitive* (1910), for example, a Confederate mother gives a Union soldier sanctuary in her home, even though he killed her own son in battle. Although she almost turns him in when Confederate soldiers come to look for him, she thinks of the northern mother's loss and spares him. At war's end the Union soldier returns to his own home and to his mother and his sweetheart, who are waiting for him.

The most positive outcome for an enemy soldier who is seeking asylum, however, occurs in *In the Border States* (1910). A young northern girl hides a

Confederate soldier in the family's well when Union soldiers come searching for him. After sparing him, she acknowledges his enemy status by refusing a kiss and ordering him to leave, thus demonstrating that she has spared him out of compassion, not ignorance of who he is or out of disloyalty to the Union. Later her own father, a Union soldier who was sent behind enemy lines to deliver a message, is chased by Confederates and is forced to return home and to destroy the letter before it falls into the hands of the enemy. The Confederate soldier comes back to the house and discovers the father, but because of the Confederate's debt to the daughter, he spares the father. Although war has entered the home, the home is still a sanctuary to both men, and they both benefit from the daughter's mercy. Furthermore, it is made clear that the Union father is not running away out of cowardice; he is given the alternative motive of preventing the message from falling into enemy hands.

The greatest threat to the moral sanctity of the home occurs when deserting soldiers forsake their duty and return to their own homes to escape the battlefield; instead of compassion, these soldiers are met with derision. In *The Battle* (1911) a Union soldier flees home from the theater of war only to be laughed at by his fiancée, who earlier in the film cheered him as he left for battle. The Union soldier is given a second chance, however, when his commanding officer comes to the house looking for deserters. The soldier leaves through the window, accidently rejoins his outfit, and serves bravely in battle. There is, conversely, no mercy or even a second chance for the Confederate soldier who returns to his own home. He, not the enemy, is seen as threatening the sanctity of the home.

In order to explain how Griffith transforms the scenes of Confederate cowardice in the early Civil War movies into scenes of heroism and honor in *Birth*, I will discuss at some length the salient filmic aspects of these early films: *The House with Closed Shutters*, *The Honor of His Family*, and *Hearts and Swords*. These films include the proximity of home and battlefield, the Confederate soldier's dereliction of duty in returning home, and the use of the Confederate point of view on the battlefield as a trope for fear, all of which will be eschewed in *Birth*. Of the three films *The Honor of His Family* provides the most extreme example of, and reaction to, southern "aristocratic" cowardice and the use of revisionist history to preserve the sullied "family honor."

In these early Civil War films a direct, head-on view of battle and the Union soldiers advancing through the smoke of gunfire becomes a trope that is associated with fear in Confederate fighters, and this shot precedes the scenes in which the soldiers flee. In *The Honor of His Family* the first cut to the battle, after the son is joyously sent off to war by friends and family, uses this point of view of the Confederate soldiers. As the Union guns fire, the son, forgetting his father's edict to "emulate those gone before you" and to "be fearless and fight," flees from the battlefield. The intertitle accompanying this scene reads simply: "The Coward."

Because of the proximity of war and home, the southern father can see the smoke of the battle as he watches through binoculars from his parlor window. The shot of the father watching is crosscut with shots of the battle and the son's subsequent escape in such a way that it seems as if the father sees the battle from the son's point of view. This deployment of point of view is unusual because of the father's distance from the scene of battle, but the technique affords Griffith the opportunity to integrate the father's values into the unfolding events in a powerful manner. As Joyce E. Jesionowski explains, the film returns to the shot of the father nine times in twenty-five shots and thereby creates the father's image as "both a point of spatial reference and the location of the affective activity in the film" (118). When a sight line is added to the crosscutting, as it is in *The Honor of His Family*, the connection between shots is even more powerful, "almost as if the concentration of attention in the look were powerful enough to draw the person being thought of back to the thinker," suggesting that the father's perceptions control "the line of activity in the world of the film just as strongly as does the war in which the soldier is fighting" (118, 162). This use of crosscutting from a static scene, usually a family "icon," creates an "Infra-film history." The subsequent activity either develops from the "spatial relationship" to this scene, or it becomes the "point of stability in the midst of constructed activity" (161).

Even as the intertitles support the father's view of the situation, there are significant elements in the film that undermine his position because the father is not the only source of "affective activity." Although the audience members are in the position of a passive spectator, like the father, they also face the gunfire of the Yankee troops. The audience can "see" what terrifies the son and might therefore have more sympathy for him when he flees the battlefield to find sanctuary in his own home, falls to his knees, and begs his father to save him. After rejecting the son's pleas, the father leaves the room, and when he returns, he pats his son on the head as though he will help him. The son's relief and gratitude is very short-lived, however, as the father takes a gun from behind his back and shoots his son. The father is triumphant as he takes his son's hand, and the dying son smiles at him and nods his head, possibly as a sign of forgiveness for his father's actions. Even if the son forgives or even agrees with his father's action, the pathos of the son's performance, combined with the father's unforgiving stance, create the potential for an alternative affective response from the audience: horror and disgust that a father would kill his own son in the name of honor. This sentiment was expressed by one critic, who wrote at the time of the film's release, "There is much to criticize besides the picturing of an actual murder—particularly the murder of a son by his father" (Simmon 170). The intertitle preceding this scene is again from the father's perspective—"That the Family's Honor may remain unsullied"—which seems to justify the father's actions, while the word *unsullied* points to the son's abjection, which threatens to pollute the entire family. The father, with the help of a black servant, takes the corpse back to the battlefield and, to perfect the charade, poses him with a sword in his hand facing the now-absent enemy. The corpse becomes the facade that props up the family honor and thereby actively incorporates abjection into the meaning of honor. The father's willingness to kill his own son to protect his "good" name is hypocritical at best, and thus the Confederate family in the film is discredited on all fronts.

Because the father's sight line does appear to connect him to the son's point of view, his actions seem all the more heartless and indefensible. Furthermore, the father's continual drinking and toasting to his absent son, even as the son faces death, also makes him a suspect character, as excessive drinking is a trope for weakness in Griffith's films (Silverman 23–30). And finally, as Scott Simmon points out, when the father leads the Confederate officers to the battlefield to prove that his son is not a deserter, two of the Confederate soldiers look at each other and smirk in reaction to the father's proof of his son's bravery, suggesting that they know that the son was not in the battle. The father has thus killed his son in vain, and his act of filicide—even more than the son's desertion—has destroyed the family's honor (169).

Throughout *The Honor of His Family* the black slave/valet serves as a witness to the events of war at each stage. In the beginning of the film it is the slave's gaze, as he stands looking out the door, that announces the arrival of the son, in his new uniform. Later, when the son has gone to war, the father turns repeatedly to the slaves as he toasts his son, as if he needs a witness to confirm the validity of his pride. The black slave, however, is ultimately witness to the guilty secret of the family, and as such, he is directly tied to the threat that abjection poses. Tellingly, at the end of the film, as the father slumps over in tears, the slave takes and pats the father's hand. But this is the same gesture that the father used after killing his son. It is not clear from this gesture if the slave is consoling the father or signaling his defeat and dishonor. After the war the former slaves, now freedmen, also have power to expose the rotting corpse for what it is and thus threaten white domination and the legibility of the corpse. *The Honor of His Family* could be interpreted as a more general indictment of the lengths some southerners were willing to go to (fighting a war and sacrificing their sons) in the name of honor.

In *The House with Closed Shutters* the slave's role in the family's dishonor is even more pronounced. He not only witnesses but also helps to perpetuate the Confederate soldier's humiliation, which extends twenty-five years after the war's end and creates a "living death" for the Confederate deserter. As in *The Honor of His Family,* the film begins with the celebration of the troop's departure to war as Agnes bids farewell to her brother, Charles, and his two friends, who are also her suitors. Agnes begins the film as a typical belle, as signaled by her white dress with layers of ruffles and her flirtation with her two suitors. Her efforts in support of the war are appropriately feminine: she proudly displays the Confederate flag she has sewn and cuts a lock of her hair for her suitor to take to war as a token of her love. But when her brother (proclaimed in the intertitle as a "A Drink-Mad Coward") returns home from the war drunk, these symbols of femininity are reversed, and Agnes, with the help of the family slave, dons her brother's uniform, cuts her hair, finishes her brother's mission, and "rescues" the fallen Confederate flag from the battlefield.[17] As the intertitle explains, "The girl goes in her brother's place to preserve the family's honor."

As she rides off on her brother's horse, Agnes is chased by the same Union soldiers who pursued her brother, but she manages to elude them, demonstrating her expert horsemanship in the process. After delivering the message from Robert E. Lee with which her brother had been entrusted, as she skillfully reins in her rearing horse, she heads off to the battlefield.[18] When Agnes reaches the battle and loses her horse, Griffith again employs the trope of the direct shot of the battlefield (fig. 1.1). As the Union soldiers advance, Agnes, too, responds in fear and starts to run away, but when she sees the Confederate

FIG. 1.1. Shot of Union soldiers advancing. *The House with Closed Shutters* (1910).

flag, she rushes into the battlefield, picks it up, and—still clutching the flag—is shot. The flag, like the cutting of her hair, indicates a gender reversal from her "proper" feminine role; instead of sewing the flag, she dies defending it.

The title of the film refers to the brother's subsequent seclusion after his mother commands him to "stay here forever for the good of the family name that the world may not know [his] sister died protecting a coward." As in *The Honor of His Family,* family honor is associated with deception and masquerade. The drink-mad coward, now dressed in his bathrobe after losing his uniform, must masquerade as the grief-mad sister, whose extreme devotion to her brother's memory keeps her from marrying. The mother and slave are left to hide the son's cowardice by closing the external and internal shutters so that no one will learn their secret shame. After the intertitle "25 years later," a now gray-haired brother, still drinking, opens the shutters and with hysterical gestures calls out to his sister's former suitors (who still leave flowers at the door as a tribute to Agnes) and then dies; the secret is finally revealed.

The ending enacts a double masquerade, which suggests other family secrets that must not see the light of day. The family's "cover story" implies a kind of debilitating incest in which the sister's extreme attachment to her brother prevents her from entering into a heterosexual marriage. The "sister" breaks her lovers' heart not because she is the stereotypical fickle and flirtatious southern belle but because she is in mourning over her war hero brother. Her extreme loyalty to the "Lost Cause," as symbolized by her grief, leaves the true war heroes, her suitors, alone and pining for their lost love. This closed circuit of loss and grief does not allow for recovery from the war, as does the North-South intermarriage in *The Birth of a Nation.* The house with closed shutters thus becomes a symbol of a claustrophobic and static South that defines its grief and its loyalty to the cause in a refusal to recover from the Civil War.

The brother's masquerade as the southern belle further invokes the infamous story—capitalized on in political cartoons—that Jefferson Davis, in order to evade capture at the end of the war, put on his wife's clothing and fled (Silber 29–38). Unlike the idealized version of Lincoln as a true southerner and "friend to the South," as the intertitle in *The Birth of a Nation* proclaims, Davis as the vanquished president is not only defeated, but like Charles, he is humiliated through his own act of cowardice.[19] But cross-dressing suggests another family secret. Because cross-dressing was associated with negative stereotypes projected onto homosexuality—which include effeminacy and cowardice—the son's sexual orientation, as well as his masculinity, are called into question. In assuming the role of his sister, Charles seems to take on her desire, just as she put on his uniform and took on his military duties. The first time the suitors arrive after the war, Charles throws open the shutters as if to receive them, but his mother throws a shawl over him, pretending he was the distraught sister. In his second attempt, when Charles opens the shutters, his mother and the (now free) black servant try to stop him. The scene cuts to an exterior shot of the suitors, in which only Charles's arms appear as he gestures out the window, calling to the soldiers. This time the suitors clearly see him, and when they rush into the house, the mother must admit the truth. In this way the brother's throwing open of the shutter and revealing his identity to the suitors takes on a double meaning, as does the symbolism of the house with closed shutters. In either case the son opens the shutters—comes out of the closet—to reveal his "shameful" secret, not only that he fled the battle but that his sister died in his place and he died taking her place as the suitors' lost love.

The mother, though she does not kill her son, as in *The Honor of His Family,* in effect buries him alive to "preserve the family's honor." The living corpse is precisely the "in-between, the ambiguous, the composite," of abjection that threatens "borders, system, order" (Kristeva 4). In relation to both films the abjection displayed by the sons that threatens family honor/identity is reinscribed by the parents' masquerade of honor, which is a simultaneous masquerade of the corpse. Beyond, or in addition to, the corpse's ability to "show me what I permanently thrust aside in order to live" (Kristeva 3), the corpses in these two cases demonstrate further what must be thrust aside (cowardice, dissipation, gender confusion) and therefore what threatens social boundaries of southernness in the films: the corpses are at the border of life/death, honor/dishonor, masculine/feminine, and heterosexuality/homosexuality and threaten the boundaries that preserve these distinctions.

Although Agnes is heroic, her actions are a direct threat to her brother's masculinity and doom him to a life of seclusion. She literally de-pants him (with the help of the slave), and her heroic death forces him to continue to masquerade as a now-unstable southern belle, while Agnes's status as heroine is predicated on her destroying the visual signs of her status as a southern belle (her clothes and her long hair).[20] The southern belle plays an even more dubious role in many of these pre-*Birth* films. In *Hearts and Swords* it is the belle, not cowardice, that distracts the aristocratic officer from his duty, while the lower-class white woman and the black slave must take on the duties of the derelict soldier. The belle in *Hearts and Swords*, Irene Lambert, is introduced from the beginning as "beautiful but calculating," and part of that calculation is based on using her skills as a belle to marry on the winning side of the war. Standing outside her home in the characteristic frilly white dress, she shakes hands with a northern soldier, who rolls his eyes in the direction of the camera as he turns his back on Irene and exits from the scene, suggesting that even the Union officer sees her as manipulative. The full impact of this scene is made clear when Irene later promises Hugh Frazier, the "son of a wealthy tobacco plantation" who is about to go to war, that they "shall marry when [he] return[s] victorious." Although the title reads, "when you return victorious," the implication is that Irene really means, "*if* you return victorious."

Juxtaposed against the treacherous belle is the humble and loving Jennie Baker, who is initially designated as "of the poor white class." At the moment Hugh asks Irene to "promise [him she] will be [his]," Jennie and her father interrupt to ask directions to Hugh's house, where they sell their fruit. Hugh's kindness to the pair is set against Irene's look of annoyance, which is further contrasted to Jennie's look of longing at Hugh in the next scene. Hugh's attachment to the traitorous Irene leads him to abandon his post and to put his men in jeopardy, as he leaves "to steal a visit with Irene." But this act also gives Jennie her "chance to prove her love," which leads to another act of cross-dressing.

In this version of cross-dressing Hugh is not stripped of his uniform in the same way that Charles is, nor does Hugh run from battle, as does the son in *The Honor of His Family*. Nevertheless, the belle is associated with Hugh's abandonment of his duty, while the lower-class woman shows her loyalty to the South and to her man. Jennie sees that Yankees have followed Hugh to Irene's, and instead of going inside to warn him, Jennie puts on his coat and hat, takes his horse, and goes after the enemy soldiers. The Yankees spot Jennie, and a chase scene ensues, as in *The House with Closed Shutters*. While Agnes had only her horse and her heroism, Jennie, the lower-class woman, also has a gun; shots are exchanged, and Jennie kills a soldier, but she is also wounded. Jennie is played by Dorothy West, who also played Agnes in *The House with Closed Shutters*, and in both films her horsemanship contributes to her prowess and her ability not just to "pass" as a Confederate soldier but to outdo her male counterpart, hinting that if women had fought for the South, they might not have lost the war.

It is not, however, only the lower-class female who must assume the duty of the negligent southern officer. As is often the case in Griffith's films, the loyal slave watches over the family for the master. While Hugh visits Irene, he not only puts his men in danger; he is also unaware of the danger to his own home by "bushwhackers." As Jennie rides to save the South, Old Ben acts to save the family. As the intertitle explains, "Old Ben anticipates the bushwhackers' attack" and removes the family strong box and buries it in the woods. The bushwhackers next set fire to the house, and Ben must rescue the father trapped inside. In the next scene, now that Hugh has lost his house and the war, Irene takes up with the Union officer. The intertitle explains, "Defeated in War rejected in love." It is Old Ben who brings about the happy ending by returning the money box to Hugh and by telling him of Jennie's heroics.

In these movies the black slaves have aided in their masters' emasculation (in *The House with Closed Shutters* it is the black slave who actually takes off the Confederate uniform), but always at the behest of either the master or the mistress. *Hearts and Swords* is one of the few films in which the slave, unbeknownst to the master, steps in and heroically saves the family (their lives and their wealth). This should, given the racist logic of the films, suggest an even more devastating form of usurpation. Hugh's role as soldier is taken, as was Charles's in *The House with Closed Shutters*, yet Hugh is able to regain his money, status, and manhood and acquire a bride. Ostensibly, because Hugh's dereliction of duty was based on love, not cowardice, he is not emasculated in the same way Charles was, and the movie's ending indicates that marrying Jeannie will not lower Hugh's status but raise hers.

Yet there is another reason that Hugh is not emasculated, which points to how race will be used in *The Birth of a Nation*. When Hugh learns of Jennie's bravery, she is hoeing in the fields, and the intertitle reads, "Hugh realizes her loyalty and her worth." Before Hugh embraces Jennie, he takes the hoe from her hand and shakes his head as if to indicate that manual labor is no longer appropriate for her now that she will be his wife; thereupon, he hands the hoe to Ben. Despite the war's end and the fact that Ben has also shown his loyalty and worth, the film's happy ending—while suspending class distinction between whites in the face of loyalty and heroism—maintains racial distinctions.

If Old Ben were granted full subjectivity and citizenship, then the film would have to acknowledge that he, not Hugh, acted as "master" of the plantation. Old Ben's role is similar to that of Freud's definition of the fetish: Old Ben enables Hugh's disavowal of his own emasculating weakness, allowing him to retain his status as a potent patriarch, without ever acknowledging his failure or Ben's help. Furthermore, Ben's postwar subordination covers over Jennie's (class) inadequacies, making Jennie "white" instead of "poor white" and therefore an acceptable sexual object and marriage partner. Old Ben, like the asexual mammy figure, is what makes the white upper-class home possible. Through marriage Jennie gains the plantation, but Ben receives only a hoe, a subordinated form of the phallus linked to his value as a laborer. The scene not only reinforces Ben's role as slave after the Civil War; it actually demotes him to the status of field slave rather than house slave, suggesting that after the war blacks are only good for hard manual labor. Jennie's class mobility and new role as "mistress" rest on the assumption that there are other black hands that will be pressed to take the hoe and do the work of running the plantation, that is, that white domination over a black underclass will continue after the war. Thus, *Hearts and Swords* uses racial subordination to shore up white status and uses marriage to remove class distinctions from white racial purity. The fickle, castrating belle is replaced by the poor but honest lower-class woman, and the black man is judged by the color of his skin, not the content of his character. But the suggested intermarriage of southern belle and northern officer is still read as a sign of the belle's disloyalty to the South as well as to her southern lover.

The "problems" that the pre–*Birth* Civil War films present are how to expunge from the story of the Civil War the flighty and/or fickle southern belle, the cowardly Confederate soldier, and the "loyal" black slave as a witness to the degradation of southern white elites. The answer is, of course, *The Birth of a Nation*. Griffith creates this transformation through the separation of home and battlefield; the elimination of the Confederate point of view of the approaching Union soldiers; the self-destruction of the belle and the effeminate younger brother; the sexualization of postwar African Americans; the replacement of both the compassion and the bravery of southern women in the figure of the heroic Confederate officer; and finally, through the victorious southern white Klansman.

THE BIRTH OF A NATION

What the early films suggest is that Griffith's initial anxiety was not solely about issues of race but about the shame of southern defeat, which Griffith localized in the image of the effete and cowardly southern aristocrat.[21] This anxiety may help to explain why he would turn to Thomas Dixon's overtly racist Reconstruction romance as the basis for one of his most ambitious cinematic projects. Dixon's play *The Clansman*, and the novels on which it is based, gave Griffith a way to restore the "proper" gender assignments and to transform the scenes of shame and cowardice portrayed in the earlier Civil War films into a depiction of the southern aristocrat, not only as brave in the face of defeat but also as victorious in his battle against Reconstruction. At the same time it allowed Griffith to transfer the signs of abjection—betrayal, fear, cowardice, and drunkenness—onto the black characters under the influence of the northern Radical Republicans. The most positive elements of the southern belle, on the other hand, were transferred onto the northern women, while the budding, yet often hysterical, belle was sacrificed as a martyr of Reconstruction by leaping to her death. *The Birth of a Nation* allows Griffith, like the father in *The Honor of His Family*, to use revisionist history to re-create the southern aristocrat as hero of Reconstruction, even if it must be under the cover of a white sheet.

In discussing his inspiration for *Birth*, Griffith told a reporter: "About the first thing I remember was my father's sword . . . As I started the book [*The Clansman*], stronger and stronger came to my mind the traditions I had learned as a child, all that my father had told me. The sword I told you about became a flashing vision. Gradually came back to my memory the stories a cousin, one Thurston Griffith, had told me of the Ku Klux Klan" (qtd. in Rogin 275). With the help of Dixon, therefore, Griffith is able to put the sword into the hand of the "Little Colonel" (not the lifeless corpse of the Confederate deserter in *The Honor of His Family*) and have him wave it triumphantly as he charges against the Union troops, outnumbered but not out*manned*. Finally, in the Klan's ride to the rescue, the Little Colonel is depicted not just as brave but, more important, as victorious.

Henry B. Walthall, as Ben Cameron (the Little Colonel), is the perfect choice for this transformation of the Confederate deserter into Civil War hero and then into triumphant Klan member for a number of reasons. Walthall was born in Alabama and served in the Spanish-American War for the First Alabama Regiment, and his father was a captain in the Confederate army, so, like Griffith, he had ties to the South and to the Confederate army. Even more significantly, Walthall played the Confederate soldier who flees home not only in *The House with Closed Shutters* and *The Honor of His Family* but also in *In Old Kentucky*. If Walthall's character in *The House with Closed Shutters* metaphorically hides behind his sister's skirts, in *In Old Kentucky*—in an act that Tom Gunning describes as "verging on incest" (143)—he literally hides under the covers in his mother's bed (while she is still in it), and it is the mother who draws her gun to prevent his Union brother from drawing back the covers. In this film the Confederate son is not shot or condemned, but his survival is predicated on his mother's courage, not his own, and when he returns home in defeat and in tatters at war's end, his homecoming is predicated on his Union brother's magnanimity. Therefore, using Walthall in *The Birth of a Nation* literally allowed Griffith to reshoot the earlier scenes of cowardice.

The scene in which Walthall, as Ben Cameron, displays his courage in *The Birth of a Nation* is one of the most elaborate battle scenes of the film. Unlike Dixon's *Clansman*, which begins with the ending of the Civil War, Griffith devotes the first half of *The Birth of a Nation* to the events leading up to the Civil War and the subsequent spectacular battle scenes. In *The Clansman* Ben Cameron's heroic battle scene is only briefly recounted by the army surgeon, as Ben lies wounded in the hospital (7–8). While *The Birth of a Nation* uses many of the same elements of the battle, as recounted by the surgeon, the two-page account of the battle is turned into an extended scene sequence featuring Ben's heroism and his humanity.

As if to facilitate the transformation of the Confederate soldier from deserter to hero, there are two important differences regarding setting and camera work in this scene from the earlier Civil War films. The setting of the battle takes place away from the Cameron home, thus eliminating the possibility of a cowardly flight home or family assistance/interference. In direct contrast to the action of the battle, the few crosscuts from the battle back to the family present a static tableau of the family praying, as if to suggest that prayer is the only aid they can give their son. This is unlike the waiting family members in the earlier Civil War film that end up usurping their son's role as soldier. The patient suffering of the Cameron family and the sense of claustrophobia in this tight tableau parallel the later series of similar family tableaux of "helpless whites" during Reconstruction, when the blacks have taken over the town.

The other significant difference between *The Birth of a Nation* and the earlier films centers on camera placement. To present the Little Colonel as valiant in defeat, Griffith takes a more oblique view of the war. Instead of the straight-on shot of the battle from the direct perspective of the Confederate soldier facing the enemy—which functions as a trope for fear (as was true in many of the early Civil War films)—the battles in *The Birth of a Nation* are typically shot either from the side, positioning the Union soldiers on the right and the Confederate soldiers on the left, or from a great distance, which allows for greater emotional detachment. The shots of the battle that are straight on depict not the approaching Union army but the Little Colonel as he advances on the Union troops. The camera thus either looks back at the Confederate soldiers advancing or views the battles from the side. The blasts from the Union artillery are clearly shown, but not from the eye-level perspective of the Confederate soldiers on the front lines. It is almost as if, to present the Confederates as heroic, Griffith had to remove the fear engendered by the direct shot of oncoming Union soldiers and the temptation to flee home that plagued the Confederate cowards in the earlier films.

While the battle in *The Birth of a Nation* shares many elements with Griffith's earlier battle scenes, the one it seems to parallel most closely is the heroic scene in *The House with Closed Shutters*, in which the sister saves the Confederate flag, except that the gender is now reversed. In both films there is a crucial dispatch from Robert E. Lee, a heroic effort to save the Confederate flag, a storming of the barricade to charge against the Union soldiers, and a wounding of the hero/ine. But with each similarity comes a salient distinction.

The urgency of the mission in both films is predicated on the import of Lee's orders. Yet while the content of Lee's message is unknown in *The House with Closed Shutters* and Charles is the messenger, in *The Birth of a Nation* we know the content and the message is delivered to, not carried by, the Little Colonel. Ben's attack is not just a brash move against all odds, as in *The Clansman;* it is part of a strategy to break through enemy lines to rescue a stranded and much-needed food wagon. Therefore, Ben fights not only for the Confederacy in the face of impending defeat but also more practically to secure food for his men, who in the "Last Gray Days of the Confederacy" are reduced to eating parched corn, as the intertitle explains.

Amid the side and extreme long shots of the battle, a series of medium and long shots single Ben out for his courage, as he either turns his face toward the camera or as the camera is placed directly in front of him. After receiving his orders, Ben rallies his troops, and although we view the Confederate entrenchment from the side and from a slight high angle, as Ben leaves the barricade in a medium shot, he faces the camera, and his image is centered and foregrounded. This scene mirrors the shot of Agnes as she stands behind the battle line, except that she wears a look of fear as she turns to face the camera, just as she is about to flee the battle. Ben, on the other hand, after facing the camera, is centered in a long shot holding his sword high in the air as he leads the attack. As both sides engage in the battle, the scene cuts to a high-angle moving shot with the camera leading, as Ben, again in the foreground medium shot, charges into battle (fig. 1.2). This shot, not seen in the earlier Civil War films, creates a sense of power, ferocity, and authority, and it is duplicated later in the moving shot of Ben leading the Klan in the ride to the rescue. In the Klan scene, however, Ben is finally able to show his prowess on horseback—as the female cross-dressers have already done—but rather than being chased, he is leading the chase.

In addition to his prowess as a leader, Ben is also singled out in a series of medium close and medium long shots as bestowing mercy, an act that in the earlier films was the purview of the women. Therefore, without cross-dressing he can adopt the feminine position in the most masculine of settings. As the battle continues, the Confederates take over two lines of Union entrenchments but are hopelessly outnumbered. Before the last charge, however, the Little Colonel stops mid-battle to give a fallen Union soldier a drink of water. The title reads, "All hope gone, 'the little Colonel' pauses to succor a fallen

FIG. 1.2. Ben Cameron charging into battle. *The Birth of a Nation* (1915).

foe," and again the camera is positioned in front of Ben as he dodges Union bullets to help a Union soldier. As the Union soldiers cheer, Phil Stoneman, Ben's old friend, calls for a cease-fire; thus, even before the romantic reconciliation of the ending, Ben lays the groundwork for a military reconciliation in which even enemy soldiers can show respect for one another.

Later, in the most dramatic straight-on shot of Cameron and one that rewrites *The House with Closed Shutters*, Ben, in a last act of defiance, plants the Confederate flag into the mouth of the cannon as if to stop its firing and to claim the final entrenchment. Moments earlier, when Ben sees the flag bearer fall, he drops his sword, not out of defeat but to pick up the flag; although he is wounded, he continues on to the final Union barricade. In *The House with Closed Shutters* it is the sight of the fallen Confederate flag that prompts Agnes to enter the battle. She, too, is shot, but the bullet kills her (figs. 1.3–4). There is also a centered, straight-on shot of her as she falls, but the difference is that we see her from the front, not as she charges into battle—as with Ben—but as she runs back to the Confederate barricade in retreat. Agnes is perhaps the most heroic character; she is the only one able to "overcome" the trope of fear and enter the battle while "looking" into the oncoming enemy, but while she dies heroically, she nevertheless dies leaving her brother to live a life of disgrace and seclusion, while Cameron lives to ride victorious in the second half of the film. Agnes dies alone, but Ben falls into the arms of his old friend and Union soldier, Phil Stoneman. Phil holds Ben in the same way that Ben

FIGS. 1.3–4. Agnes is shot as she runs back to the Confederate barricade, while Ben, who is also shot, manages to ram the Confederate flag into the Union cannon. *The House with Closed Shutters* (1910).

will later hold his own dying little sister, Flora; the two soldiers' embrace signals future North-South reconciliation, while Ben's embrace and Flora's final words, which incriminate Gus, signal the surge of the Klan.

From *House* to *Birth* we also see a reversal in the acting styles of the "brother" and the "sister." A sign of the "inappropriate" gender role reversal in *The House with Closed Shutters* is the brother's histrionic gestures in contrast to the sister's more controlled and direct action in the face of danger. Roberta E. Pearson refers to two basic styles of acting in analyzing Griffith's Biograph films from 1908 to 1913: the histrionic code and the verisimilar code.

Although, as Pearson explains, "a simple model of linear causality cannot adequately explain the transformation in cinematic performance style," the change from the histrionic to the verisimilar codes followed changes "in narrative structure, from 'pure melodrama' to a degree of psychological realism resembling that of nineteenth-century literary and dramatic realism" (53). In general Walthall's acting style is associated with the more realistic verisimilar code, but in Pearson's discussion of *The House with Closed Shutters* she explains that for the costume drama Walthall often adopted the histrionic code. Pearson's study includes only Griffith's Biograph films, and she therefore does not discuss *Birth*. But in *Birth*, despite the fact that it too is a costume drama, Walthall displays the verisimilar code; his gestures are subtler, controlled, and realistic, while Flora (the little sister), the younger brothers (both Confederate and Union), and African Americans take on the exaggerated gestures that in the earlier Civil War films were associated with the panic and cowardice of the southern soldier. From *House* to *Birth* the brother and sister have changed places, restoring the brother to his proper role of defender of the South and jettisoning the little sister, Flora, from the "realistic" story of the Klan.[22]

Flora takes on the histrionic image of the southern belle: she is exuberant and devoted yet also willful and often out of control. Because of her youth, Flora is not condemned for her actions, but she repeatedly violates the codes of proper behavior for a young lady. When she first meets Elsie, Flora rushes out of the house, grabs Elsie, and hugs and kisses her repeatedly in a frenzied manner. The northern woman is taken aback, and we can read her lips as she frowns and asks Ben, "Who is she?" Upon learning that Flora is Ben's little sister, Elsie returns the embrace. The scene is comic and shows Flora's effusive nature, but it also shows that she does not observe the polite forms of introduction. Griffith differentiates between the "tainted" belle and the southern lady by contrasting Flora and her sister, Margaret, who is introduced as an example of southern gentility, "a daughter of the South, trained in the manners of the old school." The disparity between the sisters is highlighted in a crucial scene in which the "black guerrillas" invade the Cameron home. Margaret, though upset, remains calm in the face of danger and admonishes Flora for her hysterical behavior. As the mother and daughters hide in the tight confines of the cellar, Flora, giddy and near hysteria, puts the family in danger by almost giving away their hiding place with her laughter. Her hysterical behavior in the cellar mirrors the out-of-control behavior of the black troops overhead;

both actions threaten the safety of the southern family.[23] Later, when Ben returns from the war, he warns Flora not to go out alone, but Flora insists on going to the spring to fetch water. Her childish and exuberant nature are manifest in her delight over seeing a squirrel, and instead of returning home to safety, she stays to play, allowing Gus, a former slave and a newly promoted captain in the army, to follow her to the woods.

The negative characteristics of the southern belle and the effete southern gentleman are projected onto the younger children, who are then eliminated from the movie. The two youngest sons, like Little Sister, display the histrionic code of acting. When they first meet, they frolic and play, grabbing and hugging one another, and chase each other around the house. When they meet again on the battlefield, their gaze of recognition distracts them from the conflict at hand, and each receives a mortal wound. They fall into each other's arms in an embrace that seems to end with a dying kiss. The deaths of the youngest sons and of Little Sister serve two functions: because the characters are young, they are not condemned for their actions (the homosexuality and incest are only implied, not actual), and they can be seen as martyrs to the war and to Reconstruction, respectively. At the same time it allows Griffith to redeem the southern son, removing all traces of cowardice or negligence of duty that were depicted in his earlier Civil War films.

Mimi White asserts that the incestuous overtones of the relationship between the pet sister and Ben and the homosexual implications of the two youngest sons, "culminating at the moment of their deaths," place them outside a "normative heterosexuality necessary to maintain the traditional family structure." White sees the recuperation of the family as the primary and ahistorical trajectory of the movie and the Civil War "as a purification rite, eliminating potential perversions of the 'natural' family structure" (222, 224). But the Civil War has not just purged the families of nonnormative sexuality; it has also called into question the equality of southern whites to northern whites, just as Griffith calls into question the bravery of the southern aristocrat in his earlier films. It is therefore crucial to show the equality of northern and southern whites through intermarriage, to assert that the white South was indeed fit to associate with the white North on the most intimate of personal and social terms. The obstacles to intermarriage, however, are not solely on the part of northerners such as Stoneman, who see the South as conquered provinces, but also on the part of southerners, who see intermarriage between North and

South as a betrayal of the Lost Cause. In *The House with Closed Shutters* we are presented with the "cover" story that the sister's extreme loyalty for and grief over her brother keep her from marrying at all (even a fellow southerner), while in *Hearts and Swords* the belle's willingness to marry a Yankee is viewed as a sign of greed and disloyalty.

The North-South marriages at *Birth*'s end not only symbolize a healing between North and South; they also symbolize the end of the closed world of the southern aristocrat, calling for a regional (though not racial) mixing of blood. *Birth* honors the aristocratic Old South at the same time that it dismantles it. While the North-South reunion romance was a popular literary genre after the Civil War, these novels typically portrayed a northern man marrying a southern woman. As Nina Silber explains, the reunion romance symbolically depicted northern male authority reasserting itself over the South, not through force but through sentiment. This approach reflected a northern trend in the 1870s to view the South nostalgically—rather than vindictively—as a locus of Victorian values. Southern manners could therefore restore a "sense of domestic harmony" without glorifying a southern chivalric code (6). In *The Birth of a Nation* and *The Clansman* the main romance between Ben Cameron and Elsie Stoneman reverses the genders, inserting the southern male as the standard of masculinity who wins over his bride ideologically as well as romantically (Silber 186). This reversal confirmed a new vision of the masculine southerner as patriot, forged out of the Spanish-American War (195–96).

In the secondary romance between Phil Stoneman and Margaret Cameron, however, Griffith is sensitive to the problem of showing a southern woman and a northern man together without negatively implicating the southern woman as traitor. After the war, when Phil Stoneman comes back to the South with his father, he hopes to renew his romance with Margaret, the older Cameron daughter, but she resists. The intertitle reads, "Bitter memories will not allow the poor bruised heart of the South to forget." Margaret is pictured in the private space of her garden as Phil, standing outside the fence, looks at her through the bushes and walks out of the shot; in the next shot we see him approach her across the fence. Phil speaks to Margaret and touches the white roses in her basket, at which point she pulls the flowers away, giving him a defiant look, and she too walks out of the shot but in order to get away from him. She moves further into the privacy of her garden, and her eyes widen as she crushes the rose, a symbol of love. The scene fades to black and then into an image of Wade, Margaret's brother, dying in the arms of an elderly Confederate soldier.

As in the cover story in *The House with Closed Shutters,* Margaret's loyalty to her dead brother prevents her from thinking of romance. But while "Agnes" is unable to think of any man, the implication in *Birth* is that Phil is still an enemy in Margaret's eyes and, therefore, his advances are inappropriate. This scene between Margaret and Phil is not unlike the earlier encounter between Elsie and Lynch, Stoneman's mulatto protégé. In that scene Lynch looks longingly at Elise as she arranges flowers in her father's house. An iris shot that highlights his gaze as voyeuristic frames Lynch. Later, when Gus (the black soldier) looks at Flora and Elsie, he too is framed by an iris, and his gaze is depicted as sinister. Given the racial politics of *Birth,* the gazes of Lynch and Gus are clearly depicted as more threatening than that of Phil. Phil is not framed with an iris, nor does he attempt to hide his gaze; he openly approaches Margaret and extends his hand, but when she spurns him, he withdraws. In order for the happy ending of marriage between North and South to occur, Phil cannot be seen as the victor claiming the spoils of war. Phil must prove his loyalty to the white South and to Margaret by killing a black man in order to rescue Dr. Cameron. The stumbling block to Ben and Elsie's romance is Ben's negative reaction to Stoneman's Reconstruction policies—as symbolized in Ben's refusal to shake hands with Stoneman's mulatto protégé—and by his participation in the Klan; but for Phil and Margaret the stumbling block to true love is the war itself. In both cases the marriage of the North and South cannot take place until the northern characters ostensibly admit that they are wrong about their progressive attitudes toward blacks.

There is, however, a further stumbling block to the union of North and South, and that is the image of the southern belle, as depicted by Flora, the little sister, and her relationship to Ben, the Little Colonel. Like White, Michael Rogin notes the element of incest in the relationship between the brother and younger sister. *Birth,* according to Rogin, also resolves the son's incestuous desires for the phallic mother through a series of displacements. *Birth* is located at the end of a trajectory in which Griffith "displaced sexuality from white men to women to blacks in order, by the subjugation and dismemberment of blacks, to reempower white men" (273). In response to the first step of this displacement, Rogin suggests that in *The Birth of a Nation* Griffith frees himself from the strong, sexual heroines of his earlier films, the "monstrous and chameleonlike" figure of the independent and sexual New Woman that "appears everywhere at the end of the nineteenth century, in the work force and reform movements, in literature, art, social thought, and psychology" (261, 260). To support his assertion, Rogin focuses on two earlier films starring Blanche Sweet, in which female sexuality is destructive for the male: *Judith of Bethulia* (1913) and *The Avenging Conscience* (1914).[24] Rogin's psychoanalytic reading of *Birth*, which helped to renew theoretical interest in the film, explains how Griffith projects all antisocial desire onto blacks, arguing that the attempt by Stoneman's mulatto protégé (Silas Lynch) to force Elsie, Stoneman's daughter, to marry him is a displacement of Stoneman's own incestuous desire. Likewise, when Gus (the black army officer) pursues Flora, it represents Ben's incestuous desire for his sister (280).

Rogin's analysis of the displacement of desire from white men to women to blacks does not differentiate between northern and southern white women or between black and white women. Certainly, the erasure of white "North" and "South" is encouraged by the movie itself, but the white female stereotypes associated with regions are not the same, nor are the stereotypes for black and white women the same. In analyzing Stoneman's interracial desires, Rogin astutely points out the geopolitical and racial implications of having a white northern man represent disruptive desires for a mulatto woman.[25] But in his discussion of women, Rogin looks only at white women; furthermore, although Rogin associates the New Woman with the urban, modern North, he turns around and conflates her threat with that of the passive object of desire. If the dangerous sexual character—as represented by Blanche Sweet—has been replaced by the "virginal" Lillian Gish as Elsie Stoneman (as Rogin suggests), why must the virginal image of the little sister be destroyed?

In his examples of the incestuous subtext Rogin includes the fact that in the novel *The Clansman* Ben and Phil look almost alike, as if they are brothers. Elsie's desire for Ben and Margaret's desire for Phil are therefore just as incestuous as the relationship between Ben and Flora, and, moreover, it is not mediated by Gus. In fact, these couples are heralded as the movie's happy ending and a symbol of the new nation. Why, then, is it only Flora who must die? Furthermore, concerning the theme of miscegenation, both Elsie and Flora are proposed to by black men, and both are the objects of the black male gaze. In fact, when we first see Gus leering behind the tree, he is looking at both Elsie and Flora; also, Lynch's attack on Elsie is much more direct. He actually does say that he will force her to marry him, and he not only embraces her; he has her gagged and held against her will. Flora, on the other hand, only fears what Gus will do.[26] Again, one could ask, why must Little Sister kill herself to save her honor while Elsie (the northern woman) is rescued?

Rogin's argument assumes that Flora flees from Ben's incestuous desire and Gus's miscegenational desire but not from her own desires. Although Flora is clearly depicted as a victim, her hysterical reaction to Gus's advances puts her in further danger. Rather than running home, to safety, she runs deeper into the woods and then to the top of a cliff. Through a series of crosscuts we see the brother and sister call to each other, and we know that Ben is not far away. Flora, however, does not wait to be rescued but kills herself instead. Her earlier response to the black soldiers' penetration of her house—her giddy laughter—denotes her own excitement at the transgressive breaking of boundaries between black and white. To be saved from Gus, she need only wait for her brother to rescue her, but to be saved from her own desire, she must leap to her death. In the film version, as opposed to the novel, whiteness is threatened not just from external forces, but—perhaps even more threatening—it can be destroyed by the belle's own weakness, in the form of desires that lead to the possibility of both incest and miscegenation.

The chase scene in which Flora is pursued by both Gus and Ben represents the double danger posed by miscegenation and incest, not just at the psychological level (as Rogin suggests) but also at a social level. Despite the physical similarities between Ben Cameron and Phil Stoneman, Margaret's marriage to Phil and Elsie's to Ben do not signal "regional" incest, as does Little Sister's devotion to her brother. Ben, as representative of the white South, must rid himself of the closed world of the aristocratic southern intermarriage, as represented by the little sister as southern belle, in order to fully rejoin the Union and embrace the North as ally. Likewise, the movie implies that the dangers of possible miscegenation are greater for the southern belle than for the northern woman. The incestuous and miscegenational qualities of chase are heightened by the fact that in *The Clansman* it is not Ben's sister but his former sweetheart (Marion) who jumps off a cliff, and she jumps not to prevent being raped by a black man but to prevent people from knowing that she has been raped.[27] In the novel Dixon presents a graphic account of a gang rape, in which Marion is raped repeatedly all night, while her mother is tied up and forced to watch. In the morning Marion tidies up the house, dresses in her best white dress, and takes her mother with her to the cliff. As in *The Honor of His Family* and *The House with Closed Shutters*, family honor is based on deception. Marion wants no one to know what has happened to her, so she convinces her mother to jump off the cliff with her, fearing that people will be able to read in her mother's face what has happened to Marion. Although her mother tries to come up with alternatives that allow them to live—move away, do not tell anyone—Marion is adamant that their only choice, the only way her name can remain "sweet and clean," is if they both die (305). Honor, therefore, can and should be maintained, even at the expense of truth and even if the innocent must die to protect this concept of purity. Unlike Flora, Marion did nothing to put herself in danger. She was in her home with her mother and had no possible way to escape.

Griffith also subtly taints the belle when he alters the linchpin of the southern rape complex by altering the threat represented by the black male, Gus. In *The Clansman* Dixon leaves the readers no doubt about the guilt of the assailant, and he even has Dr. Cameron go to great lengths to prove Gus's guilt. Using the latest in pseudoscientific theories, Dr. Cameron examines Mrs. Lenoir's retina and finds the image of Gus imprinted on her eye, proving that he was the ultimate cause of her death; this discovery ironically confirms, even in death, Marion's fear that people would "read" the horror of her attack in her mother's eyes. To corroborate his forensic evidence and his own intellectual superiority, Dr. Cameron uses mesmerism to get a confession out of Gus at Gus's Klan trial. The film version circumvents such elaborate evidence by having the young Flora live long enough to whisper the name Gus. Purportedly, the lynching scene was also edited, and in the existing version, after the Klan declares Gus guilty in a "fair trial," his dead body is dumped on the porch of Silas Lynch. Flora's death allows Griffith to maintain the purity of the belle while condemning the threat of the black man and brings home the concept that a belle would choose death over defilement. As presented in the film and the novel, there is no such thing (or there should be no such thing) as a rape survivor.

In his representation of Gus, Dixon also goes to great lengths, describing in elaborate detail Gus's African characteristics, even down to his "African" footprint. Griffith's Gus, however—as a white actor in black face—does not have African features, nor is he a physically imposing figure. Writing in 1898, Alexander Manly (the editor of the *Wilmington Daily Record*, a black North

Carolina newspaper) wrote a rebuttal to the pro-lynching speeches of Rebecca Latimer Felton. Manly maintained, "Every negro lynched is called a 'big, burly, black brute,' when in fact many of those who have thus been dealt with had white men for their fathers, and were not only not 'black' and 'burly,' but were sufficiently attractive for white girls of culture and refinement to fall in love with them, as is well known to all" (qtd. in Hodes 194). The anxiety and outrage produced by Manly's statements eventually led to the Wilmington riots, fictionally recorded in Charles Chesnutt's *Marrow of Tradition* (1901) and in Dixon's *Leopard's Spots* (1902), but the import of Manly's words linger in Griffith's depiction of Gus. Although we do not have the "director's cut" of *Birth,* there are indications from reviews and personal comments that the "rape" scene of Flora in the original cut portrayed Gus in a harsher light and left no doubt that he intended to rape Flora. In response to criticism that Gus (and therefore blacks in general) was being portrayed as animalistic, it appears that Griffith cut the scene and added an intertitle in which Gus tells Flora he wants to marry her, and as she flees in horror, he pursues her while calling out, "Wait, missie, I won't hurt yeh" (Lenning 117–41). As depicted on the screen, Gus is more visually characteristic of the white-fathered black men Manly refers to than to Dixon's "burly black brute." In *Birth* Gus is lynched not for raping Flora but for proposing to her, and in turn Flora must die because of the possibility of her own attraction to Gus. Rather than ameliorating the negative portrayal of African Americans in the film, Griffith's censored version of the chase actually lowers the bar for offenses that are represented as a justification for lynching and equates interracial marriage with rape.

The chase scene is crucial to setting in motion the "justification" of the Klan and the lynching of Gus, but in addition to Gus's appearance, there are other ambiguities in the staging of the chase that call into question the southern rape complex narrative. As Russell Merritt—who has analyzed the scene in detail—suggests, Gus, unlike Flora, does not display the histrionic code; he is hesitant in his pursuit of Flora and in his proposal of marriage, and it is not clear if he is pleading with her not to be afraid (as the intertitle suggests) or if it is a ploy to capture her. When Gus finally witnesses Flora's fatal jump, his reaction is "underplayed as to verge on inscrutability," leaving open the possibility of a "tragic misunderstanding." Although such a reading does not fit with the aftermath of Flora's death, Merritt maintains that these "provocative nuances" "constantly tear the fabric of [Griffith's] narrative" (228). Although

Merritt describes the chase scene as a "textbook" example of Griffith's "meticulous sense of design" in creating a chase scene with "clarity, striking pictorial composition, and irresistible forward momentum" (220), the structure of the chase scene also "tears at the fabric" of the film and of the southern rape complex. The chase scene uses geographical markers to trace Flora's flight through the woods and to show the distance between her and Gus (as he pursues her) as well as the distance between Flora, Gus, and Ben as he pursues both of them. Indeed, what Merritt describes is the perfect example of Griffith's American montage, a particular use of the movement-image as outlined by Gilles Deleuze, in which the cuts between shots indicate a geographic shift between simultaneous and interrelated actions, whose movements are therefore based on time and place.

Yet amid this "textbook" example of the cause-and-effect logic of the movement-image, there are moments of discontinuity. Merritt states that there are "no spatial gaps to permit openings between the locals," and while the characters' triangulated positions are clear at the beginning of the chase, there are indeed gaps as well as the inclusion of anomalous locals that Merritt acknowledges as "surprises." At crucial moments Ben passes through locations not covered by Flora and Gus, while Gus's progress skips several locations through which Flora passes to appear suddenly much closer. In these moments time is not attached to movement, and it is not clear who is chasing whom. The characters' frantic movements, in combination with the editing, create an abstracted rhythm of intensities of fear and panic, in which the logic of cause and effect is suspended and time is directly presented, rupturing the sensory-motor schema and the narrative of the southern rape complex. The characters "chase after each other, exchange their roles and become indiscernible" (127), and we are left with a danse macabre of fear and panic rather than the justification of the Klan or the birth of a nation. In this way the scene—especially through the affection-image of the close-up—presents the sensation of free-floating anxiety that pervades the southern rape complex (rather than narrative itself) and ties the scene to other images of hysterical panic in the film, such as Flora's hysterical reaction to the black troops but also to the black children fleeing from the "ghostly" image of the white children hiding under a sheet, which is Ben's inspiration for the Klan. The narrative of the southern rape complex suggests the former is tragic while the latter is humorous, but the images themselves visualize the similarities, as both Flora and the children run in fear from the product of their own imagination. Furthermore, Henry Walthall's fearful flight in the chase scene also links him intertextually to his earlier flights from the battle scenes in the Civil War films, the very images that the southern rape complex is meant to suppress.

The end result of the chase scene is Flora's dramatic exit from the film and her apotheosis as a symbol of white racial purity, which leaves Elsie—though a northern woman—to take on the visual signs of the southern belle and to replace Little Sister as a more appropriate partner for Ben. Ben's first "encounter" with Elsie associates her with cotton, the flower of the South. Before the war Phil has come from the North to pay his old friend a visit. As they stand in the middle of the cotton field, Ben plucks a white flower, and as he gives it to Phil, he notices the picture of Elsie in a miniature frame. Ben completes the "exchanges of women" by giving Phil the flower (which Phil gives to Margaret as a token of love) for the photo. As Phil attempts to take the photograph back, Phil shakes his head and puts the frame in his breast pocket and walks out of the shot to look at Elsie in "private." The intertitle reads, "He finds the ideal of his dream in the picture of Elsie Stoneman, his friend's sister, whom he has never seen." As Ben starts to open the picture, Flora is in the background but walks out of the shot. She is not the flower being exchanged in this scene, and she is replaced with the image of Elsie, just as she will be replaced by Elsie as Ben's true love. An insert shot of the photo shows Elsie in a series of frames: an iris shot frames a close-up of Elsie, followed by the white border on the frame, then the frame itself; within the photo Elsie's white tulle veil frames her face, and she looks off-camera in a dreamy and sentimental pose. It is this photograph that Ben, the southern soldier, takes into battle with him.

The idealized picture of Elsie set in the cotton field is in sharp contrast to Little Sister's attempts to use cotton to regain her status as belle and southern aristocrat. As a symbol of the South and its vulnerability, the belle is also emblematic of the South's troubled economic condition. In *Birth* the "insult" of Gus's proposal to Flora is preceded by a scene that ties the degradation of the belle (an image that will recur in the cinematic southern rape complex) directly to the deflated post–Civil War image of cotton. Preparing for her brother's homecoming after the war, Flora attempts to use cotton to adorn her appearance. Attaching strips of raw cotton to her dress, she kneels down to use the soot from the fireplace to create the effect of ermine. The intertitle reads, "'Southern ermine,' from raw cotton, for the grand occasion." In the

FIG. 1.5. Flora's smiles turn to tears as she realizes the pathetic image of her cotton "ermine." *The Birth of a Nation* (1915).

manner of the belle, Flora rushes to the mirror to admire her handiwork, but the sooty raw cotton on the homespun dress creates a pathetic rather than a royal appearance, and her smile turns to tears (fig. 1.5). Now that King Cotton is dethroned, it no longer has the power to ensure the social status of the southern aristocratic belle. Flora's dress is literally unrefined, in terms of both the raw and homespun cotton she wears, highlighting the fact that the antebellum South relied on cotton as an export to be processed in northern or British factories. The war has limited the South's ability not only to produce cotton but also to exchange it for costlier goods, such as the silk that Flora wore before the war. In a film that is so self-conscious about preserving white purity, Flora's impulse to blacken the white cotton out of vanity suggests that the belle is tainted by her own desires before she encounters Gus. But Flora's actions also symbolically reveal the crucial role that blacks played in maintaining white southern economic and cultural privilege.

The rape complex, with its emphasis on white purity and superiority—and its fear of miscegenation—obfuscates the South's dependence on a black male workforce. The economic mainstay of the pre- and post–Civil War South was cotton, which depended on an African American workforce, particularly the labor of young black men. The southern rape complex downplays the South's dependence on black laborers by presenting these very same black men as a threat to the society, thus justifying laws that "control" the unruly black male but also in effect attempting to force black workers to stay in the South and accept low wages.[28] As a Union soldier, Gus is not only represented as a threat to southern white womanhood; he also embodies the fear that, in the reconstructed South, African Americans will have opportunities beyond the cotton field. Although Reconstruction had ended long before the release of *Birth* in 1915, black labor, war, and the price of cotton were still divisive issues. From 1914–15 the South experienced another economic crisis with the drop in the cotton market brought on by the start of World War I in Europe, weakening southern support for President Woodrow Wilson's military preparedness proposals and causing southern congressmen to urge Wilson to provide economic aid to bolster the falling cotton prices (Grantham 74–76).[29]

While Little Sister seems to "blacken" herself with her soot-covered cotton before she ever encounters Gus, significantly, it is Elsie—the northern woman—who is able to appropriate the power of African American culture in the service of white southern men without being tainted by it. The first time Ben and Elsie actually meet, we already see the influence of the South upon Elsie: as Ben lies in the hospital bed, Elsie plays the banjo and sings. Although the film does not explain what a northern woman is doing playing the banjo, in *The Clansman* Dixon explains that "the banjo had come to Washington with the Negroes following the wake of the army. She had laid aside her guitar and learned to play all the stirring camp-songs of the South. Her voice was low, soothing, and tender. It held every silent listener in a spell" (9–10). Thus, Elsie as northern belle can safely and efficaciously appropriate black southern culture to work her own "magic" spell.

Elsie, like Flora, has strong emotions and can be quite exuberant, but Elsie can express her emotions in a more appropriate manner. After Elsie and Ben declare their love, for example, Elsie returns to her room and, in the rapture of love, jumps up and down and clutches and kisses the phallic-shaped bed poster, an act that some critics have read as blatantly Freudian. Elsie's behavior, while expressive and perhaps a bit risqué, is reserved for the privacy of her own bedroom. She shows emotions, as does Little Sister, but in an acceptable setting and in relation to an acceptable man, that is, not her brother. When she is confronted by the threat of miscegenation in the person of Lynch, who wants to force her into marriage, Elsie adapts the gestures of the histrionic code. Elsie's reaction mirrors that of Little Sister, except that Elsie has the presence of mind to try to find someone who will help her. When she finds the doors locked, she rushes to the window, breaks it, and calls out to two Klan spies wearing blackface, who bring the Klan to rescue her. Elsie, like Flora, has put herself into danger, but Elise's visit to Lynch is not a result of willful disobedience; she has gone to Lynch to try to rescue Dr. Cameron, who has been arrested as a Klan member, just as she once went with Mrs. Cameron to see President Lincoln to plead for Ben's life. Elsie's rescue indicates that she is now on the "correct" side, the white side. She is not only pleading for the release of a Klan member but more important for the racist logic of the movie, she knows a white man when she sees one, even if he (ironically, like most of the other blackfaced white actors) is in blackface. In the final scenes even Stoneman has come around to the Klan way of thinking when he is furious at Lynch for suggesting that he wants to marry Stoneman's daughter.

In the movie's climax—the double honeymoon for Ben and Elsie and Phil and Margaret—Elsie is again wearing the tulle shawl, which surrounds her in a gossamer cloud, and she now has on the white, ruffled dress of the belle. The following intertitle reads: "Dare we dream of a golden day when the bestial War shall rule no more. But instead—the gentle Prince in the Hall of brotherly Love in the City of Peace." Griffith then depicts the god of war wielding his sword and Christ superimposed over a crowd in the "hall of brotherly love." The members of the heavenly throng, like Elsie, are covered in tulle veils and shawls. In a split scene Ben and Elsie, on a hill overlooking the sea, seem to gaze out at the Celestial City as "The Star Spangled Banner" plays. Elsie's apotheosis as northern belle is complete; her ultrafeminine and "heavenly" costume make it clear that she will never try to wear the pants in this family. The final intertitle reads, "Liberty and union, one and inseparable, now and forever!" Ostensibly, the intertitle refers to the newly united states but also to the marriage. Purged of the weakness and willfulness—associated with the belle and the southern aristocrat in Griffith's earlier movies—Ben and Elsie are fit to preside over not just the new nation but also the Celestial City. The abject southern body (including the Confederate corpse, the "incestuous" and the treacherous belle, the "effeminate" men—as linked to cowardice, drink, and homosexuality—as well as freed African Americans) is thus jettisoned from the film. Heaven, which is linked to the white North-South couples—unlike even the post-Reconstruction South—is imagined as all white.

CHAPTER 2

Taking the South Out of the Southern Rape Complex in *The Story of Temple Drake*

The Story of Temple Drake (1933) is well known today as a "scandalous" pre–Production Code film. Yet before it was ever shown to a movie audience, the film was a sensation because of the controversy surrounding its literary origin, William Faulkner's novel *Sanctuary* (1931). Even in the pre-Code era, the Hayes Office demanded dramatic cuts in the film adaptation and stipulated that it could not bear the name of Faulkner's (in) famous novel.[1] The most lurid and horrific elements of *Sanctuary* include the rape by corncob of the southern belle Temple Drake and the fiery lynching of Lee Goodwin, the accused rapist, neither of which is actually shown in the film. Despite Hayes's interdiction, advertisements for the film flaunted the connection between Faulkner's *Sanctuary* and *The Story of Temple Drake*, referring to the adaptation as the unfolding of the "flaming story" of the "year's most sensational novel" (fig. 2.1). Even ads that did not specifically refer to *Sanctuary* frequently added "by William Faulkner" in the list of credits (often above the name of the director, Stephen Roberts), signaling the film's connection to Faulkner and erroneously intimating that Faulkner had written the screenplay.[2]

Reviewers, assuming that the audience knew the literary origins of the film, repeatedly commended the film for not "sacrificing any of [the novel's] essential quality" (qtd. in Ramsey 20). Writing for the *Atlanta Constitution*, Ralph Jones enthused that it was "quite a blessing" that the film "isn't deleted enough to spoil the story," and he assured all "admirers of WF and readers of his book about that peculiar gal, 'Temple Drake' (And aren't we all?)" that they "will jump at the opportunity to see their favorite story on the screen" (20). The "essential quality" of the film that censorship could not spoil is not just a story of rape but one of white identity formation that is based on the southern rape complex, a story that is told through the body of Temple Drake and the historically shifting representations of the southern belle.

FIG. 2.1. Advertisement for *The Story of Temple Drake*. The Story of Temple Drake *Press Book*. Paramount Pictures, 1933. Courtesy of the J. D. Williams Library Special Collections, University of Mississippi.

While *Sanctuary* and *The Story of Temple Drake* draw on sensational elements of the southern rape myth, they also complicate and disrupt the categories of race, gender, and region that the myth implies, redirecting the focus of the southern rape complex from the image of the black male rapist to the figure of the decadent southern belle and the violent lower-class white man. While this move is progressive, in that it undermines the racial justification of lynching, ultimately, it merely narrows previous definitions of whiteness without dismantling white racial privilege. Like *The Birth of a Nation*, the happy ending in *The Story of Temple Drake* is based on a unification of normative middle-class whiteness. Released in 1933, *The Story of Temple Drake* historically refigures the southern rape complex and the southern belle in light of the Depression and Prohibition and cinematically refigures the complex in light of the emerging genres of horror and gangster films.

THE CRACK IN THE BELLE

Unlike Thomas Dixon and D. W. Griffith, Faulkner does not present the threat to the South in the form of the black man.[3] In *Sanctuary* Faulkner rewrites the southern rape complex as a class conflict within the white community played out over the scarce resources of the Depression.[4] By the 1931 release of *Sanctuary*, the Depression-era drop in cotton prices, exacerbated by overproduction, on top of the damage done by boll weevils in the 1920s, accomplished what the Klan alone could not: it forced the foreclosure of many black-owned farms and sent even more southern blacks to the urban North in search of work. In a time of massive unemployment and falling cotton prices, the South was not as dependent on black laborers as it had been.[5] Low cotton prices and Prohibition made corn, not cotton, the South's new cash crop in the form of illegal bootleg whiskey, which was easier to transport and brought a higher price than cumbersome bales of cotton or bushels of corn. Because it was illegal, whiskey had the added advantage of being untaxed, but its illegal status also necessitated its clandestine production and distribution, making the hill country or backwoods the perfect location (rather than the working plantation) and the bootlegger/gangster the perfect distributor (rather than the elite planter class). As a result of this combination of circumstances—including the fact that over five million southerners moved into the cities from 1880 to 1910—the former plantation, now in ruins, ironically becomes the perfect secluded "hideout," the southern gentleman becomes the consumer (not producer), the belle becomes the degraded gangster's moll, and two threatening lower-class white stereotypes emerge: the urban gangster and the rural hillbilly moonshiner.

Faulkner, like Griffith, calls into question the conventions of the southern belle, but while Griffith indirectly exposes the dangers of the southern belle's vanity and willfulness, Faulkner creates an overtly flirtatious and seductive belle in Temple Drake, who many would say is (as Rhett Butler says of Scarlett) "no lady." As Kathryn Lee Seidel explains, it was Faulkner's great-grandfather, Col. W. C. Falkner, who first suggested that the threat to the belle's purity lies from within. His novel *The Little Brick Church* (1882) features the seduction of the belle by a northerner and the lynching of the same man because of his brutal and lascivious treatment of his female slave, which brings about her death. According to Seidel: "Being seduced . . . because of an innate flaw was a new trait for the belle. Beginning with this novel, she can be seduced by her own sensuousness" (140). Colonel Falkner presents lynching as a necessary means of reining in the libidinous vices of the northern male and the sexual weakness of the white southern woman. Forty-nine years later William Faulkner desecrates the temple of white southern womanhood with the brutal, "instrumental" rape of Temple. The nature of Faulkner's desecration of the belle at the hands of a white, and not a black, man points to the shift in the economic underpinning of the South as a result of the Depression.

As a symbol of the South and its vulnerability, the belle is also associated with the South's beleaguered economic condition. In both *Birth* and *Temple Drake* the belle's disgrace is symbolically related to the collapse of the plantation system. Temple's fall is, of course, linked through her name to the architectural analogy of the plantation house. The plantation house at the Old Frenchman place, a symbol of the centerpiece and foundation of the "aristocratic" southern planter lifestyle, like Temple's reputation, is in need of repairs. Also like Temple, it is now in the hands of poor whites, who tear it down bit by bit and use it as the headquarters for their bootlegging operation. Unlike that of the plantation house, however, Temple's fall is not directly related to the Civil War. Faulkner takes the belle out of the plantation and puts her in a college dorm, giving her education and independence, two important ingredients for the 1920s New Woman. But in 1931, over ten years after women gained the vote, feminism and the women's movement have stalled. Unlike the earlier image of the independent New Woman, Temple has no intellectual ambitions; she is not at college to pursue any lofty goals. As a college girl, she also has no chaperone to protect her or to enforce ladylike behavior, and Temple merely uses her freedom to sneak out of the dorm to go joyriding with the local townies. Temple more closely fits the image of the fun-loving flapper—drinking and smoking—but before the rape, she draws the line at the sexual freedom associated with the flapper.[6] Even as she violates the propriety of the belle, when she encounters a real threat, Temple attempts to fall back on her privileged background to protect, at least, her technical virtue.

Faulkner unmercifully demonstrates what happens to the belle as flapper in the wake of the Jazz Age, when the social structures that guard and limit her behavior are removed. Just as the white moonshiners have taken over and destroyed the former plantation house, it is equally symbolic that Temple's scene of degradation occurs at the hands of the white bootlegger/gangster in a corncrib and with a corncob—the abject remains of the main ingredient in moonshine whiskey. Temple herself, like the hollow corn shucks that seem to follow her wherever she goes at the Old Frenchman place, represents the abject remains of the tradition of the aristocratic southern belle and of the New Woman/flapper of the Roaring Twenties.[7]

In *Sanctuary* and *The Story of Temple Drake* lower-class whites are directly connected to the fall of the belle: they are the source of illicit pleasure, the source of censure, and the source of violation. In *Sanctuary*, Temple's fall at the hands of Popeye is preceded by her fallen reputation, which is linked to her tendency to "go slumming" with the white town boys because they have cars and can take her away from campus. Similarly, Gowan Stephen is willing to "go slumming" at the Old Frenchman place to get more alcohol from Lee Goodwin. For Temple's contemporaries in New York, the source of excitement and alcohol was often associated with Harlem and therefore linked to race. Temple and Gowan fulfill their illicit desires through lower-class whites as well as their access to cars and alcohol, two key elements associated with the freedom of the Roaring Twenties.

Another sign of Temple's fall is that those who are lower on the social hierarchy criticize her. Ironically, the characters in the novel condemn Temple not so much for being too "loose" but for not being loose enough.[8] The town boys complain that she is a tease, but Temple's harshest critic is the white lower-class former prostitute, Ruby, who judges Temple's behavior from the perspective of class and economics. Ruby does not read Temple's virginity as a virtue, or as a sign of white female purity, but as proof that Temple is a tease and an upper-class hypocrite who deserves whatever she gets. It is perhaps not surprising that a former prostitute would view sex as an economic commodity, but Ruby's critique reveals the economic basis of Temple's relationships as well, such as her need for a car.

Even as Temple violates the standards of behavior for an upper-class woman, she employs the privilege of her position, the prerogative of nonpayment. The sign of upper-class power is not the ability to pay but the ability to define the exchange rate or even to refuse payment altogether. In Ruby's speech to Temple, she chides Temple's sense of upper-class privilege: "Oh, I know your sort," the woman said. "Honest women. Too good to have anything to do with common people. You'll slip out at night with the kids, but just let a man come along . . . Take all you can get, and give nothing. 'I'm a pure girl; I dont do that.' You'll slip out with the kids and burn their gasoline and eat their food, but just let a man so much as look at you and you faint away because your father the judge and your four brothers might not like it. But just let you get into a jam, then who do you come crying to? To us, the ones that are not good enough to lace the judge's almighty shoes" (57–58). Despite the horrors Temple endures, which make her an object of pity, the novel also participates in a kind of vicarious pleasure in witnessing the belle get her comeuppance, and this is also apparent in the movie version.

In both film and novel Temple combines the frivolous elements of the flapper and belle and is forced to "pay" for her frivolous behavior through sexual violence. As Hollywood censor Jack Vizzard explains: "With the crash, the party was over. In the littered debris of confetti and tickertape, an enormous sense of guilt set in . . . In a mood of sobriety, a chastened citizenry reacted against those symbols of its great debauch and began to punish them" (38–39). In the film, however, Temple attempts to take more control over her body and her sexuality. The advertisements for the movie, included in the press book distributed to local theaters, promote the idea of Temple as a manipulator, proclaiming that she is "a girl who thought she knew how to handle men." The use of the past tense implies her downfall at the hands of a man she could not control.

The first scene of the movie presents Temple as just such a "girl who thought she knew how to handle men." In the opening shots we see only her hand on the doorknob and hear only her end of the conversation as she tells her beau goodnight. The first words we hear her speak are "Do I [s]ho' nough? Just me? Men are funny." *Sho' nough*, a phrase she repeats several times throughout the movie, is spoken with an extreme southern accent and labels Temple not only as southern but as a belle, as she uses this phrase only on men and as part of her performance as a belle—that is, as flirtatious but innocent. She drops the lilting southern drawl when her date does not take no for an answer as she barks, "I said no" and "Hey, you're too rough; let go." Once she has pushed her date safely on the other side of the door, she resumes her drawl as she smiles and says a lilting and multisyllabic "good night." Her smile fades as she looks upstairs, as if she anticipates another battle. A similar performance is enacted moments later when her grandfather meets her on the stairs, scolding her for coming in too late. "Why is it late sho' nough? I didn't know," she croons and then distracts her grandfather by asking him to help unfasten her dress and assures him that her date is a "nice boy" (i.e., he is a gentleman) who went to her grandfather's college (i.e., he is "one of us").

This opening scene is also important regarding the costuming and lighting, as it establishes the symbolic use of light and dark that is pervasive throughout the film and signals Temple's dual nature and her "dark" secret. The white crinoline dress of the belle has given way to the sophisticated, shimmering lamé evening gown that clings to Temple's body, leaving nothing to the imagination. Even after Temple turns off the light to go upstairs, her luminous dress still highlights her figure. The muted lighting of the darkened hallway, however, foreshadows the even darker tonal palate of the Old Frenchman place, and in both worlds Temple's "whiteness"—as expressed by the ability to reflect light—stands out. Miriam Hopkins seems to have been chosen for this role because of the markers of whiteness she represents, from her nimbus of blonde hair to her white skin set off by her radiant clothing. In sharp contrast to Temple is the austere, dark-toned portrait that literally stands between Temple and her grandfather as they talk on the stairs. The portrait, done in the style of the Dutch masters, is presumably a Drake ancestor, who appears to look down disapprovingly at Temple and suggests an erosion of propriety in the family.

The symbolic contrast of light and dark is repeated when Temple tries to explain to the dashing lawyer, Stephen Benbow, why she cannot marry him. Alluding to her divided nature, she explains: "It's as if there are two me's. One of them says, 'Yes, yes, quick don't let him get away,' but the other, I won't tell you what it wants, does, or what'll happen to it. I don't know myself. All I know is I hate it." The pair is standing outside on the veranda, and Stephen has his back to the brightly lit mansion where the dance is held. Temple is facing him, and though there is no source of light behind her, she is backlit, creating the radiant blonde hair as in the first scene, while her face is in shadow, suggesting her dual light/good and dark/bad character.

In the ads and press book used to promote the film, Temple's divided nature and her reputation as a good-bad girl are directly linked to an inherited

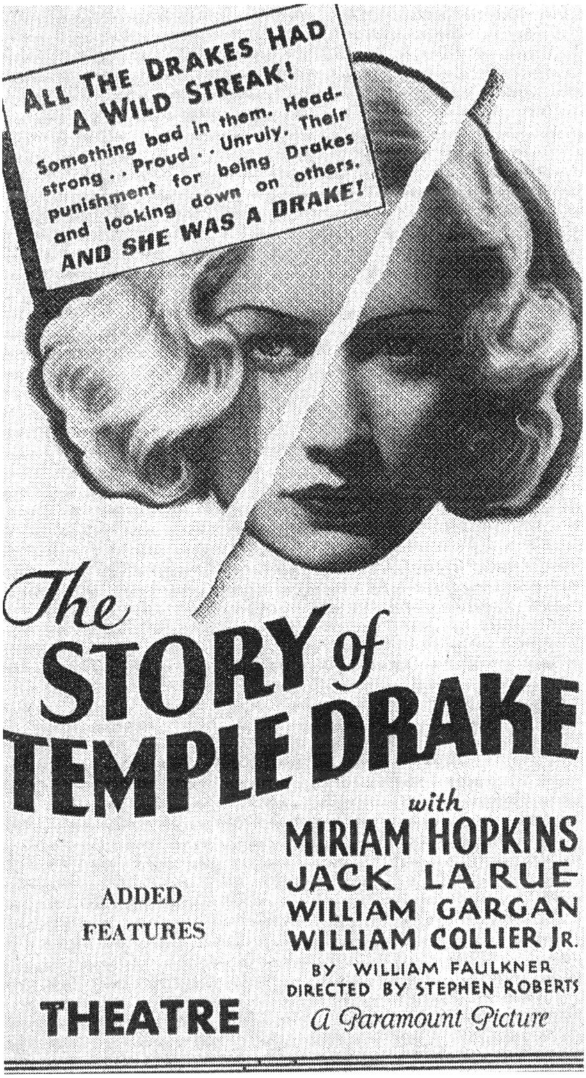

FIG. 2.2. Advertisement for *The Story of Temple Drake*. The Story of Temple Drake *Press Book*. Paramount Pictures, 1933. Courtesy of the J. D. Williams Library Special Collections, University of Mississippi.

"wild streak" in the Drake family. Like Flora in *The Birth of a Nation*, Temple is portrayed as a tainted belle even before the actual rape, and also like Flora, the threat to Temple's purity stems from both inside and outside. The ads contain several variations on the theme of the "Drake wild streak" (fig. 2.2). Some ads simply state, "All the Drakes had a wild streak," or question the source of the corruption in the family, "What was this bad streak in the Drakes?" while others indicate Temple's internal struggle: "I'm a half-good girl! I tried to be . . . longed to be respectable . . . and what? The other side of me . . . the wild Drake streak . . . it's too strong! . . . it's like there are two me's." The line in the movie from which the ads were drawn is spoken by Stephen's Aunt Jenny, who actually says, "They're a stiff-necked lot, most of them—proud and all that—but there's a wild streak in them. Every now and then one of them comes along, like Temple, with something bad in them, something wrong. Maybe she'll get over it, but not one of them that's had it that didn't end up in the gutter." The advertisements, however, extend the line to indicate that all the Drakes had a wild streak and further speculate on the nature of the streak.

Stephen, who is in love with Temple, refuses to listen, but Aunt Jenny's comments are part of a montage of gossip about Temple, beginning with the Drakes' African American maid, who, examining Temple's torn slip, laughs that Judge Drake would know more about his granddaughter if he did her laundry. Judge Drake assumes that Temple's whiteness is a sign of and a guarantee of her purity, but the maid is able to read Temple's "dirty laundry" and therefore her hidden sexuality. The gossip sequence ends with the image of a black cat, which Paula Degenfelder reads as a negative comment about the "catty" remarks against Temple.[9] Rather than simply representing criticism of the gossipers, given the negative depictions of Temple as a "bad" girl, the black cat has a double meaning, which includes a crude slang allusion to Temple's "dark sexuality"—her "black pussy"—an image of Temple's racialized sexuality.[10]

White women's purity was so exaggerated in the southern rape complex that even in the context of intraracial marriage it was unacceptable to refer to or assume white women possessed sexual desire; female sexuality was therefore projected onto black women. Richard Dyer notes the narrative ramifications of the impossibility of white female sexuality: "Whites must reproduce themselves, yet they must also control and transcend their bodies. Only by (impossibly) doing both can they be white. Thus are produced some of the great narrative dilemmas of whiteness, notably romance, adultery, rape and pornography" (30). An important element of the southern rape complex and the narratives it spawns is its obfuscation of the more common source of miscegenation in the South: white slave owners who violated their female slaves.

One of the arguments put forth by abolitionists was that slavery and the illicit relations between white masters and slave women corrupted the morals of the white family, including the daughters. Harriet Jacobs wrote in her narrative, "They [white planters' daughters] know that the women slaves are subject to their father's authority in all things; and in some cases they exercise the same authority over the men slaves" (71). Even Thomas Dixon, in *The Sins of the Father: A Romance of the South* (1912), describes the corruption of the white race: "The fact that the negro race had for two hundred years been stirring the baser passions of her men—that this degradation of the higher race had been bred into the bone and sinew of succeeding generations—had never occurred to [Mrs. Norton's] childlike mind" (85). Dixon, keeping with his racist agenda, blames African American women for their own violation but interestingly uses the language of biological inheritance to describe successive generations of whites who continued to be corrupted by "the sins of their fathers."

The visual connections between sexuality, darkness, and the Drakes' wild streak intimate that miscegenation is already part of the southern family tradition, which is precisely the unstated allusion in the ads' persistent questions about the origin of that wild streak. The anxiety surrounding the southern rape complex includes the need to limit and control the desires of both black men and white women. Unlike her forefathers, Temple's sexuality is a threat to the Drake name. Like Flora, the threat to Temple's purity as presented in the film's promotional materials comes from both within and without and includes both miscegenation and incest.

The miscegenational suggestion of the dark Drake hereditary wild streak in the press book is accompanied by a psychological analysis of the incestuous implications of the novel. Like the chase scene in *Birth*, the threat of incest follows close on the heels of the threat of miscegenation. Dr. Frank Payne, a "consulting psychologist," analyzes Temple according to his reading of *Sanctuary* in an article featured in *The Story of Temple Drake* press book. Dr. Payne declares, "Undoubtedly we have an Oedipus Complex situation between 'Temple Drake' and her father, the great and learned judge." Temple is, according to Dr. Payne, the "typical psychopathic personality which has been molded and forced into being by the repressions of our civilization, the repressions of religion, coupled with eugenic inbreeding of our so-called fine families and fine stock, which have been inbred so much that they cannot stand the pressure and tension of our civilization." In relation to Temple, Payne's comments seem to allude to the closed world of the southern aristocrat, but he maintains that this "psychopathic personality" can be seen in New York as well as the

Deep South, suggesting that class exclusiveness—inbreeding, whether it be at the lower or the upper levels—weakens the white race. Given the climate of segregation in the 1930s, it is unlikely that Payne was advocating interracial marriage, yet like Griffith and Dixon, he seems to promote intermarriages across class and religious lines as a way to strengthen white "civilization."

Payne's comments refer to Temple's relationship to her father in the novel. Although the father is noticeably absent in the movie and Judge Drake becomes Temple's grandfather, the incestuous overtones remain. In the opening scene on the staircase, we see Temple using her sexual charm to seek her grandfather's indulgence, suggesting that even Judge Drake, who turns a blind eye to his granddaughter's indiscretions, is taken in by her seductiveness. As her grandfather unzips her dress, Temple reassures him that her staying out late is not a threat to her purity because her date, Toddy Gowan, went to the Judge's alma mater. Just as the Judge assumes that Temple's whiteness is a sign of her purity, he assumes that Toddy's connections to him, through class and education, are guarantees of the young man's honor and his status as a gentleman—or least that as a gentleman he will marry Temple if he gets her pregnant, maintaining the "eugenic inbreeding of our so-called fine families" to which Dr. Payne alludes.

THAT BLACK MAN

Just as in the film Temple's sexuality is coded through the image of the black cat and the contrast of light and dark shadows, in the novel, as critics have pointed out, the rapist Popeye, though white, is also coded as "black."[11] Because of the tradition of slavery and Jim Crow in the South, at one level when we talk about race in a southern context—especially a small-town southern context—there is still the lingering myth of racial identity that on a practical, everyday level we know who is black and who is white and that these identifications have a strong bearing on where you go to church or whom you marry. But as Michael Omi and Howard Winant explain: "The effort must be made to understand race as an unstable and 'decentered' complex of social meanings . . . Race is a concept which signifies and symbolizes social conflict and interests by referring to different types of human bodies" (55). Because "race" is also signified by such things as speech, dress, and behaviors, a character can be coded as one race while visually signifying another. Although Popeye is directly referred to as a white man, the narrator describes Popeye's skin as having a "dead, dark pallor," Horace Benbow comments that "he smells black," and Temple refers to him as "that black man" (4, 7, 49). His connection to blackness is exposed even when he is being directly referred to as white. Commenting on Popeye's skittishness, Tommy asserts, "I be dog if he aint the skeeriest durn *white* man I ever see" (19. The implication of Tommy's comment is that blacks are naturally scared but Popeye's fear is unusual for a white man; that is, it is more typical of a black man.

What does it mean, then, that Popeye is coded black yet inhabits a white subject position? What happens in the slippage between black and white? Joel Williamson, in "How Black was Rhett?" argues that, in addition to *Gone with the Wind*'s black-coded references to Rhett Butler's "swarthy face" and his "springy stride of a savage," Rhett is also created as a "hipster-trickster": "independent, cocky, and insufferably yet subtly insolent" (99). Rhett's association with blackness enhances his sexuality, but his position in (and his return to) polite Charleston society ultimately marks him as "true" gentlemen. Rhett is the good-bad boy. In *Sanctuary*, which predates *Gone with the Wind* both as book and movie, Popeye's link to blackness and the lower classes only makes him a more ominous character. His connection to whiteness is not enough to redeem him fully, yet it does allow the white reader to plug into cultural and racial fantasies and stereotypes while still having the safety net of whiteness to alleviate (even more) frightening images of the black rapist (which would be offensive to the African American community and would have the added stigma of causing racial controversy, as it did in *Birth*).

Popeye's ambiguous racial coding allows Faulkner to debunk the myth of the black male rapist on more than one level. Popeye must use a corncob, an instrument, to accomplish his crime against southern womanhood. In this reading, by analogy, the myth of the black male rapist is, like the corncob, just an instrument in the hands of an impotent white culture. On the other hand, if we read Popeye as coded black, *Sanctuary* creates a countermyth that the black man, even in the position of the rapist, is impotent, as in the case of Popeye. Therefore, even if he were to attack a white woman, there is no fear of miscegenation from a corncob. Popeye' s black-white status thus allows Faulkner to invoke all the sensationalism associated with the myth of the black male rapist, discredit the myth as an instrument used by whites, and allay white fears about the "real" power of the black male.

Faulkner's use of the white-coded black man does not necessarily exonerate the black man but does shift the focus of the threat (to the South) to the southern whites themselves, especially lower-class whites. As a critic in the *American Mercury* describes it, "The thesis of this book, to the native southerner, is horrifying but undeniable: it is that the low-down southerner, with his talent for the dirt, as he calls it, is probably the most depraved of white Americans" (qtd. in Ramsey 12). The qualifying use of the word *white*, as in Tommy's statement, establishes the possibility of even more depraved nonwhite Americans at the same time that it suggests a connection; as the most depraved of white Americans, Popeye is more like a nonwhite. The connection between rural lower-class hillbilly and black man is not new, but *Sanctuary* marks a reconfiguration of urban and rural lower-class whites as a new and threatening figure, in terms of both violence and sexuality. Popeye's race and impotence doubly dispel the threat of miscegenation but not the actuality of sexual violence and murder. J. W. Williamson, who traces the history of the hillbilly in American culture, maintains that "our secret dread is that the dark, drunken hillbilly is not other, but us" (6).[12]

The historical source material that seems to have inspired *Sanctuary* further links the novel to bootlegging, rape, and lynching (Williamson, *William Faulkner* 157–58). The event that precipitated *Sanctuary* was the story of Popeye Pumphrey, a Memphis bootlegger, who was reported to be impotent but was also rumored to have raped a woman with an object (Blotner 234–35; Arnold and Trouard 5–6). The subsequent lynching of Goodwin and Faulkner's description of the murder committed by Goodwin's black jail mate both include details from the 1908 lynching of Nelse Patton that occurred in Oxford when Faulkner was a boy. Patton, also a well-known bootlegger, had been convicted on five counts of selling alcohol. While serving as a "trusty," Patton went to the home of a white convict to deliver a message to his wife, Mattie McMillan. A fight ensued, Mattie McMillan drew a gun, and Patton slit her throat, almost severing her head, though she still managed to run into the front yard.

Joel Williamson suggests that Patton was probably acquainted with both Mr. and Mrs. McMillan in connection to his bootlegging operation and that Mattie was not necessarily protecting her "honor" when she drew the gun, though this was how she was portrayed after the fact. "Somehow in the Patton case the community found itself confronting the alarming results of a commingling of race and sex with the disinhibiting effects of alcohol," resulting in a mob of reportedly two thousand men who worked for hours to break into the jail and kill Patton (161). Senator William Sullivan, the ringleader, unabashedly admitted to instigating the lynching: "Cut a white woman's throat and a negro? Of course I wanted him lynched. I led the mob which lynched Nelse Patton and I am proud of it" (qtd. in Williamson 161). In the novel the same grizzly details of the murder—including the nearly headless women running into the yard—are incorporated, but the interracial element is left out. The black jail mate in the novel has murdered his wife, not a white woman, by slitting her throat, and though he waits to die for his crime, there is no impetus from the white community to lynch him. In *Sanctuary* lower-class white men take on the sins attributed to the black man in the southern rape complex, but equally important, they—not a senator or other upper-class member of the town—also take on the violent specter of the vigilante. Even the middle-class lawyer, Horace Benbow, is not safe when the white mob threatens to lynch him for representing a rapist. The depiction of vigilante violence as a lower-class phenomenon increasingly distances the middle-class southerners from cinematic vigilantism as played out in future Faulkner film adaptations, including *Intruder in the Dust* (1949) and *The Long, Hot Summer* (1958).

THE SOUTHERN GOTHIC MONSTER AS THE "GANGSTER OF THE ID"

In *The Story of Temple Drake* Popeye, the "low down southerner," who is impotent, syphilitic, and voyeuristic, becomes Trigger, a brutal but virile immigrant gangster. Thus, the fear of the black man—as presented in the southern rape complex and promoted by Griffith and the revived Klan—is conflated with the image of the lower-class dark-skinned immigrant. Previously, in the 1920s, the gangster and bootlegger were often portrayed as successful businessmen or even as heroes who supplied a willing public with what many deemed a harmless commodity.[13] For early Depression-era audiences, during the peak of the classical gangster film (1930–32), the gangster presented an alternative model of social mobility and rags-to-riches in a time of limited opportunity (Shadoian 29), and his determination and bravado appealed to audiences. After 1932, however, the gangster became a more threatening figure, and Popeye/Trigger represents the darker side of the gangster, whose determination also incorporated the sadistic violence and authoritarianism of the protofascist dictator (Rosow 175–79; Atkinson 118–19, 141). Ted Atkinson explains that "the gangsters of post-1932 Hollywood were more like Faulkner's Popeye Pumphrey than Edward G. Robinson's Rico Bandello or James Cagney's Tommy Powers. In place of the gangster, representations of an unruly public now simultaneously reflected the longing for decisive action in the vacuum of ineffectual leadership as well as the need for civil restraint to prevent revolution" (141). Trigger, as the virile, violent gangster, however, is more of a threat than Popeye, but instead of the mob violence of *Sanctuary,* which lynches an innocent man, *The Story of Temple Drake* puts the gun in the hands of Temple, the upper-class white women, who then confesses her crime on the stand, allowing "justice" to prevail.

The Story of Temple Drake was able to take advantage of the popularity of both the gangster and the horror film and the fears that fed them during the Depression era, presenting Trigger as a combination of the dark ravisher, violent gangster, and gothic monster. David Skal explains this intersection in his analysis of the cultural significance of the horror and gangster genres. While the gangster movie "served as a lightning rod for public anger and cynicism," the "monster movies opened up the possibility of psychic lawlessness; a monster, for Hollywood, was a gangster of the id and unconscious" (114). The conflation of the horror film and the gritty realism of the gangster film is already suggested by the reviews of *Sanctuary:* "The horrors of any ghost story pale beside the ghastly realism of this chronicle" (Ramsey 12). *The Story of Temple Drake,* capitalizing on the connections, is split geographically between the dark gothic world of the rural, dilapidated plantation house (complete with "monsters") and the hard-edged realism of the urban boarding house/house of prostitution.

The Story of Temple Drake features numerous elements of the horror film, including the dark and decaying castle/mansion as the visual sign of the entrance into the southern gothic world of monsters. In the novel Temple and Gowan Stevens approach the house in daylight; in the film, however, a car accident strands the pair in the dark so that Temple and Toddy Gowan advance toward the house in the darkness of a stormy night. But even before we see the couple approach the house, the opening credits are juxtaposed with the image of the darkened plantation house intermittently illuminated by flashes of lightning. The ominous scene of the plantation house is interrupted with insert shots of the actors as they appear in the movie, beginning, of course, with Hopkins as the eponymous star, Temple Drake. The opening shot shows Hopkins before her fall, illuminated with backlights that make her blonde hair glow and bring out the lustrous quality of her evening gown. Another important change from novel to film is Temple's hair color, which in the novel is red but in the film is blonde.

Miriam Hopkins is the perfect choice for the good-bad girl. Even the whiteness of this initial view of her links her visually to both sex and violence and to both horror and gangster films. In her most important role to date—Paramount's first horror film, *Dr. Jekyll and Mr. Hyde* (1931)—Hopkins plays a dancehall girl (Ivy) who, unlike Temple, does not play hard to get. In her first scene in the movie the gentlemanly Dr. Jekyll rescues her, and to show her appreciation, she performs a striptease for him. The scene is filmed with high-key lighting accentuating the whiteness of Ivy's dress, skin, and bedspread. As she removes her garters, playfully zinging them at Jekyll, we see plenty of leg, although the camera coyly averts our gaze with cross-shots of Jekyll's amused reaction. As Ivy takes off the rest of her outfit, the camera returns to Ivy before she has covered herself with the white bedspread, clearly revealing that she has nothing on and exposing a good deal of her back, part of her breast, and her dangling leg that beckons Jekyll to join her.

Despite his gentlemanly refusal, the dangling leg—superimposed on the screen—follows Dr. Jekyll as he leaves the room and walks down the street. Later, of course, the same setting of seduction will be the scene of Ivy's murder at the hands of Jekyll's lascivious alter ego, Mr. Hyde. The horror movie had an added benefit for Hollywood in that it circumvented censorship because, as Skal points out, the Production Code did not mention monsters (117). The early horror films were typically set in Europe, with monsters that originate there, but *The Story of Temple Drake* brings the setting closer to home, complete with monsters of our own making.[14]

Moving from the horror to the gangster film, in 1932 Hopkins again plays a dancehall girl (a taxi dancer), Gloria Bishop. Again, she is the cynosure of the male gaze, as she excites the interest of a naive trumpet player and a gangster (Louie Brooks, played by George Raft). Brooks (Raft) is taken with Gloria's (Hopkins) spectacular and sensuous rendition of "St. Louis Blues," and his fascination with the song eventually contributes to his death. Predating *The Story of Temple Drake*, the advertisements for *Dancers in the Dark* also label Hopkins as a "half good girl . . . half bad girl," declaring, "Dark secrets from her past should not matter—but they do!" As with *The Story of Temple Drake*, Hopkins's "dark secrets" and her sex appeal are racially coded. Writing about Hollywood's use of "St. Louis Blues" from 1929 to 1937, Peter Stanfield argues that the song was repeatedly and consistently used "as a means to articulate racial instability in the characterization of women who represented problems in terms of their sexuality, their morality, and their (lower) class status" (84). Gloria Bishop represents all three of these things, and her performance of "St. Louis Blues" presents her as a sexual siren who lures men to their death, even if that is not her intent. Paramount capitalized on Hopkins's previous roles as a lower-class temptresses in creating the racial and class ambiguity of Temple Drake as a fallen belle, another "half good girl . . . half bad girl."

In a similar vein Trigger's role as monster is superimposed on his role as black-coded villain. The insert shot of Trigger in the opening credits links him back to Gus in *Birth*. Griffith marks Gus's sinister nature several times in the film in framing shots but particularly through the use of the iris. Before the zoom lens, Griffith uses the iris shot to highlight aspects of a shot and to create the effect of a "close-up." Gus's dangerously lascivious nature is highlighted by the use of the framing iris, which captures him leering at the innocent heroines, Elsie and Flora, and which precedes his fatal pursuit of Flora. Although an actual iris is not used in *The Story of Temple Drake*, Trigger is lit in such a way as to illuminate his face in an oval of light, leaving the rest of the shot in darkness, similar to the effect created by the iris shot. From the initial shots of Trigger in the opening credits and leading up to the rape scene, his status as monster, "gangster of the id," is created through the use of light and darkness. These lighting techniques are the work of Karl Struss, a cinematographer who began his career as an art photographer and was well-known for his artistic and technical innovations, especially in working with black and white. Struss worked with Griffith as well as with F. W. Murnau (the director of the famous German expressionist horror film, *Nosferatu* [1922]), Rouben Mamoulian (who directed Hopkins in *Dr. Jekyll and Mr. Hyde*), and Hopkins on several films.[15] Explaining his use of light and dark in *The Story of Temple Drake*, Struss commented: "For the dramatic effects such as those achieved in *The Story of Temple Drake*, we'd sort of make the actors look screwy or gruesome by having low lights hidden on the floor, behind chairs or tables, and casting them up. Large shadows would be on the wall in the back of the actors depending, of course, on how much was there and the size of the shot. And there would be variety. Sometimes we'd just have a full light directly at a 90-degree angle from one side or the other so you couldn't see anything of the opposite side of the face—there would just be half a face illuminated. Sometimes under the shadow side of the face we'd have a kicker light to outline the face" (qtd. in Harvith 16). Many scenes at the plantation house have only one source of illumination, a candle or a kerosene lamp, and the use of low angle lights creates looming shadows, particularly in relation to Trigger.

In the absolute blackness of the night after the car accident, Trigger's flashlight is the only source of light, which he uses to perpetrate his first violation of Temple. As she is lying prostrate on the ground, Trigger focuses the light on Temple's exposed legs, and when she stands up, he again uses the light to move slowly over her body from her feet up her to her face. Because of the extreme use of blackness in the shot, it is difficult to tell if the camera actually moves in conjunction with the light or if the movement is achieved only with the light. The flashlight takes on the role of the camera, imitating what Christian Metz refers to as cinema's "wandering framings (wandering like the look, like the caress)" that create "a generalized strip-tease" directing our gaze (77), as the on-screen darkness is indistinguishable from the off-screen material. And in the shot/reverse shot sequence Trigger remains invisible behind the light of the flashlight. This scene forms a visual link to Miriam Hopkins's striptease as Ivy in *Dr. Jekyll and Mr. Hyde*, but Trigger is not the gentlemanly Dr. Jekyll, who averts his eyes; he is already the monstrous Mr. Hyde.

Expressionistic use of light and dark breaks with Griffith's organic composition and instead creates shadows that form their own nonorganic life: "matter which raises itself to the point of life, and to a life which spreads itself through all matter" (*Cinema 1* 51). Throughout the film Trigger's shadow looms ominously between Temple and freedom. As Temple goes downstairs, leaving her room for the supposed safety of the barn, we see Trigger's shadow and the balustrade—with its broken and tilted spindles—projected twice their size against the wall. This scene is eerily similar to the famous scene in *Nosferatu* in which the vampire's exaggerated shadow, with its long fingernails, reaches for the innocent traveler's doorknob, as the lines of the staircase forms black bars on the wall.[16] When Temple steps outside the plantation house to seek sanctuary, we again see Trigger at an oblique angle, backlit, and in silhouette against the decaying house.

Later, when Trigger menacingly approaches the unguarded Temple in the corncrib, the lighting mirrors that of Dracula's dilapidated castle, with slits of sunlight highlighting the gloom and projecting bars onto the unsuspecting victim. In *Dracula*, however, there are parts of the castle that have been refurbished and in which a roaring fire and a series of candelabras provide a warm glow. There is no such lighting in the plantation house; it is a world of decay shrouded in shadows. In addition to the visual similarities between Trigger and his vampire precursor, David Skal's analysis of Dracula sounds uncannily similar to Trigger/Popeye and his effect on Temple: "Dracula, after all, is the ultimate charlatan and con man. He is a 'castrated' seducer who cannot penetrate in the conventional way; all sex energy is displaced to his mouth. Instead of providing stimulation, repeated encounters only drain and depress his lovers, who can barely recall his visits. Unconsummated in normal terms their passion soon becomes undead as well" (126). Shadows can take on their own nonorganic life, and the use of light and dark impacts the affective-image, concentrating the intensive series on the "Expressionist face," as the alternating patterns of light on Temple's face from the slats in the corncrib "disturb its outline and deprives it of its features," causing it to "participate in the non-organic life of things" (*Cinema 1* 92). Even in the sunlight, as Temple drives away with Trigger after the rape, her face is dead and expressionless.

Struss believed in creating deep blacks for night shots, as in the accident scene with Temple and Toddy. As he explained: "For night scenes I wanted enough underlying lights to get something on the film, because I didn't believe in pale gray for night. I wanted blacks with detail, highlights. If I got highlights, I could get blacks." Struss acknowledged that "there have been different schools of thought" but that cinematographers who use "little light" only "got grays and mushy black—they were not black, they were not night, and they had no detail in them. I just didn't like to work that way" (qtd. in Harvith 17). Struss was also willing to use total darkness for dramatic effect, as in the scene in which Ruby puts out the only source of light in Temple's room before taking her to the "safety" of the barn to hide her from men who have come "sniffing around." Before they can leave, the door opens, but we, like Temple, cannot see who has entered. The black screen is illuminated by a pinpoint of light coming from the end of a cigarette, an example of what Deleuze refers to as a rarefaction of the frame in which the shot is focused on only one element that is not just seen but that must be read, a technique that Alfred Hitchcock will employ twenty-one years later in *Rear Window* (1954) to signal the presence of the murderer (*Cinema 1* 12). Similarly, the glowing cigarette in *The Story of Temple Drake* ominously indicates Trigger's dangerous presence, as he habitually has a cigarette dangling from his mouth. Later, when Trigger attacks Temple in the corncrib, the scene again fades to black, and we hear her scream. This use of darkness, unlike the others, is not diegetic; Temple sees her attacker, but as in the novel, she never fully narrates the rape scene. The audience, however, which has either read or heard of the novel and knows that Popeye/Trigger rapes Temple with a corncob, can fill in the censored material. The fade-to-black is part of the grammar of the scene, which highlights what is omitted, so that the scene, but not the audience, is left in the dark.

After the rape scene Temple is transformed from the monster's innocent victim into the gangster's moll as the film shifts from the rural plantation house to the urban underworld and takes on the trappings of the gangster film. In the novel—in a speech similar to Ruby's earlier condemnation of Temple—Minnie, the African American maid at Miss Reba's, rebukes Temple for staying drunk and for not being grateful to Popeye: "What you want to treat him this-a-way, fer? Way he spend his money on you, you ought to be ashamed. He a right pretty little man, even if he aint no John Gilbert, and way he spending his money" (227). Minnie contrasts Popeye with the matinee idol of the silent screen, John Gilbert, who starred opposite Lillian Gish, Greta Garbo, and Mary Pickford: Popeye is not the hero but, rather, represents the antihero of the Depression, the gangster, who has money to burn.

Popeye is coded as black, but Trigger as gangster is coded as dark, both ethnically and racially. Although the studio could not get George Raft—who played opposite Hopkins in *Dancer in the Dark*—to play Trigger, Jack Le Rue, who was finally cast, had appeared in several gangster films, and his dark hair, complexion, and dark tailored suit mark him as a member of the ethnically defined gangster underworld. In early storyboard depictions of the rape scene, Trigger was referred to as "Mex," further indicating the interest in creating Trigger as ethnically other.[17] While Trigger's name rhymes with a racial slur and links him to the phallic image of the gun and the violence associated with the gangster (and he is also the trigger that precipitates the events of the movie, beginning with Temple's rape), his name nevertheless suggests sexual inadequacies, given the small size of a trigger and its propensity to fire with only slight pressure (hair-trigger) or to go off "half-cocked" (characteristics that are also associated with Popeye/Trigger). Even Trigger as gangster-rapist—though cruel and violent—does not quite measure up to the myth of black male sexuality.

The ambiguous status of Popeye/Trigger and Temple in many ways makes them a greater danger to a hierarchical system based on race, class, and gender superiority than Gus and Flora. Like the mulatto characters in Dixon's works, Popeye/Trigger and Temple, by their very existence, undermine a system based on difference. Faulkner's revision of the southern rape complex does not resolve the ambiguities; although the status quo reasserts itself in the end, Faulkner highlights the hypocrisy upon which the myth is based. In Faulkner's ending the belle is drawn back into the patriarchal society by her father and brothers, who convince her to lie about who committed the murder and therefore allow an innocent man to die. Temple gains nothing from lying, and her testimony seems to be another form of male (incestuous) violation in which she responds to her father in "rapt abasement" and is surrounded by her four "stiffly erect" brothers who "in a close body . . . passed through the door and disappeared" (290).

The Story of Temple Drake redeems the southern belle by drawing her into a "national" story of justice. The film, in opposition to the novel, has the violated belle punish her attacker and restore justice at the end of the film. Temple first lies to protect Stephen, then kills Trigger, and finally agrees to testify to defend Lee Goodwin. Because of her good-bad girl position in the movie, Temple can act as both gangster's moll and victim and takes the law (the gun) into her own hands. Significantly, the death of Tommy (the lower-class "feeb") and Temple's own violation are not incentive enough for Temple to act; it is only after Trigger threatens Stephen (the law) that she is spurred into action. She rewrites the southern rape complex because, in her degradation, she fails to personify the purity of the threatened South. Instead of dying, killing herself, or allowing herself to be rescued (as a "proper" belle should do), she stays with her attacker until she finally kills him, further circumventing the justification for the Klan to act.

In comparing the novel and movie, Degenfelder maintains that in the film version "not only did good triumph over evil, but Temple, wavering genteelly between these polarities, was, in the end, restored to her shrine" (546). While it is true that Temple is identified with good in the end, she is not restored to the shrine/pedestal of the southern belle. *Birth* jettisons the tainted southern belle and reinscribes and softens the northern New Woman as American belle. *The Story of Temple Drake,* on the other hand, recasts the belle as a male-defined New "American" Woman and redefines honor as based on truth and law, not purity and social reputation. Chivalry and the Drake wild streak have let Temple down, but American justice will redeem her.

REUNITING NORTH AND SOUTH

The Story of Temple Drake begins and ends with a courtroom scene that signals the shift from a "southern" code of honor based on white supremacy to an "American" code of justice that assumes an unproblematic, classless normative whiteness. Whereas *Birth* begins with scenes that associate the Old South and racial hierarchy with harmony, peace, and family, the opening scenes of *The Story of Temple Drake* set up a series of signifiers of southern decadence—the flirtatious belle; the drunken, effete gentleman; the racially prejudiced judge—that indict white upper-class racism and elitism. In *Birth* the final "victory" of the whites, both southern and northern, cannot restore the Old South but does suggest that the harmony equated with racial hierarchy in the beginning of the film is the key to a new post-Reconstruction national identity. Griffith was able to portray the racial model of the South as the national model for the future. In *Temple Drake,* on the other hand, the South is associated with racial prejudice, decadent belles, and "white trash" bootleggers. The film's final disavowal of all things southern, therefore, serves as the solution to the "negro problem," the "woman problem," the "class problem" and the "crime problem." The South is presented as the locus of the problems and not as a model for the solutions for Depression-era America, a move that will be especially appealing and used with greater frequency in movies that deal with the civil rights era.

In turning to a "national" legal solution for the southern rape complex, rather than a local illegal solution, the film distances itself from *Birth*'s white supremacist vigilantism but also from *Sanctuary*'s southern decadence and cynicism. To accomplish this, the movie rewrites Horace Benbow's failure as a lawyer to serve his client or justice. Just as the impotent Popeye of the novel is changed to the more virile Trigger of the film, the ineffectual Horace Benbow becomes the determined Stephen Benbow, who wins the case and the girl. In the novel Horace naively tells Lee Goodwin, "You've got the law, justice, civilization," and reassures Ruby, "You may know more about whiskey or love than I do, but I know more about criminal procedure, remember" (132,

270). Unfortunately, he actually knows less about all three, and his faith in the justice system does not take into account the reality of vigilante justice and the legacy of lynching, to which his client succumbs.

The initial establishing shot of the movie indicates what Stephen is up against in fighting for American justice by referencing the fictional world of Dixon's *Clansman*. The courthouse is not in Faulkner's Yoknapatawpha County but in *Dixon County*, and as if the audience might miss the significance of the setting, from the establishing shot of the courthouse the camera pulls into an extreme close-up of the words *Dixon County*. Inside the courthouse the silhouette of justice is displayed on the wall, but when Judge Drake speaks, we realize that justice in this courtroom is not blind. The Judge advises the jury not to blame Stephen for taking the case because the court appointed him. Stephen vociferously objects that the Judge's comments are "prejudicial to the interests of my client," maintaining that he willingly took the case. The viewer must infer the Judge's meaning, but presumably Stephen is the court-appointed lawyer of the working-class black man who sits behind him, and the Judge—assuming the defendant's guilt because of his race—is defending not justice but the white lawyer for taking the case in the first place. Stephen's partner comments that they will never win the case now, but Stephen concludes that they "never had a chance."

The southern courtroom in "Dixon County" is a place where justice is not served. As Seidel explains, in the 1930s writers "who indicted southern traditions often used the metaphor of the courtroom trial," and "most of the belles in these novels are portrayed as the daughters of judges, who represent the traditions that are on trial . . . The modern belle's father lives in town and works as a lawyer judge whose task is to preserve legal traditions—hence the easy analogy with his role as a faded inheritor of the southern past" (157). Stephen is distanced from the southern courtroom not only because of his objection to the Judge's statement but also because he does not speak with a southern accent, although he is part of the southern upper class. Unlike Temple, Stephen does not "sound" southern either in what he says or how he says it. This is reinforced in the next scene in which Stephen visits Judge Drake. The Judge, who is the epitome of the southern gentlemen, tells Stephen that he must accept the laws, which Stephen maintains are "obsolete" and "totally out of key with our times." The juxtaposition of Stephen's defense of his black client and his attack on outdated laws suggests that he condemns laws that are unfair to African Americans. Ironically, even as the Judge is chiding Stephen to follow the laws regardless of how he feels about them, the Judge produces a bottle of whiskey from his desk and proceeds to pour a drink, an act of hypocrisy that surely would not be lost on a Prohibition-era audience. The whiskey also negatively reinforces the earlier link between the Judge, Toddy Gowan, and the image of the southern gentleman. The Judge assumes that Toddy is a gentleman because they went to the same college, and Toddy insists that—as a gentleman—he was taught how to drink, but it is Toddy's never-ending search for more alcohol that takes Temple to the Old Frenchman place. Moreover, in his drunken stupor Toddy is unable to perform the function of the gentleman, to defend Temple's honor.

In the final trial scene of the film Stephen's cross-examination of Temple reconstitutes the novel's rendering of the rape, turning Temple's hallucinatory account told to Horace Benbow into a male-identified call for truth and justice. In the novel Temple never actually explains what happened to her; instead, she recounts to Horace—in an almost trancelike state and with the ubiquitous sound of the corn shucks in her mind—her delusional attempts to avoid the rape by transforming into a man and magically acquiring a penis: "That was when I got to thinking a funny thing. You know how you do when you're scared. I was looking at my legs and I'd try to make like I was a boy. I was thinking about if I just was a boy and then I tried to make myself one by thinking" (216). Temple, in her innocence, assumes that being a man will protect her from rape, a belief that Faulkner undercuts in the lynching scene.

Temple's story about Popeye's assault and his murder of Tommy should be the key to freeing Horace's client. Yet instead of empowering him as a lawyer, Horace's role as witness to Temple's degradation implicates him in her abjection. Ironically, although Temple was not able to turn herself into a boy, her story does have the effect of emasculating Horace, and he is transformed in the text into a victimized woman through a shifting of pronouns and point of view.[18] Horace runs to the bathroom to throw up in his delayed reaction to Temple's story: "He gave over and plunged forward and struck the lavatory and leaned upon his braced arms while the shucks set up a terrific uproar beneath her thighs. Lying with her head lifted slightly, her chin depressed like a figure lifted down from a crucifix, she watched something black and furious go roaring out of her pale body. She was bound naked on her back on a flat car moving at speed through a back tunnel, the blackness streaming in rigid threads overhead, a roar of iron wheels in her ears . . . Far beneath her she could hear the faint, furious uproar of the shucks" (223). Horace's transformation begins and ends with the sound of corn shucks that are symbols of abjection: the leftovers from the production of moonshine, made by people who themselves are referred to as "white trash," stored in the barn, which also serves as an outhouse and the scene of Temple's rape.

In Faulkner's novel the lawyer, rather than redeeming the belle, via purging the dark side from her, may also have succumbed to the same violation, or rather, he may have wished that they had used a corncob. After killing his client, the mob grabs Benbow and threatens to "do to the lawyer what [they] did to [Goodwin]. What he did to her. Only [the mob] never used a cob. [They] made him wish [the mob] had used a cob." Although we know Benbow was not lynched because he appears alive in the next chapter, he clearly does not take the 1:00 am train as planned and does not return home until the next evening; the time in between is never accounted for. Benbow responds to this assault the same way that he responded to Temple's fractured narrative of her rape, but this time he can hear nothing, only "a voice of fury like in a dream, roaring silently out of a peaceful void" (296).

The sound of the corn shucks signals Horace's hallucinatory descent into a place that corresponds to Julia Kristeva's description of abjection as "the place where meaning collapses" and boundaries dissolve. Abjection, the primary repression of the maternal body—though a necessary step in the formation of the self—returns to threaten identity. Corresponding to Horace's nightmare image, abjection is—as Kristeva states—a "weight of meaninglessness, about which there is nothing insignificant, and which crushes me. On the edge of nonexistence and hallucination, or a reality that, if I acknowledge it, annihilates me" (2). It is not simply a "lack of cleanliness or health that causes abjection"; it, like Popeye, is "what disturbs identity, system, order. What does not respect borders, positions, rules. The in-between, the ambiguous, the composite. The traitor, the liar, the criminal with the good conscience, the shameless rapist" (4). Kristeva's theory explains Popeye's role as the agent of abjection and his ability to annihilate all that he touches.

Popeye, because he is the most brutal character in the novel and the one who rapes and kidnaps Temple, is the most obvious source of the "logical pattern of evil" that Benbow discovers after hearing Temple's story, but as the novel's ending indicates, Popeye is just the sad product of syphilis, poverty, and ignorance. The calculating "logical pattern of evil" lies not with Popeye or with Temple as the flirtatious shallow belle but with the respectable southern belle, Narcissa, who is Benbow's sister. She is "the criminal with the good conscience" who would allow a man to be killed to prevent even an indirect taint upon her reputation, or as Faulkner would depict her in the short story "There Was a Queen" (1932), Narcissa is the belle who would actually have sex to protect the public appearance of innocence. As her name implies, Narcissa is the shallow, self-centered belle at the heart of the novel.

Faulkner totally deflates the high drama of the southern rape complex and condemns white middle-class morality by depicting Narcissa, the representative of a stuffy, white middle-class hypocrisy, as the prime mover of the rape and the lynching. It is her callous rejection of Gowan that drives him to drink and to turn to Temple for consolation, and that sets the events in motion that lead to Temple's rape and abduction. But even more important, Narcissa's desire to protect her name leads her to sabotage Horace's case by revealing information about his surprise witness to the district attorney in order to bring the trial to a speedy conclusion and conviction. Like Marion of *The Clansman*, Narcissa wants her name to remain "sweet and clean," and she is willing to let innocent people die to accomplish her goal. Rather than kill herself in the process, however, she is willing to sacrifice Temple and Lee Goodwin. Or what is even more callous, Narcissa does not know or care about the nature of the information that she gives the DA. Temple's rape, Goodwin's guilt or innocence, and her brother's sense of honor are all totally irrelevant to her. The only thing she cares about is that her brother is being gossiped about and that this in turn may besmirch her family name by linking her to the disreputable acts of white trash bootleggers. Narcissa fights to preserve her racial and class status, even if it means emasculating her own brother. Although Popeye, the real killer, is executed (albeit for a crime he did not commit), as Faulkner makes clear, it is the proper people (such as Narcissa) who are the source of corruption, and the lynching of Goodwin is only a more visible form of the systemic violence that Narcissa exemplifies.

In order to celebrate white middle-class American values, Narcissa disappears from the film, and Horace's filmic counterpart, Stephen, is able to do what Horace cannot: he extracts Temple's confession on the stand in service of his client, the law, and justice. Rather than being overcome by the abjection he encounters, Stephen restores "borders, positions, rules," and white identity.

He does so by compelling Temple "to be a man," to metaphorically acquire the phallus—the name of the father—and to tell the truth in order to "destroy the evil streak" in her: to overcome the effects of the rape; to reclaim her sense of honor; to free an innocent man; and to restore order. What finally induces Temple to tell her story to the jury is Stephen's impassioned speech that she live up to the Drake sense of family honor, their "courage, their willingness to make sacrifices, their love of truth." Stephen goes down the list of Temple's male relatives who have died for honor in battle, including not only the Civil War but also the "World War," a war in which North and South fought together against a foreign foe. He concludes: "You're a woman, but you're still a Drake. You want to act like one, don't you?" In his speech Stephen counteracts Aunt Jenny's earlier assertions about the hereditary Drake wild streak, with its implications of miscegenation, by asking Temple to live up to her "American" family lineage of sacrifice and duty. He banishes the flirtatious belle/flapper, not with an ambitious or self-defining New Woman but with a male-identified woman willing to take her place in the patriarchal order and expose her "darkest secrets" in the name of justice.

Judge Drake, as the representative of the southern gentleman, is of course outraged that Stephen would suggest that Temple testify, and he will not even entertain the thought that she could be involved in the case at all. One of the justifications for lynching in the South was the need to protect the woman's honor, not only by seeking revenge (which could easily be carried out by a trial) but also by preventing her from the shame of having to describe the rape in open court. In urging Temple to testify in order to free Goodwin, Stephen abandons the notion of southern chivalry by asking her to forget about her "honor" (i.e., her reputation as pure) and to redefine honor as based on truthfulness and justice.

The final reversal of the courtroom scene occurs when Temple faints after giving her testimony, and Stephen, carrying her in his arms out of the courtroom, says to Judge Drake: "You should be proud of her. I am." This image is significant in many ways. First, it indicates that Temple's transformation into a "man" was only temporary. It allows her to reassume the role of the innocent, fragile woman and to present Stephen as her protector. This is an important move because, before the courtroom scene, Temple has already taken the phallus (gun) into her own hands to kill Trigger and to protect Stephen. But this image also reinscribes a scene from *Birth,* in which Elsie is confronted by the threat of miscegenation by Silas Lynch (her father's mulatto protégé, who wants to force her into marriage).

The Story of Temple Drake reverses this process. In the courtroom scene Temple no longer dresses in the frivolous fashion of flapper/belle but instead wears a more sober gray suit, whereas in the novel she wears black satin with a "shoulder knot of purple" (284). In the film the disparity between rich and poor whites is neutralized in the courtroom. The sartorial class differences between Temple and Ruby that were so evident at the Old Frenchman place are no longer so pronounced; now both are modestly and neatly dressed. Ruby is transformed into the picture of motherhood, holding her child rather than leaving it in a box on the woodpile to keep it away from the rats. Even Goodwin, the lower-class bootlegger (though not wearing a tie) is transformed into the jacket-clad father/husband presiding over his nuclear family (not the dysfunctional "family" at the old plantation), an innocent man returned to the loving arms of his "wife."

In the final scene of *Temple Drake* Stephen, like Rhett carrying Scarlett up the stairs, reasserts his masculinity; he literally assumes the position of the dark ravisher—an image also linked to the horror film, in which the monster carries away the prostrate heroine—but unlike Rhett or Lynch, Stephen's actions are in support of the law. Temple's faint is not the feigned swoon of the belle; rather, it acts out Ruby's earlier statement that if a "'real man' touched her she'd faint." Stephen is the "real man," not the southern gentleman, and Temple now is a "real woman," not a southern belle. Originally, the movie version of *Sanctuary* was to be named *The Shame of Temple Drake*, but the Hollywood version has taken Temple out of a shame culture; her story is a story of whiteness preserved through the courts, not through lynching.

Walter Benn Michaels asserts that "for Dixon, racism was crucial to the reinvention of the American state; only by freeing themselves from slavery, destroying their familial bonds to blacks, and intermarrying with their racial kinsmen from across the Mason-Dixon line could whites become Americans" (34). In *The Story of Temple Drake* the perpetuation of the "American state" is based not only on the erasure of slavery and miscegenation but also on the erasure of the South as the focus of racial problems. The courtroom has miraculously been freed of racial prejudice simply by creating an ostensibly all-white courtroom, where race is no longer addressed. Temple frees herself from the dangerous threat of her incestuous and miscegenational lineage by becoming a typical white middle-class American, rather than a southern upper-class belle, and by destroying the malevolent and racially ambiguous lower-class white male. Unlike Flora, whose "dark desires" lead to her death, or Marion, whose honor and whiteness could be corrupted by a black man, Temple's whiteness is no longer an issue. Her honor—even in the face of violation by a white/black man and her own degrading behavior—can be renewed not through "spirit" or religion but through upholding the principle of truth, justice, and the American way.

CHAPTER 3

Believing in Mammy

Sanctuary, the Movie

In *Sanctuary* (1931) William Faulkner dismantles the Southern rape complex, and all it stands for, by thwarting its racial narrative and substituting an impotent white man for the myth of the black male rapist. In *Requiem for a Nun* (1951), Faulkner's sequel to *Sanctuary*, he continues to dismantle the southern rape complex by introducing Nancy Mannigoe as Temple Drake's modern mammy. If Temple's role as southern belle is destroyed in *Sanctuary* by her white ravisher, her role as southern lady is equally under attack in *Requiem for a Nun*, this time by the black mammy. While the black male rapist and the black mammy might seem to be total opposites, they are corollaries in the logic of the southern rape complex. Both symbols invoke the containment, control, and even annihilation of the black body—in other words, the necropolitics of the Jim Crow South.

In *Requiem* Faulkner makes the correlation between the mammy and the black rapist uncomfortably clear; although Nancy has not inflicted a "fate worse than death"—the crime for which black men were ostensibly and symbolically lynched—she does actually kill an innocent white girl, Temple's daughter. Yet Temple attempts to save Nancy's life by confessing that it is her own sin (her desire to return to her past by running away with her blackmailing lover, the brother of her former lover, Red) that has brought about the death of her daughter, a confession that dominates the novel. Although the image of the threatening black rapist can be safely distanced, to imagine a domestic worker as dangerous—considering her access to the most personal details of the family's life and with the care of its most precious possession, its children—is unimaginable. Neither Temple nor Stevens ever questions Nancy's motives or interpret them as malevolent. *Requiem for a Nun* vividly dramatizes just how far whites will go to "believe" in the myth of the black mammy.

Occurring, however, in between these two Faulknerian variations of the southern rape complex—the black-coded white man and the murdering mammy—was the Hollywood version in *The Story of Temple Drake* (1933). In 1933, several months after the release of *The Story of Temple Drake*, Faulkner began work on the first sketches of *Requiem for a Nun*. By this point Faulkner had already lived in Hollywood and worked on scripts and film treatments for MGM, including one, "The College Widow" (1932), that was never produced because of its feared resemblance to *Sanctuary*.[1] Although Faulkner did not resume work on *Requiem for a Nun* for many years, the novel takes up many of the elements of the southern rape complex depicted in *The Story of Temple Drake*, which focuses on race, rape, justice, and redemption and turns them on their head.

Unlike *The Birth of a Nation*, a film with which Faulkner was "quite familiar," according to Bruce Kawin (15), Faulkner's reworking of the southern rape complex in *Sanctuary* includes no dashing ride to the rescue, nor does the lynching affirm white southern sovereignty. In the place of the stereotype of the mythic black rapist, Faulkner substitutes Popeye Pumphrey, a childlike, impotent, syphilitic gangster who, though white, is repeatedly coded black, as the characters refer to him as "that black man."[2] And instead of the mythically potent black phallus, Popeye must use a corncob. Popeye's hybrid status as a white black man invokes the sensationalism of the southern rape complex at the same time it nullifies it as a tool used by whites to commit violence. Temple Drake, as representative of white southern womanhood, whose protection was the justification for lynching, has been savagely debased by the abject remains of the South's new Depression-era cash crop—corn, used to make bootleg whiskey—in a barn that is used as an outhouse, with an instrument that is often used in lieu of toilet paper. In the end Temple, the abject belle, testifies against Lee Goodwin—an innocent man—and she is then escorted from the courtroom "shrinking and [in] rapt abasement" as her father and brothers surround her.[3] After the trial a vigilante crowd sodomizes and then burns alive the innocent, white Lee Goodwin. The mob's flagrant disregard of the law in the novel is made even more evident when they threaten to do the same to Lee's lawyer, Horace Benbow (296). Faulkner therefore empties lynching of its racialized domination, leaving only the empty husk: senseless violence and terror. Faulkner himself described *Sanctuary* as "an exposition of the terror and injustice which man must face and which he must combat if he is to live with himself, in his soul; if he is to sleep in peace at night" (qtd. in Phillips 68).

If Faulkner debunks southern vigilante justice in *Sanctuary*, he also questions the possibility of legal justice. The final chapter gives us the equally arbitrary death of Popeye, who, even though he is a gangster and operates outside the law, seems to believe that justice will prevail. He does not see the need for a lawyer to defend himself against the charge of killing a policeman because he is innocent: "I told them last night I never was here before in my life" (310–11), but they hang him just the same. Similarly, Lee Goodwin does not fear the law. He has been freed in the past through the efforts of his lawyer and assumes that, because he is innocent, Benbow will be able to free him this time; it is Popeye whom Lee fears. As a well-known underworld gangster, Popeye (like the mob) is used to killing with impunity. Lee realizes that if he implicates Popeye, his death is certain, whereas in a courtroom there is a chance that he will go free: a possibility that his naive lawyer believes as well.

The Story of Temple Drake, on the other hand, creates a happy ending by taking the "southern" out of the southern rape complex and replacing the honor code, on which it is based, with a national legal standard of truth and courage. Popeye, the impotent, black-coded syphilitic is transformed into Trigger, the virile gangster; Horace Benbow, the ineffectual lawyer, is transformed into Stephen Benbow, a dashing lawyer who, in opposition to Judge Drake, rejects Jim Crow politics and "antiquated laws." Temple is transformed from vapid coed to a heroine who shoots Trigger to protect Stephen—the man she truly loves—and thereby circumvents any call for lynching by killing her own attacker. Later, at Stephen's request, she testifies on the stand to the rape and killing in order to free Lee Goodwin. But more important, her testimony gives her the chance, as Stephen implores her, to redeem herself through public confession, to eradicate the Drake "dark streak" that has kept her from marrying Stephen and to replace it with a lineage of Drake honor exemplified by their history of fighting not only in the Civil War but in the "Great War," a sign of national solidarity. As Stephen says, "You're a woman, but you're still a Drake, you want to act like one don't you?"

Temple must confess to expiate her own sins and purge her dark side, and in the process she also casts off her role as belle in terms of her appearence, her words, and her actions. It is Temple's spiritually, legally, and socially redemptive courtroom confession in *The Story of Temple Drake* that frees an innocent man as it simultaneously purges Temple's "dark side." In *Requiem for a Nun,* however, Temple confesses on three different occasions, none of which saves her or Nancy. By debunking the purgative power of the confession in *Requiem for a Nun,* Faulkner thus includes and at the same time deconstructs a crucial element of the earlier film adaptation (*The Story of Temple Drake*) not found in the original novel (*Sanctuary*). *Sanctuary* and *Requiem for a Nun* both dramatically portray the hypocrisy and perversion at the heart of the southern rape complex, which Faulkner's novels graphically depict and the Hollywood versions sensationalize even as they undercut it.

In analyzing Faulkner's relationship to film, two of the most typical approaches are to examine the influence of cinema and screenwriting on Faulkner's fiction or to analyze the filmic adaptations of Faulkner's works. While these two approaches are often used independently, I will combine them to explore how the filmic adaptation of Faulkner's work might have influenced his future novel. Specifically, I address how *The Story of Temple Drake* as the Hollywood adaptation of *Sanctuary* may have influenced Faulkner's own 1951 sequel *Requiem for a Nun.* Therefore, although almost any reading of *Requiem for a Nun* makes reference to *Sanctuary,* to understand *Requiem for a Nun* fully, it is productive to consider it as a sequel to both *Sanctuary* and its Hollywood adaptation.

There is, however, a fourth version of Temple's story as depicted in the 1961 Hollywood adaptation of *Requiem for a Nun,* entitled *Sanctuary* (1961). *Sanctuary,* the movie, includes the rape of Temple Drake (from *Sanctuary,* the novel) and Nancy's murder of Temple's child (from *Requiem for a Nun*) and therefore must be read in the context of the two novels as well as that of the earlier adaption, *The Story of Temple Drake.* There are a number of major differences between *Requiem for a Nun* and its 1961 film adaptation, entitled *Sanctuary.* Initially, in *Sanctuary* the movie, Temple is much bolder than in the novels or the earlier film, and she is much more of an overt flapper—we first see her at a rowdy party wearing a sequined, fringed red dress and doing the Charleston with Gowan. Temple also haughtily assumes her elite status will be recognized and catered to when they wind up at the bootleggers' shack, not the dilapidated mansion that figures so prominently in *The Story of Temple Drake.* But after her rape—which is unmistakably depicted as a rape—she falls madly in love with her rapist. Instead of Popeye's black-coded deviance, the rapist's "otherness," while still ambiguous, is captured by the suave Cajun Candy Man, played by Yves Montand. Furthermore, Candy Man, who is thought to have died in a crash while driving Temple's car to make a whiskey delivery, comes back eight years later to claim Pepper—his nickname for Temple—whose real name he does not care to know. Thus, there is no initial trial; Temple simply returns home when her car is found, and thus her whereabouts are discovered. But the most significant difference between the novel and film is that the adaptation seemingly resolves the ambiguity of Nancy's motives and Temple's salvation. Nancy gives a clear and Christian motivation for her act of "love," unlike her laconic and ambiguous responses in the novel when Nancy is asked why she killed the Temple's child. Temple's confession, as in the earlier film adaptation *The Story of Temple Drake,* is the key to the "happy ending." Through the suffering of confession, Temple is saved from a life of sin. Yet the ending of *Sanctuary,* the movie, also allows for a more political reading of the 1961 film, in keeping with the events of the civil rights movement, which casts doubts on Temple's freedom and Nancy's role as all-loving mammy.

What the different versions of Temple's story have in common is the tension between vigilante violence (whether perpetrated by an individual or a mob) and the legal system. Whereas *Sanctuary,* the novel, culminates in a white-on-white lynching of an innocent man, in the prologue to act 1 of *Requiem for a Nun* Faulkner traces the origins of Jefferson and its courthouse back to the town's attempt to prevent a white-on-white lynching through the power of national sovereignty. As they await the arrival of the federal marshal, the townspeople secure under lock and key a group of bandits and the drunken militia that brought them in. But ironically, the very act of federal compliance reveals a violation of federal property: as the postman points out, the lock's removal from the mailbag to secure the prisoners exposes the damage to the mailbag (federal property) made when slits were cut to secure the lock. Therefore, to avoid fines and possible jail time, the people must incorporate the town to link themselves to the very entity they have offended. Their act of naming the town Jefferson is an implicit bribe to the representative of that entity, the postman Thomas Jefferson Pettigrew.

Employing the concept of the "state of exception" to analyze the role of state and nation in *Requiem for a Nun,* Steven Weisenburger cautions against applying the term to lynching: "For while Jim Crow mobs knowingly acted outside the rule of law," they acted "according to a widely accepted, populist sociocultural warrant originating in a shared and culturally articulated white supremacist ideology," unlike recent cases (such as Abu Ghraib prison, near Baghdad) in which the torturers "knowingly violated sociocultural norms but did it on the strength of a legal writ" (742).[4] Lynching, however, is not simply an articulation of a "populist sociocultural warrant." On a political level lynching employs a "state of exception," which, according to Giorgio Agamben, is the ability to abrogate the law—to declare a "state of exception"—and it is the ultimate sign of modern sovereign power. Agamben cites Lincoln's suspension of habeas corpus during the Civil War as an example of sovereign power over and above that of the Constitution or Congress (State 20).

Lynching, although it is not an act of individual national sovereignty—as in the case of Lincoln—invokes a state of exception; the act of lynching confers state sovereignty (above and beyond national law) at the same time that it denies African Americans status as citizen subjects. The 1871 Civil Rights Act, or Force Act, effectively dismantled the Klan as a widespread southern institution; however, the reemergence and perpetuation of the lynching of African Americans constitute what Agamben refers to as a peacetime perpetual state of exception in which those who do not count (*homo sacer*) can be killed indiscriminately and without legal retaliation. Agamben asserts that this peacetime state of exception shows the true power of sovereignty, but in the U.S. South the sovereignty being invoked is not that of the nation-state but that of states' rights. The killing—while often indiscriminate as to which black was lynched, as Faulkner's "Dry September" dramatizes—is based on the fear of black economic and political equality. Lynch mobs acted under the tacit assumption that the states would use their prosecutorial discretion to overlook acts of violence perpetrated against black citizens and to select all-white juries when trials actually were conducted. Supporting these assumptions was the presence of law officials who were known to participate directly or indirectly in such violent acts. Even former U.S. senator William Sullivan openly admitted that he "led the mob" that lynched Nelse Patton, which occurred in Faulkner's hometown of Oxford, Mississippi, when Faulkner was a boy.

The state of exception creates a blurring of boundaries; it "is neither external nor internal to the juridical order, and the problem of defining it concerns precisely a threshold, or a zone of indifference, where inside and outside do not exclude each other but rather blur with each other" (23). On a psychoanalytic level, casting the black man as rapist and then castrating and killing him embodies and dramatizes the role of abjection, which also creates a blurring of boundaries.[5] According to Kristeva, abjection is a violent revolt against a threat that seems to come from "an exorbitant outside or inside" and must be expelled "beyond the scope of the possible, the tolerable, the thinkable" (1). In cases of lynching the "exorbitant outside" must be made visually manifest by an actual public spectacle, as if the threat to individual white identity was so extreme that it must be put down through public rituals that enact the very violent primitivism against which they claim to protect.

Yet as historians have chronicled, black women, too, have been lynched as well as raped and beaten—some even have had their children cut out of their wombs—and these atrocities continued well after Reconstruction. In 1894 one black mother was placed in a barrel with nails driven into it and rolled down a hill, and in 1918 Mary Turner, after voicing her objection to the arbitrary lynching of her husband, was taken from her home by a mob that hung her upside down by her ankles, cut her child from her womb, trampled it, and then poured gasoline on her and set her on fire (Allen 14; Wells 149).[6] The ferocity and cruelty of these acts, as in lynching, suggest more than violence as a political weapon. In connection with the ritualistic castration of many black male lynching victims, the murder of black mothers suggests a symbolic, if not a literal, attempt at genocide. We can see a strange link between the fear of rape and the fear of genocide in Thomas Dixon's *Clansman* (upon which *The Birth of a Nation* was based, one of the most infamous depictions of the southern rape complex). Just as Dixon used the endangerment of the white virgin as a justification for lynching black men in *The Clansman*, he also presented an equally hysterical fear of an attack on white southern mothers as a justification for violating national laws that would seek to create a "black empire" in the South. As with the southern rape myth, he positions white (rather than the black) southerners as the victims of cruel retribution: the Radical Republican Stoneman, as part of his condemnation of the South, calls for "the extermination of its landed aristocracy, that their mothers shall not breed another race of traitors" (50).

This annihilation of the black mother—like the lynching of the black male—also relates to abjection, which occurs when the primary repression of the maternal body, though a necessary step in the formation of the self, returns to threaten identity. The power of the abject is that it "confronts us . . . with our earliest attempts to release the hold of a maternal entity" that represents "a power as securing as it is stifling" (Kristeva 13).[7] Because of the use of black women as wet nurses and nannies, both before and after the Civil War, the maternal body for many white southerners was the *black* maternal body. In a society in which both women and blacks had an inferior status, the need to abject the black maternal body takes on even greater force.[8] Therefore, the relationship with the black mother had to be contained through annihilation or sentimentalized to the point that a white person's love for his/her black "mammy" became an acceptable cultural cliché.[9] Faulkner's own fondness for Mammy Callie, his family's black maid, is well documented, and his portrait of Dilsey in *The Sound and the Fury* (1929) depicts a loyal family retainer attempting to protect her white charges, as best she can, from the cruelty and neglect of their own family.[10] But even those who never had or could not afford a black nanny could still use the figure of the mammy as a link to the "old days" by purchasing the many variations of her image, from cookie jars to dolls. In the character of Nancy, Faulkner embodies the vulnerability of and dangers faced by the black maternal body; as a black prostitute, Nancy is violated on a sexual, economic, and maternal level.

The ubiquitous image of the asexual mammy who loves and protects white children functions as a screen for the white child's attraction/repulsion for the black maternal body as well as for the brutal realities of the violence done to black mothers. The mammy counteracts the fear of the wild black brute, as she is most assuredly domesticated, but by projecting all feelings of vengeance and hatred on the image of the black male rapist, the image of the mammy also negates the possibility of black female resentment or retaliation against whites. Not only is she not perceived as resentful about slavery, she herself—as popularly depicted—perpetuates the master-slave relationship. She is the enforcer of the very rules of ladylike behavior from which she herself is barred.[11] She is also depicted as willing to sacrifice her needs, as well as those of her family, out of love for her white masters. Therefore, the mammy can be embraced as "family" precisely because of her abject status; she is the black maternal body that can be symbolically incorporated because she is given only the limited power to serve and to protect her white family.

Nancy, who is referred to repeatedly as a "nigger, dope-fiend whore," is presented as an abject, self-sacrificing mammy of the white family. If the black rapist's desire for white women—or girls, as in the case of *The Birth of a Nation*—represents the most extreme threat to white society, the black mammy's love for white children represents its antidote. Unlike the myth of the black male rapist, which did not galvanize until after the Civil War, the image of the mammy was a familiar one during slavery; it was solidified in the North and South through the minstrel show and later through the commercialization of Aunt Jemima and the cinematic depictions of the loyal black mammy, most notably in Hattie McDaniel's role in *Gone with the Wind*.[12] Both the image of the asexual, yet maternal, mammy and the southern rape myth—which justifies and highlights the excessive attempt to annihilate the black male body—obscure violence against black women (a point that the black press made clear in 1923, when, days after the Dyer antilynching law was defeated in the Senate, a bill was passed to create a national memorial to the black mammy).[13] Even when sexual violation of black women is acknowledged, it is not acknowledged *as* a violation, and black women were often blamed for such acts because of their alleged licentiousness. White men held black women accountable not only for their own violation by white men but also for the violation of white women by black men. According to historian Philip A. Bruce in 1889, "Because of the sexual laxness of plantation women as a class," black men did not understand the concept of sexual violation, having never encountered resistance (qtd. in Roberts 11). Concentrating on virginal white women as victims limits victims by race and gender as well as by marital status. Part of the "tragedy" of the southern rape myth is that the white virgin is taken out of the system of exchange. Taken together, these elements of the myth obscure the practice and symbolism of systematic violence against black women and children, in particular the extreme forms of mutilation perpetrated against black mothers.

This conflicted relationship to the black maternal body is seen in the difference between the idealization of the black mammy and the vilification of the black mother. One of the many contradictory elements of the black mammy figure was that even as she was represented as smothering her white charges with love and protection, black slave mothers were depicted as literally smothering their own babies through their "great carelessness & total inability to take care of themselves," as recorded by Charles M. Pelot in the *South Carolina Mortality Schedules* of 1850 (qtd. in Johnson, "Smothered" 495).[14] After slavery black mothers, who allegedly had "none of the brooding mother-love and anxiety" of white mothers, were accused of killing their children intentionally rather than through neglect. As Eleanor Tayleur writes in 1904, "Infanticide is not regarded as a crime among negroes, but it is so appallingly common that if the statistics could be obtained on this subject they would send a shudder through the world" (qtd. in Roberts 14).

Through Nancy, Faulkner combines the loving mammy at the center of the family with the abject, murdering black mother. If Popeye embodied the abject through his role as what Kristeva described as the "shameless rapist," then Nancy equally embodies abjection as Kristeva's example of "the killer who claims he is a savior." Despite Nancy's dangerous background as a "dope-fiend whore," Temple employs her as a nursemaid. Acutely aware of the historical role of the black mammy in slavery, Temple self-consciously and self-deprecatingly explains that Nancy is no "ole cradle-rocking black mammy at all" because Temple and Gowan, part of the young, modern, smart crowd, are applauded by the "other young country-club set" for their progressive act of taking "an ex-dope-fiend nigger whore out of the gutter to nurse their children." Because Nancy's past is not that of a stereotypical mammy, her employment can be seen as an act of progressive charity rather than traditional servitude based on limited career possibilities for African American women. But the easy acceptance of Nancy's past is still based on the assumption that all black women are potential mammies, regardless of their background or training. Though they are often not seen as fit to raise their own children, black women's capacity to raise white children is not questioned. Temple's description of how Nancy came to them suggests an almost natural progression of gestation in which the arrival of the baby is followed immediately with the arrival of the nursemaid, as she explains, "Then the son and heir came; and now we have Nancy." Although Temple's tone is often mocking, her description of Nancy as caretaker is characteristic of the most sentimental descriptions of the mammy: "nurse: guide: mentor, catalyst, glue, whatever you want to call it, holding the whole lot of them together" (136). From Temple's viewpoint Nancy is the indispensable center whose only function in life is to hold the white family together.

Even though she invokes the image of the mammy, Temple reveals another more pressing function that Nancy serves, as Temple's "sister in sin" (136). In act 2 Temple prefaces her confession to the governor as an explanation for why "Temple Drake, the white woman, the all-Mississippi debutante, descendant of long lines of statesmen and soldiers high and proud in the high proud annals of our sovereign state, couldn't find anybody except a nigger dope-fiend whore that could speak her language" (105).[15] In acknowledging her tie to Nancy, Temple repudiates the proud family lineage that lawyer Steven Benbow in *The Story of Temple Drake* uses to induce Temple to confess truthfully and publicly on the stand to free herself from sin. Temple purposefully and ironically repudiates her place on the pedestal as a white, elite southern woman when she identifies her relationship with Nancy as that of the "big-time ball player, the idol on the pedestal, the worshipped; and the worshipper, the acolyte, the one that never had and never would, no matter how willing or how hard she tried, get out of the sandlots, the bush league" (137). Temple's "sports metaphor," as Stevens refers to it, also has suggestive sexual overtones, which relates back to her shared language of sin.

In the dramatic section of *Requiem for a Nun*, which most resembles a screenplay, the central question of justice—as in *The Story of Temple Drake*—centers on Temple's transformation through confession. Yet Faulkner undermines the power of the act by creating three forms of confession, none of which is public and none of which redeems Temple. Her confession does not free an innocent white man or purge her guilt (as in *The Story of Temple Drake*) because she is actually trying to free her guilty sister in sin, Nancy. And Temple—now Temple Stevens, after marrying her derelict gentleman, Gowan Stevens—does not confess in the courtroom. Although both the district attorney and the governor preside over her testimony, the proceedings are totally outside the law; Noel Polk even refers to Gavin Stevens, the district attorney and Temple's uncle-in-law, as a "one man lynch mob" (195). Temple is confessing in order to free the woman who killed her own infant daughter, but as Temple will later discover, there was never even a chance that her confession would free Nancy Mannigoe.

Temple's sexual confidences to Nancy and her confessions of sinfulness to Gavin and the governor represent, respectively, Michel Foucault's distinction between *ars erotica* and *scientia sexualis*. As "two sisters in sin swapping trade or anyway avocational secrets over Coca-Colas in the quiet kitchen" (136), Nancy and Temple exemplify the *ars erotica*, in which "truth is drawn from pleasure itself, understood as a practice and accumulated as experience; pleasure is not considered in relation to an absolute law of the permitted and the forbidden, or by reference to a criterion of utility, but first and foremost in relation to itself; it is experienced as pleasure, evaluated in terms of its intensity, its specific quality, its duration, its reverberations in the body and soul" (57). In the *ars erotica* knowledge is handed down from master to initiate. But even though Temple acknowledges Nancy's sexual expertise, Temple—by virtue of her class status—is the one in control of the conversation. In describing Nancy's role as confidante, Temple imbues her with power even as she silences her. Temple does not attempt to disguise the one-way nature of the relationship, explaining in third person that "what Temple had" was "somebody paid by the week just to listen" (138). Just before this pronouncement, Temple envisions the perfect world without war because it was "populated with a kind of creature half of which were dumb, couldn't do anything but listen, couldn't even escape from having to listen to the other half." The failure to be listened to, Temple maintains, is what creates "anti-social enemies" (138).[16] But the inequalities inherent in Temple's solution to war and perversion also describe the dynamics of slavery, which spawned both war and perversion. Temple herself acknowledges that even having a paid listener was not enough to keep her from breaking social norms, but more important, what Temple does not acknowledge is the possibility of agency or reaction on the part of the listener. Temple certainly does not acknowledge the possibility of anger or resentment. That the black mammy might hate her charges or her mistress is literally unthinkable.

Requiem for a Nun tragically depicts the consequences of assuming that the paid confidante cannot think or act. Although most critics focus on Gavin Stevens's role in compelling (or coercing) Temple to confess to her dark past and her culpability in her daughter's death, Temple's most devastating confession is coerced from her by Nancy, not Stevens, and it is about the present, not her past.[17] Gavin's desire for "Truth" clearly follows Foucault's model of *scientia sexualis,* which combines religious and scientific discourse to construct sex as the source of all problems and, therefore, demands a meticulous inventory of sexuality in order to diagnose and heal and/or punish.[18] Temple picks up on this conflation of sexual and religious discourse when she asks Gavin how much of her past (meaning her sexual past) she has to tell: "Why blink your own rhetoric? Why don't you go on and tell me it's for the good of my soul—if I have one?" (78).[19] While it is true that in act 2, scene 1, we witness Temple's confession, under pressure from Gavin, who fills in much of the narrative, when Stevens commands Temple to tell the governor the rest of the story, including the events leading up to her daughter's death, the stage is dark, and the next scene is a flashback, not a direct confession. It is not clear if this is the story that she narrates to the governor and Stevens, if this is her "private" recollection, or if this represents the actual events as they happened, but this direct dramatization does eliminate Gavin's role as interlocutor, allowing Nancy to voice her own questions.

While both Stevens—Gavin and Gowan—seem most upset that Temple enjoyed her captivity in the Memphis brothel (that it became her own captivation with sexual desire, i.e., that she "loved it"), Nancy already knows Temple's sexual secrets and has in fact been paid to listen to them. Despite Temple's assumed control of Nancy as mute listener, what we learn in the flashback is that—even before Gavin's staged confession—Nancy has already forced Temple to confess, not to having dark desires but to being a bad mother: "You don't need to make no excuses to me. Jus tell me what you must have already strengthened your mind up to telling all the rest of the folks that are going to ask you that. You are willing to risk it [never seeing her children again]. Is that right?" (169). Nancy forces Temple to confess her willingness to abandon and/or endanger her children, "to say it out in words [her]self, so [Nancy] can hear them." Nancy continues: "Say, I'm going to do it . . . If you can do it, you can say it" (164). Later (in terms of the chronology of events but not the order of narration) Temple mirrors Nancy's words when trying to understand Gavin's desire for truth for its own sake: "For no more than that. For no better reason than that. Just to get it told, breathed aloud into words, sound" (78). Temple's reluctance to confess and her doubt about it saving her soul may stem from the fact that instead of receiving absolution after her earlier confession to Nancy, she discovers her daughter's death at Nancy's hand.

In assessing Nancy's motives for killing the baby, critics often accept Temple's interpretation of Nancy as "trying to hold us together in a household, a family," even though Temple acknowledges the futility of such an act because "anybody should have known all the time [it] couldn't possibility hold together . . . even in decency, let alone happiness" (163). Noel Polk was one of the first critics to raise the "possibility that Nancy is partially motivated by revenge: against Temple, who has been no better morally than she, yet who is reaping all the rewards of virtue—husband, family, and community"; yet in acknowledging the possibility of Nancy's motivation of revenge, Polk assumes that it is based on envy, that Nancy considers the respectable middle-class elements of "husband, family and community standing" as the "rewards of virtue" that Temple has earned (202). Nancy, however, directly refutes Temple's reading: "I aint talking about any household or happiness neither" (163). As silent witness, Nancy—better than anyone else—knows that there is very little in their lives to envy, despite the outward signs of peace and prosperity: Temple's "rewards of virtue" are to be trapped in a union based on guilt and grief.

If Nancy is not motivated by envy over Temple's middle-class lifestyle and if she is not simply acting as a good mammy, is it possible to imagine any other motive for her killing a child? As both Temple and Nancy acknowledge, if Nancy really wanted to preserve the sanctity of the white family—to enforce the code of the respectable southern lady—she could have given Pete (Temple's new blackmailing boyfriend) the money and jewelry that Nancy had hidden, and he might have left with what he really came for, leaving Temple behind. As Nancy qualifies, it is the fate of Temple's two children she is talking about, not the household or Temple's happiness, and while Nancy's concern for the children is still within the scope of her role as mammy, her own relationship to motherhood has been quite different from that of Temple. During Nancy's earlier time in prison, she herself was pregnant, an event from Faulkner's short story "That Evening Sun," which is included in *Requiem for a Nun.* In that story Nancy is first pressed into service as a substitute mammy for the Compson family when Dilsey takes sick. As Temple recounts, rather than a debutante ball, Nancy "made her debut into the public life of her native city while lying in the gutter with a white man trying to kick her teeth or at least her voice back down her throat" (105). To supplement her meager income from the backbreaking work of doing laundry and to support her alleged drug habit, Nancy also works as a prostitute. But because her clients are white, respectable men, she is put in jail when she tries to collect her money from the bank cashier, who—in front of a crowd of people—kicks her in the mouth as he tries to silence her demands for payment.[20] "That Evening Sun" ends with Nancy sitting in terror but also with a kind of fatalism as she awaits—what she believes is—her death at the hands of Jesus, her common-law husband. Jesus has threatened to cut the vine of the watermelon she has under her dress because he believes the baby is the child of one of her white johns. In *Requiem for a Nun* Nancy does not die in jail, but a few months later a man kicks her in the stomach, killing her child.[21]

What Temple has—but is willing to give up—is what Nancy did not have, a mother's ability to protect her children from danger and poverty. In "One Child of One's Own" Alice Walker questions why so many white feminist artists, writers, and critics have trouble thinking of black women as women: "It occurred to me that perhaps white women feminists, no less that white women generally, cannot imagine black women have vaginas. Or if they can, where imagination leads them is too far to go . . . Perhaps it is the black woman's children, whom the white woman—having more to offer her own children, and certainly not having to offer them slavery or a slave heritage or poverty or hatred, generally speaking: segregated schools, slum neighborhoods, the worst of everything—resents. For they must always make her feel guilty. She fears knowing that black women want the best for their children just as she does . . . Better then to deny that the black woman has a vagina. Is capable of motherhood. Is a woman" (374). Temple pays the ultimate price to believe in the eternal devotion of the black mammy without fully acknowledging her as a woman and a mother.

So, what are we to make of Nancy's killing of the unnamed, white baby girl? Is it revenge, protection, or merely an expression of Nancy's fatalistic attitude? Nancy never states a clear-cut motive, but among the possible interpretations we must consider that Nancy—like the lynch mob or lawyer Stevens—creates her own state of exception to inflict punishment on Temple. It is a double form of punishment because, in killing the baby girl, Nancy takes away Temple's illusion that, as an upper-class white woman, she can protect her children. At the same time Nancy condemns Temple to live out that fantasy for the rest of her life, as though Temple's staying could automatically protect the remaining child. The sovereignty Nancy invokes, however, is not national or white state sovereignty but religious, implying that she answers to a higher order: God as the ultimate sovereign, the King of Kings. The spectators in the courtroom seem to sense this in their shocked reaction to Nancy's statement "Yes, Lord" when the judge pronounces the sentence, ending with "And may God have mercy on your soul." All the officers of the court spring into action as "the curtain starts hurriedly and jerkily down as if the judge, the officer, the court itself were jerking frantically at it to hide this disgraceful business" (45). Here Nancy does not act like a guilty prisoner upon whom a sentence has been given, but instead she presents herself as an instrument of God who is confirming his plan.

Part of the reason that Temple, Stevens, and many of the earlier critics seem willing to accept Nancy's act as moral, however, is because she combines two very powerful narratives: Christian martyrdom and the all-loving black mammy. If Nancy has learned the language of sin, she has also learned the language of Christianity, but they are disturbingly—and perhaps, as Temple indicates, appropriately—intertwined. In the final jail scene, in answer to Temple's first question, "Believe what?" Nancy replies, laconically, "Just believe." For Nancy belief and hopelessness are synonymous when she goes on to state that she knows that Temple went to see the governor and it does not matter: "I finished all that a long time back, that same day in the judge's court. No: before that even: in the nursery that night, before I even lifted my hand." When Temple tells her to hush, Nancy reiterates that it is all right, adding, "I can get low for Jesus too, I can get low for Him too" (234). Like most of the dialogue in this act, it is impossible to tell exactly what either of the women mean: the most innocuous reading would be that "get low" refers to humbling herself before Christ, but given their shared language of sin, Temple seems to suggest a more provocative reading of the line when she tries to silence Nancy again, saying, "At least, don't blaspheme," and then adds, "But who am I to challenge the language you talk about Him in, when He Himself certainly cant challenge it, since that's the only language He arranged for you to learn?" (235).

Nancy's reference to Jesus in *Requiem for a Nun* takes on a more disturbing connotation when we remember that Jesus is also the name of Nancy's razor-toting husband in "That Evening Sun."[22] In the earlier story Faulkner highlights this connection and confusion when the Compson children are not sure to which Jesus Nancy refers when, in a state of terror, she moans his name. Nancy tries to use the white Compson home as a sanctuary to save her from her husband, Jesus, and when that does not work, she tries to bring the Compson children to her house as a kind of shield, assuming that Jesus would not attack her if there were whites around. When she explains her predicament to Dilsey, she first refuses guilt or responsibility, saying, "It aint none of my fault," but later, when she concludes that even whites cannot save her, she accepts the repercussions of her action—regardless of her guilt or innocence—as she fatalistically awaits her husband's retribution, saying: "I reckon it belongs to me. I reckon what I going to get ain't no more than mine" and "Putting it off won't do no good" (307). What is perhaps more disturbing than the conflation of the name Jesus is that Nancy's hopeless resignation in *Requiem for a Nun* is identical to her fatalistic acceptance of her husband's violence in "That Evening Sun." It is, in fact, impossible to tell to which Jesus she refers.

In order to see her crime as a moral—even if misguided—act, we must understand Nancy's intentions, and that is something we never fully learn, just as we never learn the reason for Temple's only actual crime, her perjury in the trial of Lee Goodwin. But rather than determining the morality of the crime, we might investigate the possible logic of it. To do that, we can turn to Nancy's parable to explain God's relation to suffering and to her concept of heaven, apart from Steven's and Temple's interpretation of it.[23] In one sense Temple is punished by her own wish for a mute listener, as she desperately tries, in the last scene, to get Nancy to explain to her not why she did it but the nature of suffering and redemption. Nancy's parable of God as a mule owner has not received much critical attention, and it is easy simply to read it as a sign of Nancy's ignorance, as a bastardized version of a biblical parable uttered by an illiterate woman. But Nancy has in fact presented an excellent parable of the biopolitics of a jail but also more generally of the Jim Crow South. She provides an astute Marxist parable of the uses of surplus labor and an alternative version of Foucaultian surveillance, both of which seem to reflect her understanding of heaven.

In Nancy's parable her mule owner is neither omnipotent nor omnipresent; he can neither keep track of all his mules nor find useful work for them. They are his by default "because at least don't nobody else want to claim them." What he does have is a pasture fence that holds them so that "they cant harm themselves nor nobody else," and he knows where he can find them to "hem" up the ones he needs and put "the gear" on them to make them do his work. This form of containment and surveillance is imperfect, as "he's still got to be careful about getting too close to them, or forgetting that another one of them is behind him," but from Saturday afternoon until Monday morning, they can "run free in mule sin and mule pleasure" (238). If the mules are not self-policing because they have not incorporated the all-seeing eye of the panopticon, they are—like Nancy—fully and fatalistically aware that they are trapped and there is no way out. When Stevens questions Nancy's place in heaven, she replies, "I can work." Heaven for Nancy is not a place of rest or beauty but appears to be much the same as her life on earth and much the same as her parable of the mules: if you put the gear on her, she can work. It is Stevens who envisions a kind of mammy limbo where Nancy will do "the washing and sweeping, maybe even the children to be tended and fed and kept from hurt and harm and out from under the grown folks' feet" until she earns, if she ever does, her "harp" and "raiment" (239).

In a novel that focuses on the origins of towns, states, nations, and sin, Nancy's act of killing Temple's daughter makes a kind of sense, especially given Nancy's fatalism.[24] The ultimate way to protect the child, both from Temple's life with a gangster and from growing up to be like her mother—the only way to ensure that the dark streak will not be perpetuated—is to cut it off before it begins, just as Nancy's own child was killed before it could be subjected to the kind of life its mother led. Yet despite the symbolism of killing the baby girl, we cannot assume that Nancy chose to kill only the daughter. Nancy's concern is for "two children," and she is worried about Temple leaving her son, Bucky, with a father who questions his paternity. We cannot rule out the possibility that Nancy would have killed both children had she had the opportunity. But we also cannot rule out the possibility that Nancy is not actually sacrificing her own life in the usual sense of the word, but rather, her act kills two birds with one stone, or in this case kills two sisters. In "That Evening Sun" Nancy tries to commit suicide while in jail, an act that would end both her life and that of her unborn child. The end of *Requiem for a Nun* is a repetition with a difference: Nancy's act can be seen as a form of suicide in which—in killing Temple's child—she kills herself as well, knowing that she will be executed for the murder.[25] Although Alice Walker assumed that in general white women could protect their children, Nancy seems to understand what Temple does not: that whiteness alone is not enough, that Temple's protection as an elite white woman is conditional, not inherent, while Nancy's protection is nonexistent.

While Nancy seems to invoke the sovereignty of God as the basis for her state of exception—that if a mother is not fit, it is better to kill the children than to allow them to suffer—she is fully aware that within the law (national or state) she does not have the status of citizenship. She knows that no matter to whom Temple talks or what she says, Nancy will still be hanged. Temple, however, has grown up believing that she had the power and force of law on her side, which she tries in *Sanctuary* to invoke at Frenchmen's Bend by repeating that her father is a judge. It would seem safe to assume that after her rape and abduction, and now the murder of her child, the Temple of *Requiem for a Nun* would question her ability to invoke the power of the state, but as a woman of privilege—including access to the governor in the middle of the night—she assumes that her own guilt and her willingness to destroy her reputation as a southern lady (as in *The Story of Temple Drake*) should have the power to stay an execution. In other words, through her status she should be able to declare a state of exception. Temple correctly understands that the governor (who is also her father in the film), whom she refers to at one point as the "sovereign state," has "the legal power to pardon or at least reprieve" (178). But the governor, like Gowan and Temple, uses Nancy's very abjectness as a reason to accept her sacrifice: "Who am I to render null and abrogate the purchase she made with that poor crazed lost and worthless life?" (180). Because a pardon is a legalized form of "exception," it does actually signify the power of sovereignty symbolized by the power to kill indiscriminately. The governor resorts to the rule of law in punishment because, especially in a southern state, the killing of a white by a black is by definition a hanging offense; there can be no exception. An exception would place Nancy in the position of the citizen; moreover, it would grant her the status of someone capable of invoking the state of exception. As an elected official, the governor actually does not have the power to grant a pardon to Nancy because doing so would weaken the sovereignty of states' rights based on racial discrimination and therefore weaken his authority as governor.

In *Sanctuary*, the movie, the distinction between local and national justice is eliminated not by destroying the belle or erasing the South—as in *The Story of Temple Drake*—but because there is no practical difference between the two. The crowd that assembles outside the courthouse and the yell they send up after the verdict—"they're going to hang her by the neck"—is indistinguishable from that of the lynch mob. Unlike *The Story of Temple Drake*, the movie *Sanctuary* is overtly set in the South. Whereas the final courtroom scene in *The Story of Temple Drake* is all white, the initial courtroom scene in the filmic sequel opens with a wide-angle shot of the all-black balcony, a shot that will be featured so prominently in civil rights era films such as *To Kill a Mockingbird*. In the filmic courtroom scene the function of the law is associated with the whites in the courtroom. As the judge reads the sentence, we see shots of the white spectators behind Nancy (the white judge and Temple and Gowan), but when the judge addresses Nancy, a low angle shot includes the black balcony above and behind her. Although she refuses to reply when the judge asks if she has anything to say on her behalf, after he reads the sentence, unlike the cryptic "Yes, Lord," in *Requiem for a Nun,* she replies: "Thy will be done. Thank you Lord." In the wide-angle close-up we see the rails of the black balcony behind her. Nancy's association with the black balcony places providential certainty as a function of blackness, not whiteness (which is characterized by the more modern, sophisticated Temple, who has difficulty believing in anything). It is this essentialized notion of black religiosity that is the key to redeeming and reifying the black mammy.

The final jail scene in *Sanctuary,* the movie, ostensibly reveals Temple's salvation from a life of sin.[26] After cleansing herself through suffering and confession in her talk with the governor, Temple is ready to receive the final stages of forgiveness and faith from Nancy, who is already at peace. Although the dialogue confirms this reading, the composition and editing of the scene cast doubt on Temple's freedom and on what it is she actually believes. At the beginning and end of the scene Nancy is shown behind bars, but in the exchange between the two women—punctuated by a series of shot/reverse shots and close-ups and medium close-ups—it is Temple who is literally behind bars. In the film Nancy is much more forthright in presenting a Christian message, but like the novel, the real power of the scene comes from the combined imagery of Christianity and the myth of the mammy, and in the end it seems as if Temple has more belief in the latter than the former. The film heightens the drama of the encounter between Temple and Nancy by eliminating lawyer Stevens and literally focusing on the two women. Thus, instead of Stevens's attempt to interpret Nancy's cryptic pronouncements, Nancy herself fully articulates her Christian motives and her belief in salvation.

When Temple first enters the cell, both women are shown in profile with the bars behind them. Nancy, however, sits down with only the window behind her as she explains that Temple had to confess, "to suffer through the telling of it [her sins]," but that she was "suffering for something" in order to achieve salvation. Temple remains standing, clutching the bars behind her, as she defines *sanctuary* as someplace to hide. In a close-up that "removes" Nancy from her surroundings in the jail, she asks if Temple "still want[s] that Candy Man." Temple, still clutching the bars, says no, then pauses, as her face registers this revelation with a kind of surprise and relief. "Of course you don't," Nancy affirms, "that's because you're stronger now. Salvation means more than just hiding. It's a facing up to your life, your life with your husband

and your son and your children to come." In *Requiem for a Nun*, on the other hand, Nancy explains that although God does not like suffering, "He cant help Himself," and suggests that maybe it is the only way "He" can think of to keep "folks" so busy that they do not have time for "devilment" (237, 238). Suffering therefore is not redemptive but only a useful distraction devised by a deity with an apparently limited imagination.

Temple's revelation in the close-up is a perfect example of what Gilles Deleuze refers to as the affection-image, in which the movement in the shot is expressed through the face and not through the motion of the camera or the action of the characters (*Cinema 1* 102–22). The affection-image is the interval between the perception-image (the framing of the shot) and the action-image (the physical action of the shot). In the affection-image perceptions register as a sensation or emotion before they are acted upon, and therefore "the affection-image is the close-up and the close-up is the face" (85). This mental reflection and Temple's "revelation" expressed through the medium close-up signals that Nancy has indeed saved Temple from a destructive love that she repeatedly says she "can't help." Deleuze, however, differentiates between the external and internal framing of a close-up. The external framing places the close-up into relation with other shots and other types of images or actions, but the internal framing of the close-up relates it only to its own composition or in relation to other affection-images. It represents not the "state of things" but the "expressed" of the state of things. This abstracted affection-image, even if some elements of background are visible in the shot, "becomes 'any space whatever'" (96–97). The close-up "deterritorializes" the face by "abstract[ing] the image from "all spatio-temporal coordinates" and raising it to the "state of Entity" (96). The affection-image may remove the shot from its external connections to the events in the film, but Temple's hand grasping the bars behind her still suggests the contradiction within the internal framing of the shot;[27] the fear and desperation of the grasping hand is in opposition to the revelation of the face and represents the struggle between freedom and imprisonment (fig. 3.1).

As Deleuze explains, the affection-image is "impersonal" yet "singular"; it can be produced by a single close-up (affect) or can form with other affects to create a changing quality or power, a "dividual," that occurs in the act of changing but cannot be broken down into separate parts (98). The flow of affection-image shots in the scene makes up the changing quality or power,

FIG. 3.1. Temple's revelation, while visiting Nancy in jail, that she no longer wants Candy Man. *Sanctuary* (1961).

most notably in Temple's close-up reaction shots to Nancy's understanding of forgiveness and heaven. The movement across these affection-images is from the serenity of the black face to the motility of the white face, which changes from peacefulness to anxiety, to hopefulness, to gratitude, and finally not to serenity but to blankness. As Nancy says, "You just gotta believe," we see a reaction shot of Temple with her mouth open and a look of anxiety on her face. The camera later cuts to the same anxious reaction shot of Temple, after a close-up of Nancy serenely saying: "Believe all this means something. Believe that here is forgiveness just as I believe that I've been forgiven." Finally, after Temple asks Nancy for forgiveness, Nancy describes this world as only a dream that does not matter because her little baby will be waiting for her in heaven. There is a high-angle close-up of Temple as she kneels down in front of Nancy asking, "And mine Nancy, mine?" As the camera remains on Temple, Nancy places her hands on Temple's face and pronounces, "That one too." Nancy herself then speaks the lines that Stevens imposes on her in the novel: "In heaven that child remembers nothing of my hands but gentleness because I loved that baby. Even when I raised my hand against it." As we hear Nancy's off-screen voice, we see Temple's hopeful, pleading face transform into a look of relief as she closes her eyes, grasps Nancy's hand, and presses her face against it until the jailer's voice breaks in, "Time's up," and Temple turns away from the hands and toward the voice with a blank look. The ominous phrase from the voice of the white jailer breaks the spell, and Temple is set adrift. It is only when the black and white elements are combined in the composite shot of black hands on a white face that the white face is able to

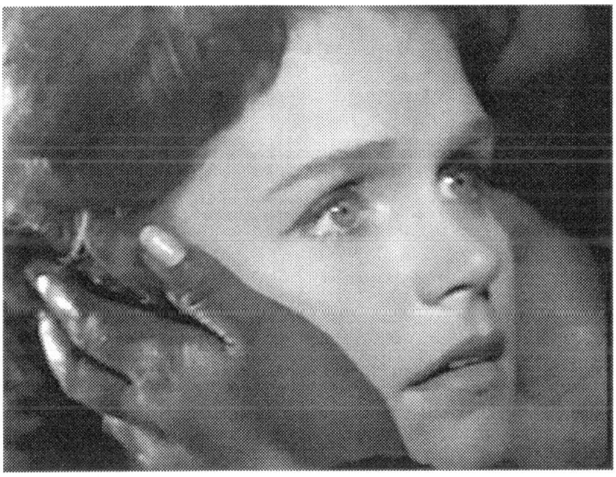

FIG. 3.2. Nancy holding Temple's face and urging her to believe in forgiveness. *Sanctuary* (1961).

register peace, so that even within the internal composition of the shot, the white expression requires the laying on of black hands to achieve stability (fig. 3.2). While Temple's face might "call forth the pure affect as the expressed," in the external composition of the shots, Nancy's black hands on Temple's white face reinscribe a racial hierarchy in which whites have faces (social identity) and blacks, as in Nancy's parable, are there to work.

If as Deleuze says the affection-image represents the expressed of the state of things (102), the comfort Temple finds in the hand that killed her child confirms the state of things in which what she needs to "believe" in is the myth of the all-loving mammy, the belief in the power and healing of black servitude. This belief is demonstrated in the novel when the black hands themselves take on the "pure affect" of a close-up. Passing the jail windows on her way to bury her child, Temple imagines the black hands as a series of images "just laying there among the interstices" of the bars: hands that are "already shaped and easy and unvanquished to the handles of the plows and . . . of white folks' cradles, until even the steel bars fitted them too without alarm or anguish." As in Nancy's parable, this description of black hands conflates work and imprisonment. The servile yet almost mystical quality of the black hands can diagnose a problem and find the cure but only for the "white one": "Even in the dark, with out even having to turn on the light, [the hands] can not only find the child, the baby—not her child but yours, the white one—but the trouble and discomfort too—the hunger, the wet didy, the unfastened safety-pin—and see to remedy it" (170). Instead of "any space whatever" in the external framing of the shot, the black hands in this

FIG. 3.3. The final shot in the film, as Temple and her husband, Gowan, recede into the background while Nancy is framed in the jailhouse window. *Sanctuary* (1961).

"close-up" suggest "any black woman whatever" can serve as mammy (just as in lynching it is any black man whatever, as Faulkner dramatized in "Dry September").

Although it has taken the death of her child, Temple is purged of her lustful desires for the only man she ever loved and leaves the jail a proper southern lady, walking hand in hand with Gavin, who has waited patiently for her outside. Because the murdered child is never seen or named, it is easier to see it as a symbol of the dark streak that, like the abject, was once "me" but now must be expelled so that Temple may regain her status. The ending, like the other Hollywood version of Temple's earlier story, creates a conservative conclusion that supports the status quo. The final shot seems to confirm this: as the camera pulls up and back from the eye-level two-shot of Temple and Gowan, they continue to walk down the street. Nancy, however, remains in the foreground, looking out the bars of the jail window. Temple and Gowan are "freed" from the jail, and Nancy is still imprisoned. The brick wall of the jail divides the shot in half, creating a kind of split screen with Nancy on the right, centered and framed by the window, as Temple and Gowan recede into the background and almost out of sight (fig. 3.3).

There are two factors, however, that work against this conservative "happy ending": the nature of Temple's "freedom" and that of Nancy's

FIG. 3.4. Temple leaving the jail as Nancy tells her simply to "believe." *Sanctuary* (1961).

"imprisonment." After the exchange between Nancy and Temple together in the jail cell, Temple leaves the jail and turns to Nancy saying, "I'm afraid," to which Nancy replies, as in the novel, "Believe." This shot should confirm Temple's final release through faith, but instead it is Temple who appears to be in prison (fig. 3.4). The point of view of the camera is from inside Nancy's cell looking out, and therefore the bars appear in front of Temple as if she is the one still in jail. As she turns to leave, we see Temple repeating "Believe, believe, believe," as if she is trying to convince herself it is possible. Although she certainly believes in Nancy, it is not clear that she believes in her own life. The reverse shot of Nancy sitting serenely is also from inside her cell and shows only the wall behind her but no bars in front of her. Again, as in the novel, the question remains: what kind of freedom is Temple returning to in a loveless marriage based on guilt and social conformity? In the novel Gowan surreptitiously hears Temple's confession and is still willing to go to the jail with her. In the film, however, he remained at home drinking for the first time since the night of the rape. Cousin Ira urges him to have the "moral courage to accept the truth," as Temple has, and then Ira gives Gowan his definition of a "true marriage": "just imagine the luxury to have one person on the earth that you could always speak the truth [to]." Ironically, Ira has just described Temple's relationship to Nancy, not to her husband, and Gowan's drunken reply, "The truth shall set you free," is ambiguous at best.

As Jay Watson persuasively argues, there is a lack of political agency for the many solitary imprisoned black characters, such as Nancy, who "haunt" Faulkner's work. Watson attributes Faulkner's reluctance to imagine peaceful, collective political action on the part of black characters as his participation "in disavowing the normative power of the civil rights movement ("Dangerous Return" 108–37). The final shot of the film, however, captures another possible reading of the film's ending that rejects the martyred mammy and suggests the reality of "collective political action" on the part of black civil rights activists. Although in 1951, when Faulkner wrote *Requiem*, he might not have been able to envision such a possibility, in 1961 the image of an imprisoned black woman takes on a meaning beyond the film's story of Temple's salvation. The 21 April 1960 cover of *Jet* features a black woman who, like the final image of Nancy, is also framed by the jail cell, but the headline reads: "Sit-In Student Freedom Fighters." Nancy's connection to the civil rights movement is even more direct, given that Nancy is played by Odetta Holmes, already hailed as the queen of American folksingers, who would inspire protest singers such as Bob Dylan and Joan Baez (Gritter). As the 1960 *Time* article explains, Odetta was known for her spirituals (the kind Nancy sings with Stevens in the novel) but also for "the anger and the protest that are part of her folk repertory," like her hard-hitting prison songs "Been in the Pen" and "Another Man Gone," both featured on her 1956 debut solo album, *Odetta Sings Ballads and Blues* ("Music: Baby in the Cradle"). In reference to these songs Odetta explained: "They were liberation songs. You're walking down life's road, society's foot is on your throat, every which way you turn you can't get from under that foot. And you reach a fork in the road and you can either lie down and die or insist upon your life" (qtd. in Weiner).

The choice of Odetta to play Nancy allows for a political counter-reading to the sacrificial black mammy, one that moves beyond the nihilist resignation of Faulkner's Nancy and beyond the plot of Temple's salvation in the film. In this reading an imprisoned black woman suggests a challenge to the state's ability to deny African Americans the rights of citizenship, rather than an affirmation of that power. In this ending shot of Odetta it is almost as if the story of Temple Drake featured in the novel *Sanctuary, The Story of Temple Drake, Requiem for a Nun,* and the movie *Sanctuary* has been dwarfed by the more momentous struggle still ahead for Odetta, not the hangman's noose but the civil rights movement. Odetta would go on to sing at the 1963 March on Washington and would be known as the "voice of the Civil Rights Movement." As a political rather than religious act, Nancy's murder of the child can signal the ultimate symbolic rejection of the role of mammy; the image of a jailed protest singer suggests another way to go when "you reach a fork in the road": to "insist upon your life" rather than to "lie down and die" to protect the sanctity of the corrupt white family. Although this is only one possible reading of what is in many ways a conservative film, the final image of Nancy in jail may take Faulkner's critique of the mammy and the southern rape complex to the next level, a step for which Faulkner himself was perhaps not ready.

CHAPTER 4

The Power of the False in *Touch of Evil*

Touch of Evil (1958) is a film noir assemblage of the elements of the southern rape complex that directly presents interracial rape as a staged event in a struggle for power and political authority across racial and geographic lines. In the film Capt. Hank Quinlan, the corrupt cop played by Orson Welles, enters into a scheme with "Uncle Joe" Grandi, the local drug lord, to employ rape—the threat against the white woman Susan Vargas—as an overtly racist plot against the authority of her husband, the Mexican official Miguel Vargas. *Touch of Evil* returns to the gang rape of *The Clansman* (which Griffith turned into a marriage proposal and subsequent chase scene) and refigures it as "staged" rape by a group of Latinos under orders from Grandi. In substituting Latinos for African Americans in his assemblage of the southern rape complex, Welles demonstrates the pliability of the logic of the complex and how it has been, and still is, used to marginalize minority groups, even as Welles undermines that logic throughout the film.

On a purely practical level, claiming (after the fact) that the rape was "faked" allows this form of sexual violence to get past the censors, while at the same time showing the terror that Susan goes through. The gang members grab her arms and legs and shut the door, preventing the audience from knowing (but not from imagining) what happens after that. Moreover, the evidence that the rape was faked remains questionable: the doctor checks Susan's blood to confirm that she was on drugs, only to find out that she was given sodium pentothal, not marijuana, but there is no indication that she was given a rape exam; therefore, we have only the word of the alleged rapist that the rape did not occur. And given what we see on-screen and the fact that Susan subsequently ends up across town naked in a sleazy hotel room, there is no doubt that a sexual assault occurred, regardless of whether or not there was actual penetration. But as the criminal perpetrators—and even her own husband—understand it, it is the appearance of violation and the appearance of purity that are at stake. Like Marion of *The Clansman* and Narcissa of

Sanctuary, Mike Vargas is adamant that his wife's name must be clean, while Quinlan, the corrupt American cop, is just as intent on sullying her name to discredit her husband. Whether or not Susan was actually raped is almost irrelevant to the plot because she, like the white southern belle, is a vehicle to forward economic and political agendas.

Touch of Evil has not typically been discussed in relation to the southern rape complex, perhaps because it is not specifically set in the South but in Los Robles, a fictional border town between the United States and Mexico. But unlike the novel *Badge of Evil* (written by Whit Masterson, the pen name for Robert Wade and H. Bill Miller), which was clearly set in California and not on the border, Los Robles could be anywhere along the vast Mexican-American border, thus creating a pervasive yet nebulous "southernscape." The indeterminacy of the southern location in *Touch of Evil* includes the possibility of Texas, a former Confederate state, but also references the history of all the border states and the struggles over exactly where the border should begin and end. Welles also makes a number of significant changes from the novel, especially in terms of nationality, that set in play the dynamics of the southern rape complex.[1] Instead of Miguel Vargas, a Mexican official, the protagonist in the novel is Mitch Holt, an American assistant district attorney who is investigating an Italian mob family, when he is called into the case of Rudy Linneker (as spelled in the novel), who was dynamited in his own home. Mitch's wife, Consuela, who goes by Connie, is Mexican, though she speaks without an accent and could "pass" as an Anglo-American. There is no staged rape, but Connie is lured to a hotel room and drugged in order to discredit Mitch and stop his investigation of the corrupt cop Leron McCoy (in the novel Hank Quinlan is McCoy's innocent partner). There are also no Mexican drug kingpins, but McCoy uses the fact that Connie's father's ranch is near Ensenada, Mexico, to incriminate her and imply that she and her family are involved in drug smuggling. As Mitch sarcastically says to the DA, it is a "perfect case" because "on top of everything else, she's of Mexican descent. You can make a lot out of that because, as every American jury knows, it's the foreign-born that cause all our crime and vice" (Masterson 180). Ultimately, Mitch proves that Linneker's daughter, Tara, and her fiancé, Shayon (no indication that he is Latino), are innocent of Linneker's murder and that they, along with his wife, were framed by McCoy. In *Badge of Evil* the evil is clearly contained in the character of McCoy.

In the context of the southern rape complex, *evil* is defined as anything that threatens purity, but in *Touch of Evil* the numerous literal and metaphorical border crossings the characters engage in prevent the emergence of any pure or unified form not simply of evil but also of race, gender, citizenship, political authority, law, justice, or even genre. As William Anthony Nericcio explains, "In the 'uncanny' border town identity is not 'fractured' but is *fracture* itself—a place where hyphens, bridges, border stations, and schizophrenia are the rule rather than the exception" (43). Nericcio briefly contrasts *Touch of Evil* to *The Birth of a Nation*, maintaining that Griffith's "ugly meditation on the fibers of racial hatred" gave viewers "a license to *think racism* and be *racist within reason*, in America," but that the obvious racism in *Touch of Evil* actually undermines racist stereotypes by "enact[ing] a scenario wherein the very fabric of Latina/o stereotypes is woven and unravels, at once, before our eyes" (41). *The Birth of a Nation* is central to Welles's unraveling of Latina/o stereotypes because it is based on an unraveling of the basic narrative of the southern rape complex, which is predicated on the power of the false, in its commonsensical and its Deleuzian meaning. Placing *Touch of Evil* in the filmic context of *The Birth of a Nation* highlights the "staged" forms that violations of the white woman have taken as justification for relegating certain ethnic or racial groups to the status of "bare life" by invoking the state of exception.

A TOUCH OF THEORY

A film can vacillate or overlap between the organic regime (characteristic of the movement-image) and the crystalline regime (characteristic of the time-image), and this is especially true of *Touch of Evil*. In particular the Deleuzian distinction between the cliché (as found in the movement-image) and the power of the false (characteristic of the time-image), which prevents the operation of the cliché, is directly relevant to the theoretical analysis of the racial stereotype that has been the focus of much of the critical debate surrounding *Touch of Evil*. According to Deleuze, we "normally perceive the world through clichés because perception is based on subtraction." We never see the entire image; "we perceive only what we are interested in perceiving, or rather what it is in our interest to perceive, by virtue of our economic interests, ideological beliefs and psychological demands" (*Cinema 2* 20). The cliché is based on an abstraction, which we automatically respond to without having to go through the process of assessing the various "sheets of past" that could correspond to different aspects of the image—as in a recollection-image—or without having to register the sensation the image provokes. The cliché almost immediately fills in the gap (the affection-image) between the perception-image and the action-image, limiting both thought and feeling, thus allowing for the simplistic use of stereotypes to disavow differences within racial and ethnic groups that work against the stereotype.[2] Laura Marks describes it as a "commonsense, hegemonic image that extends unproblematically into action" (46). But if the cliché prevents us from seeing the image, the time-image turns us into "seers."

It is precisely *Touch of Evil*'s undermining of the cliché, with its border politics and its porous racial, national, and sexual boundaries, that has made it such rich terrain for critics who counter the humanist concepts of a unified self and "objective" forms of knowledge. Numerous theoretical approaches have found in *Touch of Evil* a film that demonstrates the limitations of other forms of analysis while simultaneously articulating what their theory can uncover that was not "seen" before (Pease 79). Stephen Heath, for example, provides a semiotic analysis of *Touch of Evil*, thus helping to solidify film studies with an established methodology; Homi Bhabha uses the film to theorize the ambiguity of the racial stereotype in colonial discourse; Peter Wollen and Michael Denning both historically contextualize the film's relationship to injustice against Mexican Americans and Mexicans as well as resistance against such injustice; and Pease argues that the crime at the heart of the film is Vargas's use of the state of exception in pursing Quinlan.

Although Pease does not include Deleuze in his list of theorists who make use of *Touch of Evil*, in *Cinema 2* Deleuze singles out Welles's work, including *Touch of Evil*, stating that "Orson Welles is the first: he isolates a direct time-image and makes the image go over to the power of the false" (138). Welles achieves this effect in part by creating characters who are outside of the system of judgment characteristic of the narrative logic of the movement-image. Deleuze labels these characters "forgers," and in the time-image it is the forger (in the case of *Touch of Evil* both Quinlan and Vargas) who becomes "*the* character of the cinema: not the criminal, the cowboy, the psycho-social man, the historical hero, the holder of power, etc., as in the action-image, but the forger pure and simple, to the detriment of all action" (*Cinema 2* 132). Typically, critics have tended to employ binary comparisons between characters in *Touch of Evil* (or between couples) whose very oppositions demonstrate their similarities. While these comparisons can be productive in using one character as a foil for another, the binary coupling limits the comparison in a way the forger does not. The forger represents a power that morphs from character to character, assuming "an unlimited figure which permeates the whole film" (Deleuze, *Cinema 2* 132, 145).

Despite the theoretical differences that characterize the critical reception of *Touch of Evil*, one of the recurring issues is the role of race—and the racial stereotype in particular—in the formation of national identity. Critics disagree, however, about whether or not the film supports or subverts such stereotypes: is this a film of containment or disruption? To address this question and the role of the stereotype as it relates to the cliché, it is useful to turn to two of the most influential readings of the film: Heath's extensive semiotic reading, which helped to legitimate film studies as a discipline by demonstrating the efficacy of analyzing the film shot by shot, attending to both narrative and cinematic codes; and Bhabha's postcolonial reading, which reconfigures psychoanalytic terms—the fetish and the mirror stage—to theorize the role of the racial stereotype in colonial discourse. I examine the previous critical and theoretical uses of *Touch of Evil* not simply to dismiss them but to unpack their theoretical critiques and to recontextualize their insights from the Deleuzian perspective of the organic regime (characteristic of the movement-image and exemplified in *The Birth of a Nation*) and the crystalline regime (characteristic of the time-image and exemplified in *Touch of Evil*) in order to highlight how the film employs, yet confounds, the narrative of the southern rape complex, thus exposing the "real" intraracial crime at the heart of the film.

Any reading of *Touch of Evil* is indebted to Heath's meticulous reading of significant scenes in the film. Using the studio released 1958 version of *Touch of Evil*,[3] Heath analyzes the film's signifying codes—its "filmic system"—charting the narrative structure of the film, including a scene-by-scene analysis of the beginning and other key moments. Heath's Lacanian-influenced semiotic analysis impacted, for years to come, both film studies and readings of *Touch of Evil*. As Nericcio explains, *Touch of Evil*, in a "Tex[t]-Mex moment of epic proportions," facilitated Heath's semiotic analysis, which "ponder[ed] the fundamental dynamics of film, Subject, and culture" (42). According to Heath, the narrative of *Touch of Evil* is structured around patterns of disruption and reconstruction that correspond to desire and law, respectively. The original "violence" of the film is initiated by the explosion that kills the rich American Rudy Linnekar and his stripper girlfriend, Zita, and that simultaneously interrupts a kiss between newlyweds on their honeymoon, the Anglo-American

Susan Vargas (played by Janet Leigh) and her Mexican husband, Miguel Vargas (played by Charlton Heston).

The explosion sets in play two different investigations: one headed by Captain Quinlan (played by Orson Welles) to discover who murdered Linnekar; and the other, spearheaded by Vargas, to investigate Quinlan's propensity to frame his suspects or anyone who gets in his way. The two investigations come together when Quinlan attempts to destroy Vargas's reputation by implicating his wife in drug use, rape, and murder. These disruptions instigate numerous border crossings and exchanges, which end with the death of Quinlan and the fulfillment of the earlier kiss between Susan and Miguel Vargas that purges the couple, according to Heath, of the contaminating "mixedness," thus providing an ending of containment, both filmic and political. Susan's body represents the "lawful place" of desire, which can only be figured through repression, but "that figuration is already excessive in the narrative of that repression" (Heath 75).[4]

Heath's extensive analysis of *Touch of Evil* is instructive not only because of what it brings to light but also because of what it gets wrong. Despite the careful attention to detail, Heath mistakes the location of the Grandi hotel to which Susan is taken, which is in America not Mexico, and he identifies Zita, the stripper, who is blown up along with Linnekar, as Mexican, despite her blonde hair and American accent. Heath's analysis therefore, both directly and inadvertently, documents the difficulties the film creates in establishing when the characters are in Mexico or America and whether or not the characters are Mexican or American. It is in fact difficult to tell whether Los Robles is in Mexico or America or if the city itself is divided by the border. Heath locates it on both sides of the border, and it is referred to only as a border town throughout the film. As Vargas looks at the murder scene, on American soil, a billboard in the background reads: "Welcome Stranger! To the picturesque Los Robles, the Paris of the Border," but it is not clear which side of the border the billboard is on because even the billboard refers only to Los Robles's border status.[5]

Bhabha acknowledges that Heath's analysis differs from more "traditional" treatments of racial stereotypes and images that posit the "*origin and unity* of national identity." Heath complicates the many border crossings and exchanges in the construction of national identity through the "semes of 'foreignness,' 'mixedness,' 'impurity,' as transgressive and corrupting," which chart the "circulation and proliferation of racial and cultural otherness" (Bhabha

97). Yet despite Heath's analysis of racial difference, he tends to subsume racial under sexual difference, thereby marginalizing the very cultural otherness his analysis attempts to bring to light. As Bhabha asserts, Heath's reading of the border is "too singularly, too exclusively under the sign of sexuality"; therefore, his elaborate analysis of the codes surrounding difference still, according to Bhabha, does not "construct the polymorphous and perverse collusion between racism and sexism as a *mixed* economy" (98). The death of the father/Law that is central to Heath's reading does not acknowledge the fact that the death of Mr. Linnekar makes miscegenation both possible and deferred in relation to the two mixed-raced couples Marcia Linnekar/Manelo Sanchez (his daughter and son-in-law) and Susan/Vargas (Bhabha 99). To correct Heath's overvaluation of sexuality, Bhabha, draws on and reconfigures Freud's theory of the fetish and Lacan's theory of Imaginary identification (111).[6] Bhabha critiques theories that stress the naturalizing function of stereotypes without examining how the stereotype, like a fetish (and the southern rape complex), ambivalently functions as both recognition and disavowal, as both fixed and fantastic.

The racial fetish, unlike the sexual fetish, is not a repressed secret but is based on a "regime of visibility" that creates "discriminatory knowledge" of the colonial subject. What is repressed is the very production of the naturalness of the stereotype, that it is instantly recognizable. Yet the constant need for repeating these stereotypes points to the very thing being disavowed, that there are no consistent differences between racial and ethnic groups.[7] What Heath's theory does not address in *Touch of Evil* but Bhabha's postcolonial approach questions is "the discourses of American cultural colonialism and Mexican dependency, the fear/desire of miscegenation, the American border as cultural signifier of a pioneering, male 'American' spirit always under threat from races and cultures beyond the border or frontier" (Bhabha 98–99).[8] Although Bhabha does not proceed to address these issues in *Touch of Evil*, Welles's incorporation of the southern rape complex in the border politics of the film complements such an analysis and exposes the intersections between the domestic colonization of African Americans and the workings of U.S. "cultural colonialism."

THE MOVEMENT-IMAGE: CLICHÉ AND GENRE

Because most Hollywood movies operate under the movement-image, I will begin my analysis of *Touch of Evil* with the role of the cliché in the movement-image and its relation to the use of stereotypes in the film as they relate to race, ethnicity, nationality, and the southern rape complex, which is based on the fear of biological and social border crossings. Captain Quinlan is the most overtly racist character in the film, and he fully embodies a belief in the national and racial superiority of Anglo-Americans: referring to people as "speaking Mexican," slapping around Sanchez during the interrogation while letting the Anglo-American Marcia Linnekar exit with her lawyer, and referring to Vargas as "that Mexican" and refusing to acknowledge his expertise as well as resenting his very presence. Quinlan also demonstrates how the stereotype, in establishing discriminatory knowledge of the postcolonial subject as natural, justifies colonial domination that is predicated on that very knowledge. Quinlan even uses the word *naturally* throughout his interrogation to establish Sanchez's guilt and to discredit Vargas. Sanchez picks up on this usage and sarcastically mimics Quinlan:

> Quinlan: Naturally he [Linnekar] objected to having a Mexican shoe clerk for a son-in-law, so naturally you . . .
>
> Sanchez: (*overlapping*) Naturally!
>
> Quinlan: . . . you had to put him out of the way.
>
> Sanchez: Naturally! (*Sanchez then walks away speaking Spanish to himself*)
>
> Quinlan to Vargas: Just because he speaks a little guilty, that don't make him innocent, you know.

Naturally therefore justifies racial prejudice on the part of whites because the "natural" assumption is that Sanchez is guilty. Although Bhabha posits mimicry as a potential tool of the postcolonial subject to undermine colonial discourse as natural, Quinlan refutes Sanchez's overt use of mimicry as a ploy to hide his guilt.

While white prejudice is deemed natural, Quinlan asserts that Mexicans are naturally prejudiced. When Vargas refutes the existence of the planted dynamite in the shoebox because only moments earlier the shoebox was empty, Quinlan again asserts his knowledge of Vargas as postcolonial other:

Quinlan: I know how you feel.

Vargas: Do you?

Quinlan: Sure I do. You people are touchy. It's only human you'd want to come to the defense of your fellow countryman. (*As Vargas leaves, Quinlan calls after him*) Vargas. Vargas, don't worry.

Vargas: Why should I worry?

Quinlan: You go right ahead and say anything you want to. Folks will bear your natural prejudice in mind.

Here racial prejudice itself is declared natural. As a Mexican official, Vargas challenges Quinlan's assertions more directly than does Sanchez, but Quinlan's reference to "you people" points to the power of the stereotype to assume natural similarities within a racial group.

During this famous interrogation sequence shot, in which Quinlan roughly questions Sanchez, both the racial and sexual fetish are repeatedly invoked, but this scene also demonstrates the Deleuzian fetish associated with the impulse-image, and all three revolve around the image of a shoe. Quinlan assumes that naturally Linnekar would not want a Mexican shoe clerk for a son-in-law. In this statement both Mexican and shoe clerk are accepted as naturally undesirable qualities in a son-in-law, thus drawing on both the sexual and racial fetish. Sanchez is repeatedly associated with shoes, especially with helping women try on shoes. He suggests his own shoe fetish in his role as "the best shoe clerk the story ever had," who first met Marcia when she was trying on shoes, adding that he has "been at her feet ever since."[9] Sanchez literally positions himself in an inferior position, which not only overvalues Marcia but also betrays his own castration anxiety. The shoe as fetish, therefore, both masks and betrays this anxiety. But Quinlan betrays his own fascination with shoes when he declares that he wants to know everything, "the works," but he wants to "start with the shoe store."

Quinlan introduces another aspect of the fetish in relation to shoes when he tells Sanchez: "There was an old woman on Main Street last night picked up a shoe . . . and the shoe had a foot in it. We're going to make you pay for that, Sanchez."[10] Quinlan's description is the perfect example of when a shoe is not a fetish . . . when there is a severed foot in it. If a fetish is supposed to compensate for the missing body part, the presence of a missing body part negates that possibility. From a Deleuzian perspective what Quinlan describes is an example of the fetish as seen in the impulse-image, in which the fetish is "torn away" from the originary world that pervades the world of the film. The impulse-image, which is a special form of the movement-image, occurs between the affection-image and the action-image. The impulse-image creates an impression, rather than an expression of thought or emotion, and operates not on logic but according to the law of the "steepest slope," in which "all the parts converge in an immense rubbish-dump or swamp, and all the impulses in a great death-impulse" (Deleuze, *Cinema 1* 124). The impulse-image cannot exist separately from the specific historical and geographical milieu of the film that constitutes the action-image in which thought and feelings are actualized; it can only make itself known in the determinate milieu but as "symptoms" that materialize through the fetish as a sign of an undercurrent that exhausts and degrades the world. Quinlan is angrier about the discovery of the shoe with a foot in it than with the death of two people, calling attention to the affective intensity surrounding this image.

If Quinlan is the quintessential bigot, Susan Vargas, as a proper young woman from Philadelphia who married a Mexican, would seem to have overcome racial prejudices, especially because, as the southern rape complex indicates, intermarriage between racial or ethnic groups was considered to be one of the most taboo forms of interracial interactions, and any form of intermarriage was considered a legal form of interracial rape. Yet Susan exemplifies the contradictory blend of discriminatory knowledge of, and power over, the postcolonial subject and at the same time an aggressive fear that the other will violate mythic white purity, by returning the gaze of the other in place of white identity, a fear that is manifest through the use of a mirror to mediate the confrontation between Susan and Grandi. On her way back to her hotel on the Mexican side, Susan encounters one of Grandi's nephews. She is instantly suspicious of him, even after he prevents her from being hit by a truck as she walks into the street, and this suspicion—in keeping with the logic of the southern rape complex—takes on a sexual connotation, leading to the threat of violent retaliation. Susan pulls away when the Grandi nephew hands her a letter for Vargas and speaks in Spanish. An elderly man translates,

"Lady, he says you don't understand what he wants," to which Susan replies: "I understand very well what he wants . . . Tell him I'm a married woman and my husband is a great big official in the government ready and willing to knock out all those pretty front teeth of his." Despite her assumed "understanding" of what the nephew wants and her threat of violence, Susan agrees to follow the young man to meet his uncle, Joe Grandi, brother of the drug kingpin who her husband is going to testify against the following week and the man who will later plot against her with Quinlan. After reading the note out loud, Susan shrugs and asks the bystanders, "Well, what have I got to lose?" She clearly already has the rape narrative trajectory in mind when she responds to her own question, "Don't answer that," and then turning to the nephew says, "Lead on, Pancho."

Susan's reference to "Pancho," and the encounter that follows, demonstrates the ambiguity behind the stereotype: what must be ignored in order for it to operate as a cliché but also the limits of postcolonial discourse. When asked by Uncle Joe why she called his nephew Pancho, Susan responds, "For laughs, I guess." Her flippant response reinforces the stereotypical import of the name as a generic and demeaning term for a Mexican man; the fact that Susan has not given it any thought, and that she never bothered to ask his name. (The film seems to follow suit, and we never learn the young man's name. Even in the credit he is listed only as Pancho.) For Uncle Joe Grandi and his nephew the name does not function as an automatic cliché, and they question its meaning, asking Susan twice why she called him Pancho. From the perspective of 1950s U.S. pop culture, "just for laughs" suggests the comical sidekick Pancho in the recent popular television show *The Cisco Kid* (1950–56). But even this explanation does not allow for an easy cliché. Pancho and Cisco are border crossers and "outlaws," but like *Zorro* (another popular TV series [1957–59]), they come to the aid of the defenseless against both corrupt officials and criminals. Both Pancho and Cisco are represented as Mexican through their clothes and accents, but while Cisco is a brave, dashing figure who speaks standard English (much like Vargas), Pancho displays many of the comic elements of minstrelsy in his disheveled clothes, exaggerated accent, malapropisms, mangled grammar, and comical reactions of fear and apprehension. For a Latino audience, however, *Pancho* has a potentially different connotation but one also linked to border politics. Pancho Villa, one of the most famous generals of the Mexican Revolution, also commanded military, political, and economic power in the Mexican state of Chihuahua, which borders both Texas and New Mexico, and Villa made border crossings of his own. Although he made an alliance with the United States, after the partnership broke down, he sent his army to Columbus, New Mexico, in 1916 to raid the Thirteenth Cavalry Regiments and successfully evaded the U.S. army's attempts to capture him ("Buffalo Soldiers").

In "hailing" the nephew as a stereotype of a Mexican, Susan must ignore the fact that he actually dresses like Marlon Brando in *The Wild One* (1953), listens to American rock and roll, and as we later learn, speaks unaccented, standard English. It is Uncle Joe, not his nephew, who most resembles the comic Pancho. Uncle Joe has a strong accent, is short, fat, and wears a toupee that falls off at various points in the film, forcing the nephews to run after him with his "rug." Welles presents Uncle Joe as a stereotypical figure but immediately complicates the cliché when Uncle Joe explains that he is an American businessman, that Grandi is not a Mexican name, and that the family does business on both sides of the border. The very belief in the ability to know the racial other through the lens of stereotypes produces ignorance of subaltern knowledge, whose existence is disavowed; therefore, Susan does not have the cultural contexts necessary to "get" or to be "in on" the joke. When Uncle Joe asks if Susan knows him, she refers to his nightclub, Grandi's. He explains that the name of the nightclub, Grandi's Rancho Grande, is "kind of a joke . . . Get it?" As he says this, he brandishes his gun, and Susan replies, "I can't say it's the funniest thing I ever heard." Just as Uncle Joe does not get Susan's "joke" about Pancho, neither does she understand his. In part Susan is, of course, responding to the implied threat of the gun, but this conflating of joke and threat exhibits the splitting/multiplicity of racial stereotypes that Bhabha theorizes.

The obvious joke is that *Grandi* is a homophone for *Grande*, but as Joe explains, "Grandi is not even a Mexican name." The name, however, as well as Joe himself, is easily mistaken for its Mexican counterpart. Furthermore, because the Rio Grande River separates Texas and Mexico, it is an appropriate name for a border town establishment. Rancho Grande has an additional connotation for those familiar with Mexican film, which is part of the "joke." *Alla en el Rancho Grande* (1936), directed by Fernando de Fuentes (dubbed the Mexican John Ford by the *New York Times* review), was one of the first Mexican blockbusters, received national and international awards, was credited with creating the genre of the *comedia ranchera,* and produced a song by the same name. The film was so popular that in 1946 Fuentes made a more lavish color version of *Alla en el Rancho Grande,* helping to popularize the movie's theme song, which would later be covered by American singers such as Bing Crosby, Dean Martin, and even Elvis Presley. The allusion to Fuentes's film also suggests a connection back to Pancho Villa. In the same year that *Alla en el Rancho Grande* came out, Fuentes made *Vamanos Pancho Villa,* the last film of his famous Mexican Revolution trilogy, which, like *Touch of Evil* itself, went on to be a critical, if not box office, success. Rather than presenting Villa as a dashing hero, as he was often portrayed in films, Fuentes avoided the cliché and painted a more complicated figure, as a man who could be ruthless, even to his own men.

Susan's continued assumptions about the difference between America and Mexico lead her to play into Uncle Joe's scheme to destroy her reputation when she decides to go to an American motel for "safety" and "comfort," not realizing that Uncle Joe actually owns it and that he has sent Pancho to carry out the "fake" gang rape. Susan's reaction to Pancho as both a dark ravisher and a comic figure is further complicated by the fact that she references her Mexican husband as her defender, which clearly works against the politics of color integral to the southern rape complex. However, Vargas/Heston's status as Mexican is complicated by his use of another facet of minstrelsy (which is also a feature of *The Birth of a Nation*), the use of the blackface, or, in *Touch of Evil,* brownface. In *The Birth of a Nation* blackface draws on the stereotypes propagated through the popularity of minstrelsy, but it also calls for a more willful suspension of disbelief. As Michael Epps argues, the problem in theorizing minstrelsy is "the complex address of the viewing subject implicit in any staging or restaging of the form" (17). Epps demonstrates the form of address to the white audience in *The Birth of a Nation* by citing a particularly strange diegetic use of blackface in which two white characters disguise themselves through blackface to spy on the African Americans who have taken over the town. Because Griffith chose to use white actors in blackface for all the principal parts, to avoid any "race mixing," these white spies are visually indistinguishable from the other supposedly black characters, yet Elsie, the endangered white woman held captive by the scheming "mulatto" man, is still able to recognize them as white and yell for help. In order to confirm their belief that race is always visibly recognizable, the white audience members are asked to suspend their disbelief and pretend that there is a difference between a black character played by a white actor in blackface and a white character in blackface pretending to be a black man.[11] The white audience, therefore, can pretend to be "duped" by blackface because they are "in" on a joke that supports the idea of white racial superiority.

The address to the audience in *Touch of Evil* is equally complicated: is the white audience encouraged to be duped and accept Charlton Heston as Mexican in order to negate the negative stereotype of the corrupt Mexican official; or does it invite viewers to be "in on" the joke and ignore Heston's brown face, "knowing" that he is white and therefore a "suitable" hero as well as an acceptable husband for Susan (the reverse of *The Birth of a Nation*); or as Pease says, does the film show "how Mexicans should look before they could acquire Vargas's lawful authority" (86)? Further complicating the use of brownface in *Touch of Evil*, unlike *The Birth of a Nation* as a silent film, is the role of sound. One may attempt to account for Charlton Heston's lack of accent, as Welles did in persuading the reluctant Heston to take the role, explaining that Vargas has had an elite American education and so, with only makeup and wardrobe, Heston could "pass" as Mexican. But even this scenario (which is never mentioned in the film) cannot account for Heston's lack of fluency on the occasions when he does speak Spanish in the film; one does not have to have an accent to speak Spanish, but the ability to actually speak fluently is still necessary. Welles tackles this problem head on in the film by calling attention to it and using it as an opportunity to show Quinlan's racism when he says to Vargas: "You don't talk like one, I'll say that for you. A Mexican, I mean." But the Latino actors in the film can switch effortlessly from Spanish to English (a skill that Mitch Holt attributes to his Mexican-born wife in the novel), which only highlights Heston's halting use of the language. This contrast is most notable in the scene in which Vargas/Heston invokes the power of exception behind the southern rape complex.

When Vargas discovers that Susan is missing from the motel and learns that Grandi's nephews have abducted her, he rushes to Grandi's Rancho Grande to confront them. Here the calm, cool Vargas relinquishes his official status and resorts to violence. Ironically, as Heston tries to yell passionately in Spanish, asking where his wife is, Risto, Grandi's other nephew, responds by saying, "Talk English, can't you." On the one hand, Risto's call for English seems to indicate that he does not speak Spanish, a sign that he is asserting his Americanness, yet his incorrect use of *talk* for *speak* suggests that English is not his first language or that he speaks a border mix of Spanish and English. But in the context of Heston's halting Spanish, this request comes across as an almost comical commentary on the actor's inability to speak fluent Spanish (that a true speaker of Spanish could not understand him), thus undermining the violence of the scene as well as Vargas's own status as Mexican.[12]

Vargas's use of extralegal violence in this scene, however, is a more extreme version of Quinlan's rough treatment of Sanchez during the interrogation. While Quinlan is willing to invoke a state of exception to employ "enhanced" interrogation, and even to frame a "guilty" man, Vargas, as if to deny the link, explains, "Listen, I'm no cop now, I'm a husband." In refuting his status as a "cop," Vargas implies that, unlike Quinlan, he is not abusing his legal authority because, as an injured husband, he can "legitimately" invoke the state of exception associated with the southern rape complex: the ability to use violence, to break the law, without fear of retaliation to protect the "honor" of a white woman. Despite Vargas's abhorrence of Quinlan's corruption of the law, even he feels justified in circumventing the law when defending his wife's honor. Vargas's reaction is in direct opposition to that of his counterpart, Mitch, in the novel *Badge of Evil*. When Connie, Mitch's wife, is arrested for drug use, the police surgeon refuses to test her blood because it is a "clear-cut case of marijuana" based on the presence of marijuana in her purse and the smell on her breath. The doctor assumes the "natural" prejudice of a husband (rather than a Mexican), telling Mitch "As her husband, you're entitled to believe in her innocence, I suppose." To defend his wife, Mitch counters: "I'm not speaking as her husband . . . I'm speaking as her attorney. I demand the examination be made. If you won't do it, then I'll call in an outside doctor" (Masterson 142–43). Mitch invokes the law, not the state of exception, to protect his Mexican American wife.

For Pease, drawing on the theories of Giorgio Agamben, Vargas represents not only a touch of evil but a "radical evil" in his acting out the "emergency state's obscene enjoyment of the violation of its own rules" (99). Placing the film in the context of Cold War politics and its effect on border politics, Pease makes the connection between Vargas's powers to police the border for illegal substances (as the head of the Pan American Narcotics Commission) and a program called Operation Wetback, which deported over a million migrant workers who entered the country illegally. At the height of the McCarthy anti-Communist campaign, illegal immigrants were linked to enemy infiltration, and the McCarran-Walter Act of 1952 was used to sanction these massive deportations. To make his claim about Vargas's radical evil, Pease takes his argument a step further, asserting that Vargas assumes the powers of the state of exception in his pursuit of Quinlan: "Vargas assumes the emergency power to take whatever means necessary to accomplish this purpose. Schwartz authorizes him to enter Quinlan's private property without a warrant, to obtain access to his police files, to interrogate him without counsel, and to plant a wire to gather evidence against him" (93). The problem with this argument is that Schwartz, not Vargas, goes to Quinlan's ranch to look for the dynamite. Vargas looks only at public records concerning the sale of dynamite and the trials of Quinlan's past cases, and it is Menzies, Quinlan's partner, who wears a wire.[13] While it is true that Vargas invokes a state of exception, it is not in his legal capacity, or through his extended power on the border as part of the Pan American Narcotic Commission, but as a "husband" and it is based not on the law but on the logic of the southern rape complex.

A TOUCH OF FILM NOIR: MARCIA, MARCIA, MARCIA

The logic of the southern rape complex is most clearly delineated in the use of "rape" as a political tool in the case of Susan and Vargas, but its logic is also at work in the relationship of Marcia and Sanchez. As Pease argues, *Touch of Evil* operates under the logic of film noir, in which the knowledge necessary to discover the real "crime" at the heart of the film cannot be acknowledged "or must [be] disavow[ed] as the precondition for its coherence" (80). While Pease argues that the real crime is Vargas's invocation of the state of exception in his investigation of Quinlan, I maintain that in *Touch of Evil* what is disavowed is the interracial narrative of the southern rape complex (the large form) as a pretext/diversion that obscures the real situation of the small form: that the murder of Linnekar and Quinlan's planting of evidence are both intraracial and intrafamilial crimes that are based on greed and jealousy.[14]

Like detective films, film noir fits into what Deleuze describes as the small form of the movement-image (Action Situation Action), in which an initial action occurs that must be explained or clarified as the situation reveals itself. Either the cause or meaning of the action is unknown (index of lack), or the action could have multiple meanings (index of equivocity) (*Cinema 1* 160–77). The initial action, which opens *Touch of Evil,* is the planting of the bomb (we do not know who Linnekar is, why he was killed, or who did it); however, as the film progresses, Vargas and Quinlan seem to lose interest in solving this crime, as the struggle between the two men takes precedence. Welles actually abandons the generic film noir plot when he lets Marcia, the femme fatale and the mastermind behind her father's murder, literally walk out the door about a quarter of the way through the film, never to be seen again. The novel, on the other hand, "resolves" each action before moving to the next: Mitch Holt proves that Linneker's daughter and her boyfriend Shayon are innocent and gets the confession from the real killer, Ernest Farnum—a disgruntled employee—before dealing with the planted dynamite. The film therefore presents a series of actions (typically combined with some form of border crossing) whose meaning or partial meaning is suggested but without actually presenting a fully resolved new situation.

After Marcia exits the film, the discovery of the planted dynamite in Sanchez and Marcia's apartment creates a new storyline, one more in keeping with the large form (SAS) of the movement-image (often associated with the western). Deleuze holds up *The Birth of a Nation* as an example of the "large form" in which the protagonist is presented with a situation that builds until the hero must act to bring about a new, and hopefully better, situation. In *The Birth of a Nation* a situation (growing animosity between North and South) causes an action (the Civil War), which, from the perspective of the southern whites, forms a new and negative situation (Reconstruction), which in turn brings about a new action (the formation of the Klan) that is resolved—again, from the perspective of the white southerners—by restoring racial hierarchy. In *Touch of Evil* the developing situation is Quinlan's abuse of power and open racism (the very situation that *The Birth of a Nation* tries to obscure through stereotypes of happy slaves and benevolent masters). This building situation leads Vargas to question Sanchez's innocence and to launch his own investigation. Vargas's hunch that Sanchez is innocent, which he is unable to prove, actually reflects the ending of the novel in which the assistant district attorney, Mitch Holt, listening to his wife's intuition about the young couple, proves that Linneker's daughter and her boyfriend have an alibi but refused to give it because they were embarrassed to admit that they had spent the night together at a motel. In *Touch of Evil* the situations that could explain the reasons for both narratives—the killing of Linnekar and the planting of evidence against Sanchez—are never fully revealed because the small form of film noir is abandoned and the final situation is never presented. Quinlan's and Menzies's deaths do not ensure an end to racism (we have no idea who would take their place), nor does the reunion between Susan and Vargas resolve the tension that has surfaced throughout the film regarding their split loyalties to and attitudes about Mexico and the United States.

Just as the critical confusion over the characters' geographical location or national identity indicates the ambiguous borderland the film creates, the critical confusion over Sanchez's relationship to Marcia occludes their real motives for killing Linnekar. Although Heath acknowledges that we learn that Marcia and Sanchez have been secretly married, he refers to Sanchez as Marcia's boyfriend because he maintains that Sanchez is positioned as a "boy." But Heath forgets his own knowledge of events in saying that when "the father prohibits the sexual relation of daughter and boy[,] they kill him" (92). Heath—following Quinlan's theory of the case, not the facts as they play out—actually reverses the order of events. Marcia does not want her father killed so that she can marry Sanchez; she marries Sanchez so that she can manipulate him into killing her father, so that she can inherit his money. Furthermore, the marriage has the added advantage of providing Sanchez with a clear motive because as a husband he would also inherit Linnekar's money. Quinlan assumes that the use of dynamite indicates a personal desire to annihilate Linnekar, and while this may be true, the very public and spectacular way that Linnekar was killed ensures that it cannot be mistaken for an accident, that the police are motivated to find the killer, and that Sanchez, who worked for her father when the dynamite was stolen, will be the prime suspect. In the famous interrogation sequence scene Marcia, her father's "slick" lawyer, and Sanchez move in a unified triangulated relationship as they nervously await Quinlan's questions (fig. 4.1). However, when Quinlan starts to question Marcia, her lawyer (even Sanchez realizes that this is not his lawyer too) breaks up the triangle as he moves to Marcia's side, warning her to say nothing and then escorting her out of the room, leaving Sanchez to fend for himself. At the end of the film, when Assistant District Attorney Al Schwartz mentions, almost as an aside, that Sanchez has confessed, there is no mention of Marcia.[15] Ultimately, the marriage and the use of dynamite allow Marcia to get rid of both father and husband.[16]

Kelly Oliver and Benigno Trigo acknowledge that Quinlan is blind to the fact that Sanchez is "but the tool of the femme fatale," Marcia, who is "the true evil force behind his actions." Nevertheless, they turn their critical focus toward Susan, not Marcia, as the femme fatale who "will bring [Vargas] down just as Marcia Linnekar brings Sanchez down with her" (126). Part of the

FIG. 4.1. At the beginning of the scene Marcia Linnekar, Manelo Sanchez, and the lawyer stand together awaiting Quinlan. *Touch of Evil* (1958).

problem with this comparison is that there is no indication that Marcia is brought down. If Marcia's name does not remain "clean," in that she married a Latino who confessed to killing her father, her knowledge and use of racism are what make possible her "clean get away." In focusing on Susan as the femme fatale, Oliver and Trigo, like Heath, stress that she must be recuperated as the good object and proper wife with the final embrace of Susan and Vargas. But while Susan is complicit with assumptions of white superiority and her privileged place as a white American woman (as was often true of the white southern women whose honor was used to justify the lynching of black men), she is never a destructive, sexually manipulative schemer who endangers her husband. Instead, she is the one who is endangered by her husband because of her position as a political pawn.[17] Marcia is the femme fatale, the bad object that cannot be reconstructed.

By the conventions of film noir the femme fatale—because she violates the codes of femininity by using her sexuality to manipulate men—must be punished, killed, or sent to jail. Marcia, however, is rewarded rather than punished because her "seduction" of Sanchez has more to do with money and marriage than sexual desire. As Sanchez explains, "If it hadn't been for the money I wouldn't have given her a tumble," but he also makes clear that Marcia openly pursued him, that "instead of the man chasing the girl, suppose she was the one, suppose she asked him to marry her." But even more important, Marcia uses her race to achieve her ends, assuming that no Anglo-American would believe Sanchez instead of a rich white woman. In other words, her being tainted by the dark other does not threaten the system of white superiority because Marcia acknowledges racial stereotypes in using Sanchez as a fall guy, which allows her to fall back into her role as a grieving daughter, a victim of the "devious" Latino. Like the blackfaced white spies in *The Birth of a Nation*, Marcia crosses over the color line only to reinforce it.

In the film noir plot Marcia is clearly the mastermind behind her father's murder: Sanchez sums it up nicely during the interrogation scene when he exclaims, "If I had that kind of power [to hypnotize Marcia and make her kill her father] I wouldn't be where I am today, believe me!" Therefore, what appears to be an interracial murder (Sanchez-Linnekar) is really an intraracial and intrafamilial murder based on greed (and perhaps revenge): Marcia's murder of her own father. There is, however, another seemingly interracial murder (Quinlan's wife and the "half-breed" who kills her), which, according to Quinlan, instigated his propensity to plant evidence against those he decides are guilty. This murder is never visualized; instead, a drunken Quinlan relates the details of the murder to his partner, Menzies. Yet the way Quinlan describes the murder and his own subsequent interracial murder of Grandi, using a similar method, raises the possibility that Quinlan himself killed his wife and that her murder is also intraracial and intrafamilial. While Quinlan's hatred/prejudice toward Latinos and his desire to take the law into his own hands by framing Sanchez could certainly stem from his inability to "catch" the half-breed who killed his wife, Quinlan's version of events raises more questions than answers about who killed his wife, where, with what, and most important, why: leaving open an alternative narrative of events. This alternative version of Quinlan as murderer reveals what is an important part of the passion fueling the southern rape complex and the taboo on intermarriage: the fear that white women will choose the "dark" man and that white men will lose their exclusive "possession" of white women.

To begin with, it is not at all clear why Quinlan suspects the unnamed half-breed in the first place because no apparent motive is ever given. The location of the crime also raises questions: Quinlan asserts that his wife was killed in the factory where she worked, but if his wife were at the factory during the day, there would have been witnesses, suggesting either that she was in a secluded spot or that she was there after hours, both of which support the possibility of a secret tryst. For Quinlan to know who committed the murder, as he claims, he would have had to have been there himself, either because he followed his wife or because he discovered the affair and the secret meeting. The method of the murder also raises questions. The killer's use of binding cord could suggest that the murder was spontaneous and that the murderer used anything at hand, rather than bringing a weapon, yet Quinlan himself attributes premeditation to the choice, calling it the "smart way" to kill because "rope doesn't leave fingerprints."

Equally incongruous is the detached way Quinlan discusses his wife's murder in reference to the Linnekar case. In the middle of a conversation, in which Menzies tells a drunken Quinlan that Vargas is accusing him of planting dynamite, Quinlan says, "He was a fool." Menzies assumes that Quinlan is talking about Vargas, but instead this seeming non sequitur actually links planting evidence and his wife's murder, as Quinlan dispassionately analyzes the method of the Linnekar murder:

> Quinlan: No, I mean Sanchez. Dynamite's no way to kill. Did I ever tell you the smart way to kill, Pete?
>
> Menzies: Sure, sure . . . strangling.
>
> Quinlan: Clean. Silent.
>
> Menzies: You told me all that . . .
>
> Quinlan (*over*): That's how my wife got it.
>
> Menzies: Come on, finish that coffee.
>
> Quinlan: I don't usually talk about my wife.
>
> Menzies: Never, when you're sober.

Quinlan's praise of strangulation as "clean" and his flippant reference to his wife's death as "how she got it" do not indicate a man overcome with grief, again opening the possibility that in Quinlan's view his wife "got" what she had coming to her. It is hard to imagine someone admiring the manner of his wife's death unless he was the murderer (or as in Marcia's case, unless he got someone else to do it). Just as Vargas wants his wife's name to be clean, Quinlan's reference to "clean" and "silent" may refer not just to the method of his wife's death but also to his wife, whose death would stop the affair, allowing her name to remain clean and preventing her from leaving Quinlan or making him a public cuckold. Given Quinlan's ability to twist events to suit his purpose, as we see throughout the film, he may well hold the man accountable for "causing" Quinlan to murder his own wife. In equally twisted logic, we know he interprets the man's death on the battlefield of World War I—which would make him an American hero and patriot—as divine retribution: "The good Lord done the job for me." Quinlan, therefore, is just paying back the favor by framing men whom he decides are guilty, further justifying his own "divine right" to administer justice, the ultimate state of exception.

This alternative version puts a new light on Quinlan's murder of Uncle Joe Grandi and his framing of Susan as a repetition of past events. Quinlan has Vargas's gun and could have used it to kill Grandi, thereby framing Vargas for murder as well as ruining his wife's reputation, but Quinlan is more interested in punishing the Anglo wife who is in love with a Mexican. Quinlan uses Susan's stocking to strangle Grandi, in a protracted and violent struggle. Susan then becomes a substitute for Quinlan's wife (who can now be exposed and punished by the law), and it is his rival, Vargas, not he, who will be humiliated. Furthermore, Grandi takes the place of the half-breed, allowing Quinlan to finally get his revenge by killing him, rather than waiting for God to do it. The stocking, like the binding cord, suggests a crime of passion and a weapon of opportunity, but this is actually a premeditated murder in which Quinlan forces his victim to call the police, knowing that by the time they arrive, Grandi will be dead. In addition to this repetition with a difference, Grandi's death also makes him "silent," so that Quinlan's partnership with Grandi cannot be revealed and he, like Marcia, can get away clean. Quinlan, however, does get what is coming to him when, after shooting his own partner, Quinlan is shot in return by Menzies, perhaps because both men have violated the cardinal rule of film noir: never double-cross your (white male) partner.

Quinlan, however, does not want to punish Marcia, who also marries a Latino, perhaps because her marriage is a cynical attempt to exploit racial stereotypes in order to inherit her father's money; she is using Sanchez as a fall guy in the same way that Quinlan tried to use the "half-breed." In planting the dynamite in Sanchez's apartment (ignoring the fact that Marcia lived there too), Quinlan completes the crime that Marcia instigated when she conned Sanchez into stealing and then planting the dynamite in her father's car. Marcia uses Quinlan's reputation and his prejudice to make sure that Sanchez, not she, will take the fall. In the staging of evidence, like the staging of a rape, racial stereotypes are used to allow whites to break the law even as they claim to enforce it. Marcia demonstrates how racial superiority trumps racial purity, the latter being only a convenient tool to maintain the former.

POWER OF THE FALSE

Welles's use of the power of the false in *Touch of Evil* is in keeping with his break with the movement-image of the film noir plot. In a typical film noir the guilty party is exposed as a liar or traitor, but in *Touch of Evil* the forger "is not a localized liar, but an unlocalizable and chronic forger in paradoxical spaces" because "the forger exists only in a series of forgers who are his metamorphoses," while "the power itself exists only in the form of a series of powers which are its exponents" (Deleuze, *Cinema 2* 132, 145). Although Quinlan is exposed as a crooked cop who perverts the law to impose his own justice and Vargas is on the side of truth and the law, Deleuze maintains that both Vargas and Quinlan are "forgers" who share a will to dominate. For Deleuze the most positive form of the forger is the artist who moves beyond judgment to embrace the Nietzschean "innocence of becoming," which is "beyond good and evil" but not beyond good and bad (132).[18]

There is, however, another side to the forger, and that is the desire to move beyond good and evil in order simply to dominate, not to "become." And ultimately, in *Touch of Evil* the will to dominate drives the film. Quinlan most obviously displays the desire to dominate by setting himself above the law to decide who needs to be punished, but Vargas, who appears to be "the epitome of the truthful man," is willing to use the law for his own "strange motives," such as revenge: Vargas is willing to ignore his wife, putting her in danger, because he is more interested in gathering evidence against Quinlan, his enemy (Deleuze, *Cinema 2* 136–37, 140). This desire to judge, therefore, for both Vargas and Quinlan, turns into a will to dominate.[19] And Vargas, like Quinlan, uses the logic of the southern rape complex as a pretext to "take down" his nemesis. The variations of this will, "an irreducible multiplicity," appear in other characters who are "now valid only as transformations of each other," as in the "chain which unites those in *Touch of Evil*." Although Deleuze does not articulate this chain, we can see that Linnekar exercises his will in his status as "a big deal in this town," Marcia wants her father's money and his power, and Joe Grandi wants to take over when his brother is prosecuted, while the nephews feel they should take over after their father is in jail. Deleuze also sees a pattern between Quinlan and Menzies, maintaining that there is "always a character destined to betray the other," as "Menzies must betray Quinlan," because "the other is already a traitor, and betrayal is the link between forgers throughout the series" (*Cinema 2* 145). Quinlan, of course, also betrays his "partner," Grandi.

Having Quinlan and Vargas in the role of the forger, as a series of powers or qualities outside the system of justice that morphs from character to character, is paramount in understanding the time-image in *Touch of Evil* and in Welles's films in general. Unlike Fritz Lang or Bertolt Brecht, who put the system of judgment in crisis, for Welles "the system of judgment becomes definitively impossible, even and especially for the viewer."[20] Welles fights against a system of judgment in his films by creating characters that are "unjudicable." Quinlan is the ultimate forger, not only in his penchant for planting evidence but also in his ability to shape facts into his own falsifying narrative not linked to the cause and effect of an organic narrative, which proceeds "according to legal connections in space and chronological relations in time" (Deleuze, *Cinema 2* 139, 133). When Vargas complains that his wife was accosted on the street by "Pancho" and intimidated by Uncle Joe, Quinlan immediately reframes the situation, asking if Vargas's wife is in the habit of being picked up on the street by strange men. Before anything has happened between Vargas and Quinlan, Quinlan has already created a story of cuckoldry (a possible connection to his own wife) that impugns Susan's reputation as a respectable wife. Quinlan thus lays the groundwork for the frame he and Grandi will later perpetrate against Susan, before he has any logical motivation to do so. Furthermore, Quinlan's narrative sets into play the counter-narrative to the southern rape complex—and perhaps the real fear that is always lurking behind it—that the white woman was asking (looking) for it.

In addition to the role of forger, Deleuze's description of the falsifying narrative in the time-image relates directly to the perverted role of the law in *Touch of Evil*, in which "investigators, witnesses and innocent or guilty heroes will participate in the same power of the false, the degrees of which they will embody, at each stage of the narration." Even a "truthful" man like Vargas "ends up realizing that he has never stopped lying." The inability to judge the "truth," the breakdown of the system of judgment, is what creates the falsifying narrative, and in the absence of such truth, or the ability to judge good and evil, what is left are simply forces or powers "always referring to each other and passing into one another" (*Cinema 2* 139, 137). By the end of *Touch of Evil* these forces are manifest in the conflict between Vargas and Quinlan, regardless of other issues of justice. What is at stake is not the truth but reputation, which is the social manifestation of a person's power within or (as in the case of Quinlan) outside of the system, irrespective of right or wrong. When Joe Grandi first gets the idea to smear Vargas, so that he and his wife will wish they had never been born, Grandi sneers defiantly, "He's got a reputation!" When Vargas accuses Quinlan of planting evidence, Quinlan's response is: "I've got a position in the town. A reputation! Who's Vargas?" Menzies sums up the zero-sum game between Quinlan and Vargas when he replies, "Vargas is kinda important, too, Hank. Somebody's going to have to give in on this thing." And even after Susan has been cleared of all charges and the Grandi nephews have confessed, Vargas still wants to bug Quinlan, to prove him guilty. Using the logic of the southern rape complex, which justifies vengeance upon the pretext of defending a white woman's honor, Vargas maintains that he cannot leave until his wife's name is clean and that he must bug Quinlan to get his confession, even though he hates "spying" and "creeping around." In the final chase scene Vargas both literally and figuratively creeps around and gets dirty in order to prove that Quinlan is a dirty cop.

REFRAMING QUINLAN AND VARGAS

In *The Birth of a Nation* there is a series of chase scenes (or rides-to the-rescue) in which the Klan rushes to protect "innocent" whites from the black "menace." The first is a three-way chase in which Gus pursues Flora while her brother Ben rushes to try to save her but arrives too late. This unsuccessful chase is followed by a more elaborately choreographed crosscutting Klan ride to free the besieged whites in an isolated cabin, which is intercut with a second ride-to-the-rescue to free Elsie from the clutches of the mulatto, Lynch, and a third to protect the whites in town from the black Union soldiers. What all of these chase scenes have in common is that the chase involves freeing an innocent victim. Welles, however, just as he abandons the final scene of the noir plot (revealing the guilty femme fatale), also leaves out a crucial element of the chase scene: the innocent white victim. Throughout the film Vargas is so blind to the danger his wife faces that it becomes almost farcical. Indeed, Welles blatantly signals Vargas's blindness when he calls his wife (after leaving her on their honeymoon) from a store owned by a blind woman. Later, in what should be a rescue scene, he drives down the street in his convertible oblivious to the fact that his wife, who has been abducted and drugged by Grandi, is standing on the fire escape wearing only a sheet and screaming for help. Instead of rescuing his wife, Vargas participates in an elaborate chase to prove Quinlan's guilt. This final crosscutting montage "chase scene," in which Vargas surreptitiously carries the recording device that "captures" Quinlan's confession, reimagines both the famous opening sequence shot of *Touch of Evil* and the crosscutting chase scene in *The Birth of a Nation*. The scene demonstrates how Quinlan, Vargas, Sanchez, and even Menzies operate as a series of forgers connected by betrayal and guilt.

In the crystalline regime the forces that act upon one another are represented through cinematic style as well as through content and, in the case of Welles in particular, through montage and the sequence shot. According to Deleuze, both Welles's montages and sequence shot create a "shock of forces," but the montage presents a series of bodies in succession as forces that act upon each other, while the sequence shots present simultaneously the relation among the forces as the camera's constant reframings create a "proliferation of centres and multiplication of vectors" (*Cinema 2* 139). In the opening sequence shot and the final chase montage, Welles combines the two forms by contrasting the role of sound and vision. The camera in the opening sequence shot provides real-time continuity between the planting of the bomb and its explosion, which creates the first cut in action. The camera (not editing) creates a seamless continuity in time and space as it takes the viewers on our first border crossing, from the Mexican side to the border checkpoint and then to the American side (fig. 4.2). All the while, with the camera leading, it charts the crisscrossing path of the car carrying the bomb (Linnekar and Zita) and the newlywed couple walking down the street (Vargas and Susan). At

FIG. 4.2. The couples, Susan and Miquel Vargas (*on foot*) and Rudy Linnekar and Zita (*in the car*), who are tracked in the sequence shot, come together at the border crossing. *Touch of Evil* (1958).

times the camera follows the couple as the car continues out of camera range, but the camera also pulls ahead and stops to wait for the car and the couple to catch up, as it negotiates the crowded streets, including a herd of goats. But even as the camera provides continuity, through its constant reframings to keep the characters in view, it "throws up a jumble of vanishing centres" (Deleuze, *Cinema 2* 142).

While the camera creates continuity, the musical montage indicates the clashes of competing cultures. The 1958 studio release of *Touch of Evil* changed Welles intended soundtrack, using Henry Mancini's opening theme song as the background for the sequence shot; the 1998 version, however, re-created Welles's opening sound montage, with abrupt shifts in the music (using Welles's detailed, fifty-eight-page memo to the studio and the preview version, discovered in 1976).[21] As the couples walk/drive past the open doors of the various establishments that line the streets, the music pours out, creating shifts that are sometimes abrupt (like direct cuts), while at other times the sounds overlap (like a dissolve). The effect is a jarring cacophony of divergent sounds (both diegetic and nondiegetic) representing the competing cultures that populate the border town and subsequently the movie itself: rock and roll from the radio in Linnekar's car, the seductive bump and grind from the strip joint, traditional mariachi music, Latin-inflected jazz of the opening theme, or even the sound of goats and the mix of Spanish and English. Sound is a particularly appropriate way to indicate the inescapable mix of cultures on the border because sound cannot be "fenced off" or even limited visually. Off-screen sound (unlike off-screen space, which can only be imagined) can dominate the on-screen space, even drowning out the on-screen dialogue.

The final chase scene with Vargas, Quinlan, and Menzies, in contrast to the opening sequence, presents a visual montage through the use of abrupt cuts but creates aural continuity through the running, real-time recording of the conversation between Quinlan and Menzies. In this inversion of the opening sequence, Vargas, with his tape recorder, creates continuity through his constant aural "reframings," to keep the characters in earshot, but to maintain this sound continuity, he, like the camera in the sequence shot, must stay out of view (of the characters). The chase scene therefore dramatizes the "behind the scene" recording of the sequence shot, by revealing the recording device and the man operating it. But Vargas's use of a recording device also mirror's Sanchez's use of a timing device.

The opening sequence shot begins with a medium close-up of a man's hand setting the timing device of the bomb for three minutes (the time of detonation but also the approximate length of the shot). As the man (whose face we never see but later learn is Sanchez) turns to his right, the camera pans left to reveal in the background, through deep focus, the targets of the bomb: Linnekar and his "date," Zita, the stripper. The man crosses back and forth in front of camera, keeping out of sight of his targets, then runs to plant the bomb before the couple reaches the car. Because it is a sequence shot, this occurs as part of one fluid moving shot. In the chase montage these elements are duplicated but fragmented through editing: Vargas in a medium shot is shown holding the tape recorder, and as Vargas turns to his left to keep his target in sight, we see in the background, through deep focus, Quinlan and Menzies. A medium close-up also shows Vargas setting the dial, not to control the time of the shot but to control the sound of the recording. Vargas and Sanchez (who we later learn planted the bomb) therefore share a similar space in relation to the camera, and both are using a mechanical device to "destroy" an American white male authority figure (figs. 4.3–4). Vargas occupies the place of Sanchez, but while Sanchez exits the scene after planting the bomb, Vargas remains to

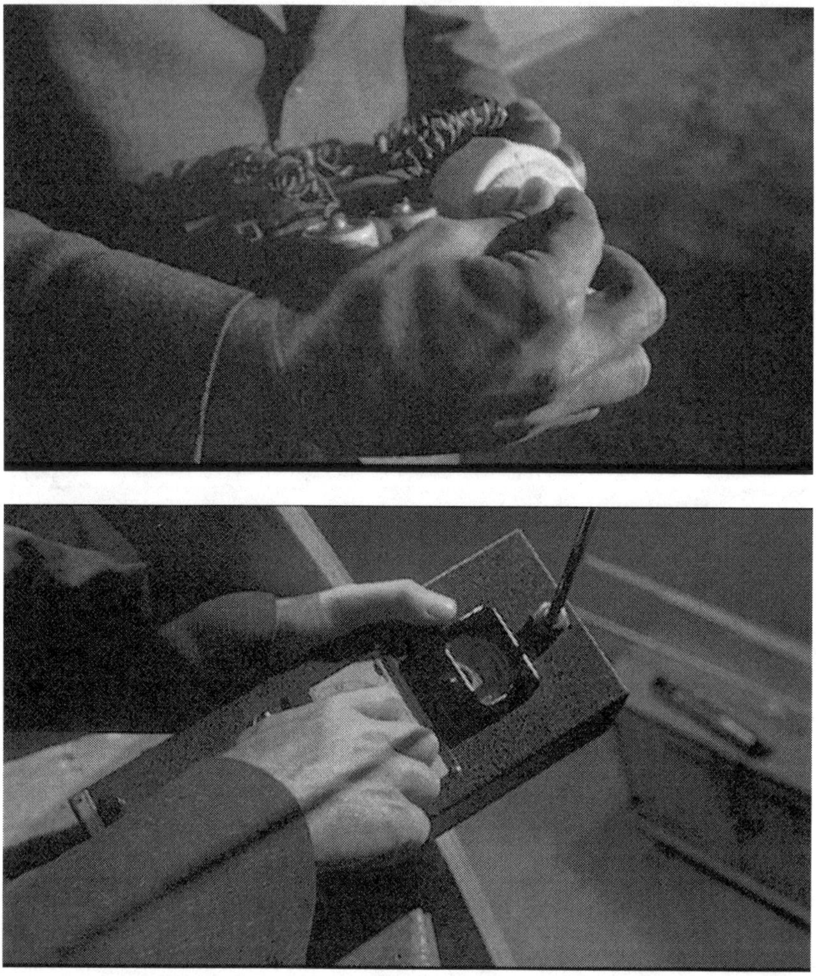

FIGS. 4.3–4. Sanchez setting the timer for the bomb and Vargas setting the dials on the recorder. *Touch of Evil* (1958).

record the entire scene, thus taking on the role of the camera in the famous opening scene sequence.

The final chase montage also reimagines the chase scene in *The Birth of a Nation.* Whereas in *Birth* the characters' geographical position relative to one another is obscured as the chase continues, unmooring them from the logic of the chase (the motor schema underlying the crosscutting) and therefore decoupling movement from time to expose pure affect, in *Touch of Evil* the relative position of the characters to one another is clear; it is the geographical perspective, the border space vis-à-vis the camera, that is in question. The scenes in both films involve the triangulated relationship of the three characters but in very different configurations. In *The Birth of a Nation* Flora is pursued by Gus, who is pursued by her brother, who sets out to rescue her. The crosscutting isolates the three figures, and the only clues we have to understand their relative positions are the geographical markers that they pass by. These markers, however, as discussed in chapter 1, become increasingly obscure, to the point where it is difficult to tell who is chasing whom, and time is released from movement, creating a time-image.

In *Touch of Evil* Menzies and Vargas are in pursuit of Quinlan not to catch him physically but to capture his confession on tape. The politics of color are also reversed, as it is the Mexican Vargas who pursues the Anglo Quinlan. In order to do this, Menzies, who is wearing the wire, must lure Quinlan out of Tanya's and away from the overpowering sound of the pianola, whose music has punctuated the stages of Quinlan's investigation and the descent of his career (during Quinlan's last visit Tanya has even predicted that his future is all used up). Vargas must follow with the recording device, keeping enough distance not to be seen and at the same time following closely enough to keep the recorder in range. Unlike in *The Birth of a Nation*, it is not the physical relation between the three characters that is in question; Menzies and Quinlan are walking together, and we often see Vargas in the same shot, though at a distance, thus establishing their relative positions. Although it is clear at the beginning of the chase that Quinlan and Menzies are in Mexico, as they have just left Tanya's establishment, as the montage continues and the characters both cross and then go under a bridge, it is increasingly difficult to tell which side of the border they are on; indeed, they appear to be literally *on* the border, the very borderland that the film has complicated throughout. The camera placement exacerbates this blurring of boundaries by violating the continuity of the 180-degree rule (that the camera always stays on one side of an imaginary 180-degree line vis-à-vis the characters, in order to establish their relative position in space). Welles employs the Soviet montage style, in which the shots purposefully clash and conflict with one another, creating dissonance, not continuity, among the shots. These clashing images are shot from a dizzying array of distances and angles, often using canted shots, which further add to the disorienting effects. Even when we do know which side of the border the characters are on, we often cannot tell on which side the camera is placed, and therefore the camera itself creates a borderland perspective.

Only Vargas remains sure about which side of the border he is on when, in the final standoff between Vargas and Quinlan (not a "Mexican" standoff because only Quinlan has a gun), Vargas, with unswerving, if naive, belief in the law and his own position on Mexican soil, confidently declares that Quinlan cannot touch him because Quinlan has no legal authority in Mexico. The viewers at this point have little reason to believe either of these assertions, as we have just witnessed Quinlan shoot his own partner, Menzies, whom he loved, leaving little doubt that he is also willing to kill Vargas. This idea is visually reinforced when the mortally wounded Menzies, in a two-shot with Quinlan, literally falls out of the frame to reveal Vargas in the background, who now takes Menzies's place in the line of fire. Quinlan, the ultimate forger, proceeds to fabulate a new scenario in which he not only frames Vargas for Menzies's murder (Quinlan uses Vargas's gun) but also is "forced" to shoot Vargas "in self-defense." Quinlan claims (for good reason, considering his previous successful frame-ups) that "they always believe me" (regardless of the truth), despite Vargas's continued assertion that Quinlan will never get away with it. But Quinlan has already "framed" the real killer of Grandi, by "planting" evidence—the cane he leaves behind, which Menzies finds, just as he did the dynamite and all the other planted evidence. Welles highlights the irony that Quinlan frames himself by featuring a close-up insert shot of the sign on the motel door instructing patrons to take all personal property with them. Appropriately, at the end Quinlan and Vargas change places; if Vargas had to slog through the detritus under the bridge to clear his wife's name, it is Quinlan whose body ends up in the trash-filled waters of the borderland, marking it (as was Gus's body in *The Birth of a Nation*) as the ultimate abject body, which cannot be made clean but which (unlike Marcia) also does not simply disappear, as Tanya says of the bloated, floating corpse, "Isn't somebody going to come and take him away?"

Ultimately, what *Touch of Evil* demonstrates is that in border politics it is difficult to take a side without creating artificial boundaries. A case in point is the character Sanchez: all the characters, and even some of the critics, attempt to turn him into something he is not—an innocent man (Vargas), the mastermind behind Linnekar's murder (Quinlan), a migrant worker (Pease), a boyfriend (Heath)—in order to fulfill their plans or their readings of the film. But as Welles presents Sanchez, it is just as possible that he, like Uncle Joe, is an American citizen who speaks Spanish and who had a white-collar job as a salesman before Marcia turned him into a husband, a construction worker, and finally a murderer. The border politics that *Touch of Evil* enacts is the refusal to define boundaries or solidify national identity. The final kiss that ends the movie does not, as Heath asserts, reconstruct or fulfill the interrupted first kiss on American soil. After the final embrace Vargas says, "Let's go home," but given the confusion that occurs between the two throughout the movie, it is not clear that "home" means the same thing to both characters. When Vargas says "us," he refers to Mexico, while Susan understands it as referring to them as a couple, and Susan refers to America as her country (where she can be safe), and Vargas refers to Mexico as his country (the place where he would like to be able to keep Susan safe).

One final example of a time-image in *Touch of Evil* speaks to another form of the power of the false that circulates through the characters, a form of becoming that, like the politics of the border and the racial fetish, is always mixed. When Pancho first takes Susan to meet Uncle Joe, as Pancho puts his arm around Susan, another Grandi nephew snaps a picture. To get Susan to "pose" for the camera, a Latina woman holds up a baby and says in Spanish, "Look at the baby" (fig. 4.5). Later a letter is delivered to Susan at her hotel, which contains the photo and a note reading: "A souvenir with a million kisses. Pancho." An insert shot shows the photo first and then the message. The letter appears to be an unspecified form of blackmail, indicating an affair between Pancho and Susan, similar to the story Quinlan made up about Susan being "picked up" on the street. A souvenir photo from a honeymoon should be of the husband and wife, but the off-screen element of the insert shot, the Latina woman with her baby, suggests another kind of honeymoon souvenir that marks a future nine months from now as well as a past event.[22] The insert shot of the photo creates a time-image that conflates past, present, and future, the actual and the virtual, off-screen and on-screen, and stasis and movement. The photo captures Susan's face in the present as a memento of the past, but her gaze is on her virtual future. The photo, therefore, is a souvenir of Susan's future as the mother of a "mixed" baby: a form of "mixedness" that the final kiss foretells rather than forestalls. But, because we only have Pancho's word that the rape did not happen, if Susan does bring home a souvenir from her

FIG. 4.5. A woman holds up her baby to attract Susan's attention while her picture is taken with "Pancho." *Touch of Evil* (1958).

honeymoon, it still could be a sign of interracial rape. The movie, like the picture of Susan and Pancho, the souvenir of the future, affirms the unavoidably mixed nature of Vargas and Susan's future lives and the impossibility of establishing racial purity, whether or not the rape was real or "faked." Combining the static image of a photograph within a moving image, the picture works as a microcosm of the entire film by documenting a staged assignation between Susan and Pancho and, at the same time, marking the permanent mixedness of the final kiss between Susan and Vargas. The southern rape complex, like the powers associated with the forger, morphs throughout the film, working in a variety of often contradictory ways. Although various characters attempt to use it for their own purpose, it also takes on a power of its own. As the film indicates, however, the desire for racial purity is only a useful tool, not the actual goal; the real power at the core of the complex is the power to dominate at any cost.

CHAPTER 5

"A Man Like that Doesn't Deserve Civil Rights"

Systemic Violence in *Cape Fea*

IN THE CINEMATIC depictions of the southern rape complex discussed so far, the issue of who should or should not be able to create and enforce laws is an integral component of vigilante violence. The justification for lynching in the South, as put forth in *The Birth of a Nation* and *The Clansman,* was that the end of slavery also abolished the master-slave relationship that was necessary to "control" blacks and that the national laws (as martial law) arising during Reconstruction did not protect its white citizens—particularly its white women. The logic of this argument is that equality under the law cannot be extended to those who are not fit to be citizens. Therefore, it is only after blacks have been stripped of their Second and Fourteenth Amendment rights that national law can be reinstated at the film's end. Although the dramatic emphasis in *The Birth of a Nation* is on the attempted "rape" and subsequent death of Flora as the affective motivation for the lynching of Gus, the formation of the Klan actually predates Gus's "attack."[1] The initial inspiration for the Klan's creation occurs after Ben Cameron's account of injustices against whites during Reconstruction. These injustices are attributed to all-black juries (who free guilty black men); to northerners who "buy" black votes, prevent white citizens from voting, and stuff the ballot box; as well as to the majority black state legislature, whose first order of business is to pass a law legalizing intermarriage, which is denounced as a form of legalized rape. Yet despite these "injustices" and the emotional impact of Flora's death, the film still attempts to legitimize the lynching of Gus by going through the motions of a Klan trial in which Gus is declared guilty before he is executed.

During the civil rights movement of the 1960s, the vexed relationship between the law, rape, and race reemerged as a topic of great—even if at times somewhat deflected—literary and cinematic concern. *The Story of Temple Drake* anticipated many of the forms this deflection would take: the creation of a black-coded white male as rapist; a greater emphasis on the lawyer, rather than the Klan, as the arbiter of justice; and the courtroom as the center of the drama. As we saw in *The Story of Temple Drake,* the conclusion of the trial is actually the romantic, as well as the dramatic, climax of the film: Stephen Benbow is both lover and lawyer, and he is successful in defending his client and winning the "girl." Likewise, in *Sanctuary* Ira, Nancy's lawyer and Temple's uncle-in-law, is unable to save his black client, but he "saves" Temple's soul by instigating and arranging her confession and her subsequent reunion with her husband.

The lawyer plays an even more important role in two 1962 films, *Cape Fear* and *To Kill a Mockingbird,* in both of which Gregory Peck plays a southern lawyer who struggles to maintain his faith in the law.[2] Surprisingly, the films manage to conflate Faulkner's ineffectual Horace Benbow in *Sanctuary,* the heroic Stephen Benbow in *The Story of Temple Drake,* and the sagacious Ira Stevens in *Sanctuary* (the movie). The southern lawyer in *To Kill a Mockingbird* and *Cape Fear* is both heroic and impotent, wise and obtuse, just as the law is both sacred and ineffective, both absolute and bendable. Peck as Sam Bowden in *Cape Fear* tries to use the law to defend himself, and more important his wife and daughter, against the guilty black-coded white rapist. Conversely, Peck as Atticus Finch in *To Kill a Mockingbird* tries to defend an innocent black man on trial for raping a white woman. *Cape Fear* and *To Kill a Mockingbird* thus demonstrate the seemingly opposing yet interrelated fears that laws either do not protect black men from the false charge of rape or do not protect white women from the threat of rape. In both cases, despite the heroic efforts of the lawyer, the law itself is lacking.

When we compare *To Kill a Mockingbird* and *Cape Fear* as two sides of the same coin, Gregory Peck's characters play out the limits not only of the law but also of liberal tolerance. Taken together, the films produced during the height of the civil rights movement return to many of the same issues that arose during Reconstruction: the racial makeup of juries, due process, and the role of vagrancy laws (which are an amended holdover from the Black Codes). While *To Kill a Mockingbird* asserts that a black man has a right to competent counsel, it does not address the issue of full citizenship: the right to vote, which is directly related to the right to a jury of one's peers, as juries are typically drawn from the voter registration files. In *Cape Fear,* on the other hand, Peggy Bowden pointedly declares of ex-convict Max Cady, "A man like that doesn't deserve civil rights." While *To Kill a Mockingbird* is circumspect about who actually deserves due process and who is still above the law, *Cape Fear* openly tackles the issue in the way it treats and disposes of the black-coded Max Cady.

CAPE FEAR

Cape Fear is based on the novel *The Executioners* by John D. MacDonald, to which Gregory Peck bought the film rights for his production company, Melville-Talbot Productions. Although Peck realized that the Max Cady figure would dominate the film, Peck cast himself as Sam Bowden (the epitome of the good citizen and dutiful lawyer) and cast Robert Mitchum, who had demonstrated his ability to play a captivating psychopathic killer in *The Night of the Hunter* (1955), as a violent ex-convict who terrorized the Bowden family. If *Touch of Evil* demonstrates the impossibility of assessing the "truth" of the southern rape complex by presenting a "real," faked rape, *Cape Fear* animates the southern rape complex by sending the middle-class white family the embodiment of their own fears and desires but in an even more frightening form. It is more frightening because, as a bestial, white male rapist, Cady evades the restrictions of Jim Crow segregation. Significantly, his menace is manifest first by his intrusion into the public, but completely segregated, leisure spaces of the white family: the bowling alley and the boating club. Cady is a fearful "dark" stranger, an ex-con who plays out the paranoid fantasies of "polite" white society, most significantly because he systematically targets white women. As a white male who has educated himself about the law, he has the ability to evade and invert Jim Crow–inspired laws.

An ex-con looking for vengeance against Sam Bowden, Cady's brand of violence appears to represent "subjective violence," which has a clear, individual agent whose violence masks the systemic violence that facilitates "normal" everyday life for more privileged citizens (Žižek 1). But by 1962 the civil rights movement had increasingly brought to public attention the systemic violence of racial discrimination, not only the sensational violence of lynching but also everyday acts of humiliation and discrimination triggered by racial segregation of public and private spaces, which for many white Americans was accepted as normal. Therefore, even as Cady's subjective violence dominates the foreground, Sam's use of legal and extralegal means to eliminate

Cady pointedly and repeatedly exposes the background of systemic violence upon which peaceful small-town life is based. Cady invokes his own freedom from harassment, a freedom that allows him to legally terrorize the proper, law-abiding, middle-class white family, a "legal freedom" that whites had consistently exercised against African Americans, both during and after slavery. By exposing liberal tolerance, which is actually based on the right to maintain a safe distance from the other and is fueled by an "obsessive fear of harassment" (Žižek), Cady, like the police dogs and fire hoses that will be used in Birmingham, Alabama, not long after the release of the film, makes visible and palpable the violence occluded in everyday life.

From a Deleuzian perspective *Cape Fear* would seem to be an example of the large form of the movement-image (SAS), which often takes the form of a duel or struggle between opposing forces. In the film there is a clear narrative in which a situation (S: Max Cady's threat to Sam's family) triggers an action (A: Sam's legal and extralegal attempts to protect his family), but whether or not Sam's action creates a new situation (S') in which the family's safety is restored and the law triumphs is unclear from the film's ending. Although Cady certainly directs his violence against Sam, or rather at Sam's family, his violence goes beyond a simple act of revenge because no mere act can fully actualize or satisfy Cady's raw, violent impulse. Cady's corrupting presence in the film, therefore, goes beyond the cause-and-effect violence of an action-image and is characteristic of a special aspect of the movement-image: the impulse-image.

Whereas in *Touch of Evil,* in which the impulse-image—the corrupting force that pervades the world of the film—is ultimately superseded by the protean power of the false, in *Cape Fear* the impulse-image dominates the film from beginning to end.[3] Donald Pease characterized Vargas in *Touch of Evil* as "radical evil" because of his relationship to the state of exception, but it is Cady who produces what Deleuze describes as a "very special kind of violence" associated with the impulse-image, a radical evil (*Cinema 1* 124). Unlike the active violence of the action-image, which is a reaction against a "milieu, against society, against the father, against poverty and injustice, against solitude," the violence of the impulse-image is not just a reaction to a situation but, like subjective violence, is internal to the character: "This is no longer an acted but a compressed violence, from which only abrupt, effective and exact, often terrible acts which show a raw impulse, derive" (135). This is just the type of violence director J. Lee Thompson found in Robert Mitchum, who told Thompson, "This part is a drunk and a rapist and a violent man and I live my parts." Mitchum was, according to Thompson, a man with a chip on his shoulder and a "bitterness against the whole place" who "might explode at any minute and sometimes did," which "was great for the part" (*Making of* Cape Fear).

Occurring between the idealism of the affection-image and the realism of the action-image, the impulse-image, which is "naturalism's most important element," rather than being opposed to realism, uses the realist actions that occur in a specific geographical and historical setting and exaggerates them into "an idiosyncratic surrealism." The mere presence of an originary world, however, does not constitute cinematic naturalism; if the two worlds (originary and determined milieu) remain separate, despite the number of naturalistic elements, a film would not be considered naturalistic. The impulse-image in many ways signals the crisis of the movement-image that triggered the time-image because the impulse is not rational and therefore does not lead logically to the action-image; instead, it has a very specific relationship to time. The impulse-image resembles the time-image in that it operates according to impressions and impulses, not a causal narrative; the form of time in the impulse-image is the originary image of time, capturing the state of formlessness and chaos of the beginning and the end, "causing an originary image of time to rise, with the beginning, the end and the slope, all the cruelty of Chronos" (Deleuze, *Cinema 1* 124). Although time is made apparent in the impulse-image, what keeps it from revealing pure time, apart from movement, is that time is tied to the impulse and can only be grasped as the "destiny of the impulse and the becoming of its objects." Typically, time in the impulse-image is associated with the negative effects of time, time as entropy: "attrition, degradation, wastage, destruction, loss, or simply oblivion" (127). The impulse challenges the causal links between affection and action, but it still has a continuity and consistency all its own.

A good example of the difference between realism and naturalism, as set forth by Deleuze, is the difference between the novel, *The Executioners*, and the film itself. In the novel, though Sam describes Cady in animalistic terms—"Sullen, vicious and dangerous" with "dark hair" which "grew low on his forehead. Heavy mouth and jaw. Small brown eyes set in deep simian sockets"—Sam also provides a "rational" explanation for Cady's rape of the fourteen-year-old girl based on Cady's war experience. In 1943, when the rape occurred, Cady was twenty-five, had served seven years in the army, and was on furlough in Australia after two hundred days of combat in the Pacific Islands, known to be some of the bloodiest battles of World War II: "He'd been pulled out with a bad case of jungle rot and jungle nerves and sent to a rest camp near Melbourne. It was his first trip into the city. He was drunk. She looked older, and she was out on the street at two in the morning"—to get help for her sick father. Sam goes on to explain that Cady's resentment toward him is based on a kind of class distinction between commissioned and noncommissioned officers: "Sam could tell what Cady was thinking. A nice clean non-combat lieutenant. A meddler in a pretty uniform who'd never heard a shot fired in anger. So the pretty lieutenant should have backed right out of the alley and gone on his way and left a real soldier alone" (MacDonald 6). Given the army's reluctance to prosecute white soldiers for the crime of rape, Cady is justified in assuming he would never have been convicted nor given a life sentence (which was reduced to thirteen years after his sentence was reviewed), if not for the presence of another white officer who was willing to testify. These "rational," if unacceptable, motivations for Cady's crimes suggest the negative impact of the war on returning veterans and the army's reluctance to prosecute sexual assaults.

The film, on the other hand, does not mention Cady's war experience and limits Cady's jail time to eight years, well after the end of the war, thus removing his "acceptable" motivation for his later crimes. Sam ultimately concludes in his conversation with police captain Mark Dutton that Cady is "psycho," thus making him an aberration rather than a social problem. Like the typical character of the impulse-image, the filmic Cady operates according to the "destiny of the impulse," which is "to take possession through guile, but violently, of everything that it *can* in a given milieu, and, if it can, to pass from one milieu to another. This exploration, this exhaustion of milieu, is constant" (Deleuze, *Cinema 1* 128–29).[4] Cady's off-screen violence, the rape of the fourteen-year-old and his kidnapping and raping of his ex-wife, suggests just such an exhaustion of the milieu and an ability to move from one victim (and one milieu) to another.

The differences between the novel and the film also have a bearing on their connection to the southern rape complex and civil rights. The novel is not set in the South and does not have the same relation to issues of race and civil rights; the law, as applied to property rights, eventually allows Sam to kill Cady as he flees from the house. In the film Cady, as an agent of the impulse-image, exemplifies the corruption and violence that lurks under the veneer of normal middle-class America. Rather than being Sam's opposite, Cady is merely his darker double, someone who uses the law to protect his "way of life." Thus, *Cape Fear* is able to capitalize on Cady's dual nature as a black-coded white man who violates as well as uses the law to enact the struggle between subjective and systemic violence.

A more subtle distinction between realism and naturalism (than between the novel and film) occurs between the final screenplay (27 March 1961) and the film as shot and released in 1962. The differences in dialogue and camera direction between the two consistently push the film in the direction of the impulse-image and its effect on the everyday world of the film; the screenplay exemplifies realism, while the film is an example of naturalistic cinema. Throughout the discussion of the film I will therefore point out the impact of what are often small but significant differences between the screenplay and film, differences that additionally heighten the connection between Cady and issues of civil rights in the film and blur the lines between personal vengeance and law.

Evidence of the originary world in *Cape Fear* is manifest through symptoms, the energy of the impulse, and fragments, which Deleuze defines as fetishes torn from the originary world. In *Cape Fear* Cady himself, especially his gaze, represents the symptom, the energy of the impulse, as everything about him is tied to the "diabolical intelligence" of the impulse, while his ever-present cigar and rakish Panama hat (the two distinguishing features that Sam uses to describe Cady) serve as fetishes of the originary world, objects that are "supercharged" with primitive power. The dominance of Cady's gaze is appropriate to the impulse as it goes beyond a feeling, is still less than an overt action, but has its own force. Amid a peaceful scene of a sleepy southern town, Max Cady's mere presence disrupts or disconcerts all those he comes in contact with as he moves from the town square to the courthouse in the opening credits sequence.

The opening shots of *Cape Fear* demonstrate Cady's embodiment of the impulse-image, which pervades the ostensibly normal functioning of everyday life. The force of Cady's presence is signaled as the camera is instantly drawn to him, and what was a static shot of a town square with numerous people walking by turns into a moving shot that singles out Cady and labels him with the film's title, *Cape Fear,* in bold white letters with black shadows that convey both a 3-D effect and a feeling of movement. (This scene is one of the few extended uses of the long and extreme long shot.) In addition to the ominous opening music and the title, our next visual clue that something is wrong here is Cady's attire. While the other white men are wearing suits and ties, indicating their respectable, middle-class workday attire, Cady appears in khakis, a Windbreaker, and a straw hat set at a rakish slant. At this point we do not know who Cady is or why he is going to the courthouse. Yet his mere presence and the power of his gaze so pervade the world of the film, apart from the narrative, that they establish a situation that the hero, Sam Bowden, must react to, which is characteristic of the large form.

Using only his gaze, Cady signals his contempt for and challenge to middle-class norms and authority. He openly ogles two young women, turning his head to stare pointedly at their derrieres, yet as he climbs the stairs in the courthouse, he totally ignores a middle-aged woman whom he bumps into (perhaps intentionally), knocking over the precariously high stack of law books she carries. At the top of the stairs he stares defiantly at a suit-clad man and then at the framed picture on the wall outside the courtroom, which the screenplay identifies as a picture of the presiding judge. Although Cady is clearly looking for something, he refuses to ask for help from the whites with whom he exchanges looks.

Cady's first words in the opening, "Hey, daddy," said to the black janitor, suggest a kinship not only through the use of the word *daddy* but also through the implication of a shared hipster language that sets them apart from the conventional white characters. Cady's assumption of kinship with the janitor codes him as black at the same time that the janitor's polite use of the word *sir* in his reply to Cady distances him from Cady. The janitor therefore presents himself, as Atticus Finch says of Tom Robinson in *To Kill a Mockingbird*, as a "humble, respectable Negro." The use of *daddy*, however, is not included in the screenplay, and the position of Cady and the janitor are reversed. In the screenplay Cady is in the foreground, and the janitor is in the background, making him only a minor character, but in the film the janitor dominates the foreground, while Cady appears much smaller in the background, thus highlighting Cady's attempt to create a connection and the janitor's formal "rebuff" (fig. 5.1).

Cady is twice associated with a janitor, but unlike the forger of the time-image who morphs from character to character, Cady's relationship to these

FIG. 5.1. Cady hails the janitor, "Hey, Daddy." *Cape Fear* (1962).

characters indicates his difference from them, setting up limit positions of acceptable behavior of lower-class men, both black or white. Cady is related not with blackness in general but with a certain type of black man, one who does not know his place in middle-class white society. Cady's status as black-coded troublemaker is confirmed later in the film, when the police chief repeatedly calls him "boy" and tells him to get out of town. The various charges of vagrancy that the sheriff uses to try to intimidate Cady into leaving are characteristic of the Black Codes used to control black men during Reconstruction,[5] but they have been revised to be race "neutral" and thus are applicable to any "undesirable."

But it is not just his hipster lingo or his dress that links Cady to undesirable blackness; he is also willing to stand up for his rights. The signs of harassment at the hands of the police that Cady's lawyer outlines are also true of the police's conduct toward blacks in general, the very issues that the civil rights movement addresses. As his lawyer explains, Cady "has been constantly harassed by the police, subjected to mental cruelty and public degradation—even denied an adequate place to live." While the issue of race is not as pronounced in the novel, the differences in citizenship are. The good news Sam gives Carol (the name of his wife in the novel) to offset the bad news of Cady's appearance is that, even though the firm handles corporate law, estate work, and taxes, Sam has "friends in the police force" and is "one of the boys. And the boys take care of their own," which means that the police will find "so many ways on the books to lean heavily on an undesirable citizen that he departs for more comfortable areas" (MacDonald 12, 13), or as Chief Dutton says in the film, "Just remember, there are legal ways to convince Mr. Cady that this can be a pretty poor place to live in."

These legal ways prove not only futile but dangerous as they set Sam on what he calls a "war of nerves" with Cady, a war for which Cady is both legally and physically more prepared. Each time Sam, via the police, tries to invoke the law to get rid of Cady, Cady anticipates and counters his moves. After Cady shows up at the bowling alley and watches Nancy and Peggy, Sam gets the police to pick up Cady. They strip-search him but find nothing illegal (though Cady mockingly tells them he has a couple of jolts of horse under the collar). When the captain finds only seven dollars in Cady's wallet, he threatens Cady with vagrancy, only to find that his bankbook contains fifty-four hundred dollars. Cady follows his successful outmaneuvering of the police with a more direct attack on Sam when he kills the family dog, demonstrating his violence and his ability to come and go on Sam's property undetected. When the police prove ineffectual, Sam hires a private investigator, Sievers, who tails Cady and Diane, the woman he picked up in a bar, to her place. The PI acknowledges that Diane is over eighteen, but he phones the police to tip them that they can arrest Cady on lewd vagrancy. Cady has already spotted Sievers tailing him, and he uses the occasion to again demonstrate his violence and his ability to elude the police. Cady, like the impulse-image, has a kind of intelligence, "a diabolical intelligence which leads each to choose its part, await its moment, defer its gesture, and borrow the outlines of form which will best enable it to perform its act" (Deleuze, *Cinema 1* 124), a description that perfectly captures Cady's modus operandi as he drives Sam further and further away from the law. At first Sam relies on the systemic violence of the law, and then, when that does not work, he engages in illegal violence in the name of protecting his family.

Although the film repeatedly upholds democratic principles of freedom—that you cannot arrest a man for what you think he has done or what he says he might do—increasingly, the film presents a situation in which vigilantism seems to be the only recourse. Perhaps the best example of the equivocal nature of this relationship between democracy and vigilantism, in a film in which the impulse-image dominates, occurs in the scene after the killing of the dog in which Peggy emphatically declares, "A man like that doesn't deserve civil rights." The final screenplay depicts this line as occurring during a conversation between Sam and Peggy as they attempt to reason out what to do, but the film presents a dream sequence in which the conversation between the two is superimposed in an out-of-focus shot over an image of Peggy in bed, tossing and turning. A dream-image, like a time-image, can suspend the laws of cause and effect, but a dream-image is not typically considered a time-image if it can be accounted for within the narrative of the film. In this instance, however, the relationship between the dream and reality remains unclear. Is Peggy dreaming about a "real" conversation that she had with Sam earlier that day, or is Peggy dreaming about what she wishes she had said or what she fears that she really believes? The film, like the dream, leaves the audience in a state of legal and emotional limbo: rooting for the white family regardless of the law; or siding with civil rights and due process, regardless of Cady's threat; or questioning their own beliefs about civil rights.

Regarding the relationship between democracy and vigilantism in *Cape Fear,* Juliet Flower MacCannell maintains that "modern Law makes its *noir* entrance in the guise of a 'criminal' demand: Max Cady's demand for satisfaction" (49), which enacts the dilemma of modern law: how to fulfill a universal right to enjoyment without infringing on others' rights to enjoyment. But despite this dilemma, the film is not a "brief for 'vigilantism' as a necessary supplement to a modern law that wimpily lets criminals go free or paroles them to 'do it again.'" Instead, the film presents "the limits of the Law not only toward, but within the subject" (62). The conflict is between patriarchal law and modern law, but the problem is that the characters themselves still believe in patriarchal law. Cady, MacCannell argues, does not represent mindless violence because he operates (even if unintentionally) as an enforcer of patriarchal laws concerning women's behavior, and even the victims of his violence unconsciously incorporate and accept these laws. But Cady does not simply represent an antiquated model of patriarchal power; he represents the power of the white, landowning patriarchy upon which American democracy was founded. Ultimately, *Cape Fear* is a brief for vigilantism based on the southern rape complex because it pretends that in a democracy rape is virtually unprosecutable and that nothing can legally be done to protect (white) women; at the same time it pretends that both legal and illegal means are not used to limit the freedoms of African Americans on a daily basis.

The tension between patriarchal and modern law, for MacCannell, is most pronounced in Cady's attack on Diane Taylor. In beating up Diane, Cady has done the "dirty work" of patriarchal law: keeping women in their place. In Cady "Diane has run up against Freud's reality principle, the limit of pleasure, and Benjamin's 'law-preserving violence'—the thuggish arm that keeps patriarchal order in force" (MacCannell 56). Diane assumes that Cady's animalist tendencies are a sign of his rejection of patriarchy: "She expects Cady, as a fellow 'animal,' to become her ally in resisting the rules that pattern the female's response to the Law, and shape her uneasy relation to the unconscious *jouissance* her body contains" (54). But in invoking the differences between ancient and modern laws, MacCannell does not address issues of class standing and citizenship, both of which have historically been linked to ownership of property, including land, as well as people and things. Diane does not simply assume that as a "fellow animal" Cady will help her resist patriarchy and get in touch with her "unconscious *jouissance*"; she clearly considers herself superior to Cady based on her class background.

MacCannell assumes that Diane is putting down small-town propriety in mentioning her status as a former queen of the Veiled Prophet's Ball, but because we only hear this secondhand from Cady, it is not clear if it is Diane or Cady who is putting it down. Given that she has known him only for a short time, it is significant that this is one of the first things Diane tells Cady about herself, suggesting that it is still very much a part of her identity, and it is also possible that she says it to delineate the differences in their status. Diane sees herself as possessing knowledge of, and appreciation for, beauty and culture that sets her apart from Cady as an animal. As she says to Cady: "What would you know about scenery, or beauty, or any of the things that really make life worth living? You're just an animal. Coarse, lustful, barbaric." Diane may be attracted to Cady's brutal, animal nature, but rather than a fellow animal, she acts more as if she were visiting the zoo, a place where Cady is expected to stay in his place while she is free to come and go. As she explains, what she likes about him is that he is a sign of her *choice* to "go low" and that "they don't go much lower than Max Cady." She seems to assume that because of his inferior status, he is lucky to be with her and that he will "take" her insults as the price to pay for her favors. What Cady graphically demonstrates is that her class will not protect her in the "wild" and that she *can* "go lower" than just having sexual intercourse with him. Cady leaves her bruised and beaten and unwilling to say what he did to her, suggesting that Cady's attack went beyond Diane's concept of sexual freedom.

Although MacCannell employs Lacanian theory in her analysis of *Cape Fear,* she maintains that her reference to patriarchal law is not the Lacanian "name of the father" but actual ancient law. In combining Lacan and law, MacCannell seems to agree with Deleuze and Guattari that all desire is social and not limited to the "family romance." Although Deleuze obviously appropriates the language of psychoanalysis in defining the death drive of the impulse, there is a significant distinction. "Fetish" for Deleuze is not a compensatory object to screen the fear of castration; it is a fragment of the originary world. Furthermore, Deleuze's objection to psychoanalysis, in his work with Guattari, is that it limits desire within the confines of the psychosexual family dynamics: "Drives and part-objects are neither stages on a genetic axis nor positions in a deep structure; they are political options for problems, they are entryways and exits, impasses the child lives out politically, in other words, with all the force of his or her desire" (Deleuze and Guattari 13). For Deleuze all desire is social; as the southern rape complex graphically demonstrates, the familial and the social are inextricably intertwined. Desire cannot be divorced from the economic and political dynamics inherent in the complex (just as the term *complex* includes yet exceeds a psychoanalytic definition). An analysis of the impact of the impulse-image in *Cape Fear* does not preclude an analysis of the social dimension of the film; the two are in fact intertwined.[6]

MacCannell acknowledges that Cady's actions "challenge Bowden's democratic law to be more consistently applied" to blacks and women but only because he "draws out the 'irrational' and nonsensical remainders of paternal power that remain in place even under democracy" (61). MacCannell locates these remainders in small-town America, but they are not irrational or geographically limited; they are the basis of democratic law in America, which considered slavery constitutional, limited voting by gender and race, and, fearing the "mob," created the electoral college rather than one *man*–one vote. What *Cape Fear* demonstrates is that whom vigilante justice purports to protect can be limited not only by race but also by geography. Sam makes this clear when he tells Cady that he may be able to push around a "little drifter" like Diane Taylor but that Sam, as a respected male member of the community, will not stand for it and will use extralegal means to stop Cady. Although Sam wants Diane to testify against Cady to protect his "own" women, because Diane is not a member of the community but only a "drifter," even vigilante justice will not extend to her, and she must return home to find legal or extralegal protection. *Cape Fear* demonstrates that the 1960s white male–dominated lawmakers themselves create the need for vigilantism as the only means to protect women by their refusal to pass laws that would protect the privacy of rape victims or laws against stalking.

After the brutal rape of Diane Taylor, Cady's appearance at Nancy's school and the number of parallels between the two scenes heighten the audience's expectations of sexual violence against Nancy, but just as with Flora in *The Birth of a Nation,* the parallels also hint that Nancy is already tainted. In the previous scene Nancy has her first look at Cady and stares directly at him as her father pulls her away, just as Cady and Diane share an exchange of direct looks in the bar where he first picks her up. Nancy's stare dissolves into an extreme long shot of the street in front of her school where she and Cady will have their first "encounter." Nancy is at first obscured in a high-angle long shot of a group of teenage girls walking down the stairs leaving school. The camera seems to simulate Cady's predatory gaze in zeroing in on Nancy, even though Cady is not yet in the scene. As the crane shot moves down to street level, the bars of the black wrought iron fence frame Nancy in the center of the shot, mirroring the shot before Diane's rape as the camera looks through the posts of the bed frame to capture Cady standing over Diane (fig. 5.2). Director J. Lee Thompson worked with art director, Robert Boyle, who had previously worked with Hitchcock, to perfect these two scenes. As Thompson explains, in the bedroom scene Boyle knew just what he wanted in using a single light to create shadows and shooting the scene through the bed railings. When it came to shooting the school scene, Boyle painted the fence rails black because they were not dark enough to create the contrast Thompson wanted to achieve (*Making of* Cape Fear). Once again, Nancy is in the "position" of Diane outside the school when, finding the family car empty, she gets in to wait and looks around expectantly. Nancy moves to the middle of the front seat to turn on the radio, sitting just where Diane sat with Cady on their date. The jazz music Nancy turns on also links her to Diane and to the bar where Cady picks her up. As Allison Graham points out, "Hollywood had for decades appropriated black music as a marker of white illicitness, and by the 1940s it found a complementary iconography in an underlit fantasy world of downtown dives" (45).

Cady's almost mesmeric power is evident in the chase scene, which is

FIG. 5.2. Cady after the attack on Diane. *Cape Fear* (1962).

unique in that Cady does not actually chase Nancy, confirming the power of his mere presence to disrupt ordinary life. Despite the power of Cady's gaze, the camera rarely shares his actual point of view; instead, we witness the effects of his gaze on his prey. From a medium side shot of the car, we see the moment of recognition, as Nancy sits up and gazes out the windshield. We then watch Nancy watching Cady from an actual point of view shot in an extreme long shot and from a psychological point of view shot from a long to a medium shot, showing Cady larger (i.e., closer) than a strict point of view shot. The stationary camera allows Cady to grow larger as he approaches, until he is briefly in a medium close-up. Even the camera distance in *Cape Fear* occupies the in-between space of the impulse-image; the medium shot dominates *Cape Fear* instead of the close-up, which is associated with the affection-image or the medium long shot characteristic of most action shots or the extreme long shot of the perception-image. Only a few extreme long shots are used to signal Cady's approach in the opening and the chase scene with Nancy, and the limited number of close-ups tend to be medium close-ups.

Even before Nancy sees Cady, the camera picks him out. As in the opening, he appears simply to be walking down the street in a tranquil southern town as he passes by a beautiful fountain in the park, but even the fountain, which features sculptures of tritons blowing their horns, portends the violence to come.[7] Characters associated with the impulse-image typically convey

FIG. 5.3. Cady as he stands outside the fence of Nancy's school. *Cape Fear* (1962).

something animalistic or not quite human. They are like animals "not because they have their form or behavior, but because their acts," based on impulse, "are prior to all differentiation between the human and the animal. These are human animals" (Deleuze, *Cinema 1* 124). The fig leaf–covered triton with the head and chest of a man, who instead of legs possesses a powerful tail, is a fitting image for Cady, especially because it is on and in the water that he poses the greatest danger to the family in the final chase scene. The portion of the anatomy covered by the fig leaf may also be that of an "animal," and it is Cady's threat from the waist down that the camera uses to "fool" the audience during the chase scene.

Unlike Diane, who assumes that her class standing will protect her from Cady, Nancy already knows to be afraid of him, and seeing him approach, she runs from the car back into the school; however, both Diane and Nancy would have been wise to stay in the car. As Nancy enters the school, the bars again frame her, bringing home the fact that she is trapped by Cady whether she is leaving or entering the school. The reverse shot shows Cady behind bars, but rather than being a comforting image, the terror behind the scene is the knowledge that those bars do not confine him (fig. 5.3).

The suspense and terror of the chase scene at Nancy's school are predicated on the fact that Cady's clothes are indistinguishable from those of a janitor. If Cady does not fit into the white middle class or the black working class, his inappropriate attire indicates where he does "fit in," or rather where he should "belong" according to the logic of the film—in the white working class. Although the screenplay features only shots of Nancy running through the school rooms and into the basement, the film intensifies this scene by the crosscuttings between Nancy's desperate attempt to evade him and the slow steady approach of "Cady," who is shot from the waist down, as if to highlight his sexual danger but also to hide the identity of Nancy's pursuer.

Nancy's hysterical flight takes her into the basement of the school, the perfect secluded place for Cady's violence, but she is finally able to open a window and squeeze through. When the camera finally reveals the attacker's face in a medium shot, it is actually the janitor, and the tension is momentarily lifted. The frightening monster, when put back in his proper place, is instantly seen as harmless. It is at that point that we learn that Cady has not been following her at all; he remains outside the school, and she runs into his arms as she flees, and breaking away, she runs into the street and into the path of an oncoming car. We could interpret Nancy's actions, like Flora's, as a product of her own fearful fantasies but also as an indication of the power of the impulse. Cady has reduced her actions to mere impulses, in this case flight rather than fight. In the previous scene Cady provokes her father to fight, when Sam punches Cady in public for his lascivious description of Nancy, which only furthers Cady's charge of harassment.

Given the overtones of civil rights issues the film employs, the fear produced by the very possibility of Cady entering the school invokes the fears around school integration after *Brown v. Board of Education* in 1954. As we see from the earlier shot of Nancy's school, she goes to a segregated, all-white girls school; the girls do not wear uniforms, and there is no indication that it is a parochial school or that the Bowdens are Catholic, suggesting that this is not a religious decision and that the Bowdens have already found a way to subvert the ruling on integration. The fear of integrating the neighborhood school was that it could allow for integration on the basis of class and race, and Cady represents fears about poor whites as well as about blacks. Resistance to integration belies the Enlightenment arguments about the civilizing power of education to produce good citizens. The fear is not that blacks and the lower classes cannot be taught but, rather, what they will do with their knowledge. The real fear is that they will expect to be treated as full citizens with equal protection under the law, a point that Cady vividly brings home. Cady is the product of a public education, though in his case it was a prison, not a school, but his education makes him a danger whether or not he has access to Nancy's school.

The "attack" on Nancy prompts Sam to explain why laws on rape are virtually unenforceable: they cannot protect a woman's privacy and her good name. MacCannell argues that, especially concerning rape, there is a tension in the 1962 *Cape Fear* between ancient proscriptive patriarchal law, in which the patronymic (the father's name/status) was the "backbone of political and legal structures," and suprafamilial democratic law, a system that—since Rousseau's theory of the social contract—has stressed individual universal freedoms, which, despite the emphasis on individual rights, assumes a homogeneous society of like-minded citizens (57). But the film demonstrates that neither form of law actually protects women. The attack on Nancy, as well as on Diane, makes it clear that in the case of rape you also cannot try a man for what he has done. Sam explains to Peggy that Cady knows they would never put Nancy through the ordeal of a trial because of the stigma of testifying about sexual matters in open court. And as Diane says when Sievers tries to talk her into testifying because of Cady's threats to the Bowdens: "I'm somebody's daughter, too. I could never repeat the things he did to me." Rape, therefore, except in the case of a third-party eyewitness, as Sam was in Cady's trial, is a crime in name only if it cannot be prosecuted. The film, through the conversation of Sam and Peggy, takes this presumption at face value, as an insurmountable obstacle, and it is this legal obstacle that prompts Sam to use extralegal violence against Cady.

THE STEEPEST SLOPE

Unlike an action-image, the impulse-image does not operate according to logic, yet it maintains a "perfect consistency and autonomy." As mentioned, it operates according to the law of the "steepest slope," in which "all the parts converge in an immense rubbish-dump or swamp, and all the impulses in a great death-impulse" (Deleuze, *Cinema 1* 124). The film captures Sam's downward spiral each time he tries to combat Cady, culminating in the ending in which Sam and Cady fight a primitive battle on the swampy shores of Cape Fear. The difference between the film's ending and that of the novel and the final screenplay again demonstrates Deleuze's distinction between naturalist and realist film. As stated earlier, if the originary world of the impulse and determined milieu are kept separate, the film is not dominated by the law of the steepest slope. The novel and screenplay both reassert this division in their endings by the presence of the law, which clearly supports Sam's version of events. In the novel the husband and wife set a trap for Cady (the children are sent away to keep them from danger), and the trap is not in a swamp but in their own home. Although there are moments of tension in which Cady gets into the house undetected and attacks Carol (Sam's wife's name in the novel), in the end Sam fatally shoots Cady. Because Sam has lured Cady to his home, he can legally shoot him as an intruder, no matter how premeditated the killing was, and the local authorities are even willing to lend an officer to assist in the stakeout. Both justice and the law are upheld, and therefore Cady, though a threat, has not brought down the family, and time is not presented as the destiny of the impulse. Cady and Sam enact the duel associated with the action-image—good/lawfulness triumphs over evil/lawlessness—and the two worlds remain separate. Sam acknowledges that he should feel differently now that he has killed a man, but instead he claims a greater clarity about the law: "I was idealizing my profession, and leaning on it too heavily. Now I know it's just a tool. You use it like any other tool. Use it wisely and it can help you. And when it's of no use to you, you take a course of action that will be of use" (MacDonald 213). Even though the law alone (the police) could not save Sam, his actions are still within the confines of the law.

The novel, also, does not make the same link between Diane and Nancy, as daughters of upstanding white citizens who are threatened by Cady. In the novel Bessie McGowan (not Diane Taylor) is a middle-aged, blousy barfly, who is described as "grotesque, ludicrous and incredible . . . in the great bawdy tradition of the mining camps and the frontiers" (MacDonald 147). Bessie relates that Cady picked her up and then beat her up (there is no suggestion of sexual assault) not because she insulted him or to send a message to Sam but for a more "practical," even if slightly paranoid, reason: because she asks him too many questions about himself. It is Sam who seeks her out, and she assumes that he is trying to pick her up, until she discovers that he wants her to testify against Cady. Although Bessie was once Miss Indiana, according to the bartender, unlike Diane, she does not identify herself as such, nor does she express the need to return home to seek protection. Instead, she describes herself as "girl graduate of Dannemora," a prison in New York State. Bessie realizes that because of her lack of class status, regardless of her race, the police will not protect her against Cady or take much interest in his assault against her. As she explains to Sam when he asks her to come to police headquarters: "In the first place I've seen the inside of that place too many times already. In the second place they wouldn't listen to anything Bessie McGowan says" (152). Thus, as Bessie confirms, it is not simply that the law cannot protect women; it is also that it is only interested in protecting certain types of women.

While the differences in the film's and novel's endings distinguish realistic from naturalistic cinema, in the final revised script the ending is more neatly resolved according to realistic cinema: Cady, subdued and tied down, is delivered into the hands of the police, and the family unit is restored to "normal." The directions in the script describe a shot in which Cady, strapped to a stretcher, is taken away in the bow of the sheriff's boat (Webb 233). As the boat leaves the dock, the camera "picks up" the Bowdens in the stern; Sam and Peggy are draped with a blanket, while Nancy, "well-wrapped," is sleeping peacefully between them. As if to restore the normalcy of daily life, a deputy comes into the shot with a cup of coffee, which Peggy hands to Sam, "both of them smiling slightly that all of Nancy's troubles are so soon forgotten." A final reverse shot shows the dawn and the cruiser speeding away, "with the river winding away into the distance" as the scene fades out (Webb 109).

The film's ending gives no such return to normalcy and law and order; Cady is never shown restrained or in custody. From the pull-out shot of the final confrontation on the shore with Sam holding a gun on Cady, there is a straight cut to Nancy, Sam, and Peggy siting in the boat wide awake but with a stunned look (fig. 5.4). No one talks or smiles, and no representative of the law brings a comforting cup of coffee. Unlike the stage directions of script, there is no sense in this shot that Nancy's troubles will so soon be forgotten. The final dialogue of the film is Sam's vow of revenge, sending Cady to jail not as a form of justice but in order to make him live like an animal for the rest of his life. Because Max is such a horrifying character, however, the "liberal" audience is affectively in the uncomfortable position of "rooting" for Sam to use extralegal means to get rid of Cady once and for all. Although Sam stops short of killing Cady, by the movie's end Cady's malevolence pervades the entire film. Cady literally brings Sam down to his level and forces him to "get dirty," thus implicating the white middle class in the violence of systemic violence and effectively erasing the line between the two. Sam spares Cady's life not out

FIG. 5.4. Cady's impact on the family is still present even after they are rescued. *Cape Fear* (1962).

of mercy or a belief in the law but as a form of cruel and unusual punishment that will treat Cady "like the animal [he] is." The law in the end, therefore, is exposed as a form of personal vengeance. Significantly, the representative of the law, the deputy who in this case participates in an extralegal stakeout, must be sacrificed in order to bring Cady to justice. It is his dead body that will be used to put Cady behind bars for life because, as we learn early, attempted rape will not put Cady away for long.

SYSTEMIC VERSUS SUBJECTIVE VIOLENCE

Cady, a known rapist who stalks, kidnaps, rapes, and beats up women, does not simply demonstrate that the law does not work; he shows *how* the law works and, more importantly, for whom. Cady represents a dangerous new class, not based solely on race or economic class: an educated underclass that does not share middle-class norms of propriety and property. Even as Cady will force Sam not only to witness but also to participate in the manipulation of the law and the extralegal measures he takes against Cady, there is another form of systemic violence that remains invisible and that serves as the normal background against which subjective violence is viewed. Cady appears to be the disrupting influence in the courtroom as he enters just as Sam is in the middle of a court case. Ostensibly, this scene sets up the proper course of justice and also demonstrates that Sam is a good and just attorney fighting for the rights of his client. The trial Sam is working on is not part of the plot and is indeed presented only as a backdrop, a contrast against which the later violence is highlighted as aberrant. But this scene, far from innocuous, demonstrates the acceptable manipulations of the law, which totally undermine its universal application.

Although in the novel Sam's firm works on corporate issues, estate work, and tax matters (MacDonald 12), in the film Sam is fighting for the "little guy" against an insurance company. In this initial court scene the judge tries to persuade Sam to agree to the defense's motion for a third postponement of the trial because allegedly one of its eleven witnesses is ill. Rather than argue for the merits of the motion, the judge explains that in the summertime the courtroom is "hot as an oven" and that Sam might create a hostile jury if he forces them to sit through the trial rather than postponing it until the fall. This could be a metaphor about how justice is meted out in the South and that the jury may be hostile if the case is seen as "too hot to handle," as we see in *To Kill a Mockingbird,* but the judge's actions could also be interpreted as a form of collusion, in which he intercedes for the defendant by delaying the case, a tactic often used by wealthy companies or defendants to exhaust the time and money of the complainant. Sam insinuates that the defense's motion is just such a delay tactic as he comments that the case has already been postponed twice but also suggests the difference in resources between the defendants and the complainant. As Sam points out, the earlier delays were always because a defense witness was sick, and even if the witness cannot make it, there are already eleven defense witnesses while his client only has one: "Eleven against one should be enough, no matter how sickly and decrepit those eleven happen to be." Sam objects to the postponement because his elderly client "has money due him" and is "in bad need of it," and his only witness is also elderly and might not be alive in the fall. Although the judge rules in Sam's favor, this seemingly innocuous scene demonstrates how easily the law is (legally) manipulated for the powerful.

Sam's final invocation of the law to put Cady away until he "rots" also requires extralegal measures. Given Cady's knowledge of the law and his ability to hire a good lawyer, the case against him remains largely circumstantial. The only crime that will put Cady away for good is the killing of the deputy, but as Cady makes clear as he pats the lifeless body of the deputy, "There's not a mark on him." Because Cady takes the deputy unaware and holds him under the water, there is nothing to prove murder rather than drowning—no fingerprints, no marks, and in this case no eyewitness. Cady does not actually sexually assault Peggy or Nancy, nor does he have a chance to kidnap Nancy.[8] Even Cady's brutal assault on Diane, had she testified, would only, according to Sievers, have warranted six months in jail (in the novel Cady only serves thirty days for striking an officer). Cady, on the other hand, is the only one with proof of a crime. Whereas in the novel the private investigator is careful to make sure that no one can trace the order against Cady back to him or Sam, in the film Cady has an eyewitness to confirm that he was hired at the behest of Sam to do a "hospital job" on Cady, and disbarment proceedings have begun against Sam, proceedings that Sam has skipped out on in order to stake out Cady.

What might sway a jury is Sam's testimony as to Cady's harassment, but again, it is Cady who can establish a pattern of police harassment instigated by Sam's complaints; Sam has no proof. Furthermore, if Sam testifies about Cady's harassment and assault on his family, he will have to disclose the trap he set for Cady, using his own wife and daughter as bait (something a jury might not believe or, if they did, might find repugnant). Just like the all-white juries that turned a blind eye to the murder of African American men (or children, as in the case of Emmett Till), Sam would have to count on a jury that would ignore the circumstantial facts of the case and convict Cady of murder and another jury (and the ethics committee) that would ignore the evidence in order to free Sam, using the state of exception—a man's right to protect his family—to plead exigent circumstances.

Sam's refusal to kill Cady seems to distinguish him from the impulse-image as Sam calculates his decision, but instead it only serves to dramatize the similarities with Cady. Sam repeats Cady's own words that killing is "too fast." As Cady explains, for seven years he wanted to kill Sam, but by the eighth he wants instead to make Sam suffer the "thousand cuts" of Chinese torture. That Sam counts on the law (despite the lack of physical evidence) to believe his side of the story over Cady's only reinforces what Cady himself embodies: the systemic violence necessary to maintain a "peaceful" white middle-class world and to quiet white middle-class "obsessive fear of harassment."

CHAPTER 6

"Blind Spots"

The Visual Logic and Historical Context of *To Kill a Mockingbird*

The Birth of a Nation's overt racism and justification of the Klan arguably have had the greatest impact on the cinematic representation of the southern rape complex. But, because of its overt racism, the film is no longer rereleased nationwide, and therefore, its influence is invisible to many contemporary moviegoers. The film *To Kill a Mockingbird*, based on Harper Lee's 1960 Pulitzer Prize–winning novel of the same name, on the other hand, still exerts a direct and discernible impact on the American public. It has become deeply embedded in American culture as a symbol of courage, justice, and tolerance, precisely because it was one of the first films to confront directly the relationship between the law and the southern rape complex through the use of an innocent black man who is accused of raping a white woman.[1] Rather than being relegated to an embarrassing or outmoded view of race relations (as is the case with *The Birth of a Nation*), *To Kill a Mockingbird* has actually gained in popularity over the years. In 2008 the film still ranked number one as the best courtroom dramas in American Film Institute's "10 top 10" and number two for most inspiring film of all time in the "AFI's 100 Years . . . 100 Heroes & Villains." And the role of the lawyer Atticus Finch, for which Gregory Peck won the 1962 Academy Award for best actor, was voted the number one all-time film hero in 2003.[2]

As discussed in the previous chapter, both *Cape Fear* and *To Kill a Mockingbird*—released during the height of the civil rights movement and starring Gregory Peck as a besieged southern lawyer—address the issue of who does and who does not deserve civil rights based on the state of exception of the southern rape complex. *Cape Fear* uses the "cover" of the black-coded white man to allow the audience to agree that the vicious rapist Max Cady "doesn't deserve civil rights," as Sam Bowden's wife exclaims. *To Kill a Mockingbird*, set during the early 1930s in Alabama, seems to be the first post-*Birth* film to eschew the black-coded white man and to reimagine the southern rape complex with an innocent black man, Tom Robinson, who is wrongfully accused of raping a young lower-class white woman, Mayella Ewell. In assessing the role of the southern rape complex in *To Kill a Mockingbird*, however, we must keep in mind that Mayella Ewell and Tom Robinson are not the only characters that are relevant to such an analysis. Set against the fabricated, but nonetheless lethal, accusation against Tom is the real danger posed by Mayella's father, Robert E. Lee Ewell. As the counterpart to the innocent Tom Robinson, Ewell, as the negatively black-coded white man, is a danger not only to his own daughter (whom he beats) but to the young middle-class white girl (Scout Finch)—a situation we have seen in *The Story of Temple Drake* and *Cape Fear*. *To Kill a Mockingbird* therefore turns out to be the exception that proves the rule.

Typically, in the southern rape complex the black man was cast as a menace to white southern identity and power; in *To Kill a Mockingbird*, however, Tom Robinson represents the "humble, respectable Negro," who, because of his compliance with middle-class values, deserves (some) civil rights. Bob Ewell, like the other black-coded white attackers, combines the negative qualities of both racial and class stereotypes: he is lazy, violent, dirty, drunk, lives in squalor, has too many children who, like their father, are also uneducable, and (in the novel)—most damning from the perspective of Depression-era anti–New Deal rhetoric—Ewell is willing to take charity and assistance but is not willing to work. Therefore, while the film and novel suggest that Tom Robinson does deserve a fair trial (but not full citizenship), Bob Ewell does not deserve any civil rights. The doubling of victim and attacker, one of which is false (Tom/Mayella) and the other real (Ewell/Scout), allows the film and novel both to debunk and to draw on elements of the southern rape complex, to dismiss the image of the black rapist as merely the product of Mayella's lies based on her "ignorance and poverty" and at the same time to see her father's violence, also based on "ignorance and poverty," as the true danger. In both scenarios, however, it is the lower-class characters who pose a sexual threat, either to the black man or to the white middle-class girl.

READING ATTICUS

Given Atticus Finch's status as a paragon of integrity, it is not surprising that most of the early criticism about *To Kill a Mockingbird* extoled its message of racial justice. For decades *To Kill a Mockingbird* was more often analyzed in law journals than in literary or film journals, with Atticus held up as a model to be emulated.[3] As late as 1992, Monroe Freedman's critique in *Legal Times* of Atticus's performance as a lawyer raised a firestorm of angry rebuttals from critics who defended Atticus, arguing that he cannot be judged by late-twentieth- and twenty-first-century standards of racial equality.[4] But critics on both sides of the debate often assume that Atticus's actions and values represent those of Harper Lee (and therefore those of the novel as a whole), especially because Atticus is based on Lee's father, Amasa Coleman "A. C." Harper, a lawyer who was both the editor of the local *Monroe Journal* (1929–47) and an Alabama state legislator (1926–39).[5] But if we look past the loving portrait of a father and lawyer, a systematic critique of Atticus emerges within the novel and its historical context that demonstrates Atticus's lack of sympathetic understanding and calls into question even his abilities as a lawyer.[6] More recent approaches have critically examined *To Kill a Mockingbird* in the context of both the 1930s (when it was set) and the events of the civil rights movement (when it was released). Yet despite the more developed historical analyses of the novel, most critics still do not credit the novel itself with providing this form of critique.[7]

Eric Sundquist has provided one of the most extensive legal, political, and literary analyses of the Depression-era setting of the novel, including the infamous Scottsboro trial, as a backdrop for the events taking place in the civil rights movement at the time of the novel's publication: the murder of Emmett Till and *Brown v. Board of Education*.[8] But despite his attention to history, Sundquist maintains that by situating the novel in the past, Lee displaces the conflict of the civil rights movement onto a "simpler" time ("Blues" 88). Furthermore, he states that *To Kill a Mockingbird* is ultimately constrained by its genre—juvenile literature—because of Harper's "cute framework" of the Boo Radley plot and the easily digestible "moral" of tolerance based on Atticus's dictum to imaginatively stand in someone's shoes (Sundquist, "Black Skin" 230). And finally, Sundquist accuses Atticus of lying to the children when he says that the Klan is a thing of the past. Sundquist attributes the "lie" either to Atticus's desire to shield the children from racism or to Lee's desire to shield "southern readers from a confrontation with their own recalcitrance" ("Blues" 88).

The nostalgic use of the past, as Sundquist asserts, may seem to valorize Atticus as a heroic precursor to liberal racial politics in the South; however, the more we fully place the events of the novel in the past, the more apparent the critique of Atticus becomes. While the novel can be read on more than one level and certainly it has been deemed appropriate for young readers, rather than simply refusing to confront the southern reader, the novel actually challenges an adult, educated southern audience, especially regarding the issues Sundquist raises. Harper Lee pointedly makes no reference to the Scottsboro trials from 1931–37 in which nine young black men were accused of raping two white women. At the same time the novel invites such a comparison because of the significant similarities between the historical trials and subsequent retrials of the infamous Scottsboro case and the facts of Tom Robinson's case. These similarities include the questionable testimony of lower-class women; the lack of medical evidence; the defendant's physical limitations, which call the charges into question; and the jury's bias. Furthermore, although the novel does not refer to the cases, it does repeatedly refer to the specific newspapers that Atticus reads each night, newspapers that reported the landmark Supreme Court rulings in the Scottsboro trials. As the narrator explains, "Atticus subjected every crisis of his life to tranquil evaluation behind, *The Mobile Register, The Birmingham News,* and *The Montgomery Advertiser*" (240). By looking back at those very papers, we can "see" the discrepancies between the actual Supreme Court ruling against all-white juries in the Scottsboro cases and Atticus's limited views on racial justice and the jury system. We can see what Atticus should have seen: that without full rights as citizens (the right to vote and the right to serve on juries), there could be no justice or due process for African Americans.[9]

In the late 1920s the same newspapers also reported the anti-Klan movement in Alabama and the editorials of Grover Cleveland Hall in the *Montgomery Advertiser,* which helped to sway public opinion against the Klan. Atticus's dismissal of the Klan, which he ridicules as a group of cowards harassing the Jewish grocer,[10] reflects this history in which planters, industrialists, and professionals sought to end the violence—but more important, the populist power—of the second Klan movement, for which *The Birth of a Nation* served as a recruiting tool. (Even Thomas Dixon did not support this second movement and its attacks on Jews, Catholics, and immigrants, which he saw as being very different from the Reconstruction Klan that he glorified in his novels.) Atticus's dismissal of the second Klan is therefore not simply a lie in the early 1930s; it is part of a more complex history of the Klan in Alabama.[11]

And being against the Klan in the 1930s meant something very different than being against the third movement of the Klan, which was a backlash against the civil rights movement.

The plot involving Boo Radley also bears a more complicated relationship to the Klan, which is key to how the film and novel both support and dismantle the southern rape complex. Boo, the neighborhood recluse, in saving Scout and her brother, Jem, by killing Ewell, serves the function of the Klan in *The Birth of a Nation* but in the guise of a harmless "mockingbird." Boo is a nostalgic trace of a brutal past but one that the children understand they need not fear because it only appears when they are in danger. This view of vigilantism suggests that it still has a role to play in the South, though it is up to men such as Atticus and Sherriff Tate to decide when it can and cannot be tolerated.[12]

Ultimately, what the novel portrays in Atticus is a good but flawed man who tries to live by a motto that he never fully understands: how to "consider things from [the other person's] point of view," which you cannot do "until you climb into his skin and walk around in it" (Lee 33). Atticus, however, can neither put himself in the skin of a black man nor that of a lower-class white man, and this failure puts both his children and his client in danger. Atticus underestimates the men who come to lynch Tom Robinson, underestimates Bob Ewell's capacity for violence, underestimates the jury's ability or willingness to understand his closing arguments, underestimates how devastated Tom Robinson is by the verdict, and, most important, is blind to the possibility that Tom was shot in cold blood, not while trying to escape. Because Atticus's maxim about sympathetic understanding is so frequently cited as the source of Atticus's lessons of tolerance, his own inability to live up to it also points to the limits of progressive tolerance, for which, ironically, the film and novel have been praised. Atticus's characterization of Mr. Cunningham (in the novel), even after he attempts to lynch Tom Robinson, is equally applicable to Atticus himself: he's "basically a good man . . . he just has his blind spots along with the rest of us" (Lee 179).

Rather than simply shielding the southern audience, the novel shows its readers how to love and even admire Atticus, as a father, friend, and lawyer, despite the fact that he is wrong about important historical and political issues, and the novel shows us over and over just how wrong he is. Atticus sums up this very position of tolerance for other people's blind spots (including their own racism) when he explains to the children, in reference to the "war" they will fight against racial prejudice: "'It's different this time,' he said. 'This time we aren't fighting the Yankees, we're fighting our friends. But remember this, no matter how bitter things get, they're still our friends and this is still our home" (Lee 87). Therefore, Atticus may be a portrait of a loving father and dedicated lawyer, based on Lee's father, but he is also a portrait of a character who is on the wrong side of history, not only from the perspective of the novel's publication during the civil rights movement in 1962 but also in light of the Supreme Court rulings of the 1930s taking place during the time of the novel/film. While Lee might be shielding children and uninformed readers from this critique, it is precisely Lee's own father (a lawyer, legislator, and newspaper editor) and informed readers like him (who know the history and politics of Alabama) who would best be able to understand Atticus's shortcomings as a lawyer.[13]

Early critics' blindness to the novel's critique of Atticus is due in part to the force of Gregory Peck's dignified and heartwarming performance and the film's omission of significant passages that call into question Atticus's judgment, if not his good intentions. When analyzing a filmic adaptation, we often assume that the influence goes only one way—from the novel to the film. But because of the force of Peck's performance of Atticus, the filmic Atticus is often seen as indistinguishable from the character in the novel,[14] and the fact that Harper Lee gave Peck her father's watch after his death—which Peck brought with him to the Academy Awards—only reinforces the connection between Peck, Atticus, and Mr. Lee (Shields 231). As one of the producers of the film, Peck also had considerable clout in shaping and enhancing Atticus's role, and at times Peck's vision trumped that of Horton Foote, the writer who won an Academy Award for best screenplay, as well as that of the director.[15] But the blurring of the novel and film goes beyond the depiction of Atticus. Rachel Watson argues that analyses of the film tend to focus on its narrative features and therefore they treat the novel and film as "interchangeable texts." Furthermore, Watson maintains that critics have approached the film as a cultural artifact, not as an aesthetic one, and have therefore left the "visual logic" of the film "virtually unexamined in favor of its historical occasion" (Watson, "View" 419). As a remedy, Watson therefore examines the film exclusively. But rather than bracketing out the novel, or treating the film and novel as interchangeable, or favoring the historical occasion over the visual logic, it is possible to place the film in its historical context, as alluded to in the novel, to see that the visual logic of the film reinforces many of the novel's more historically specific critiques.[16] Drawing on Deleuze's concept of the perception-image, with its emphasis on point of view, camera consciousness, and off-screen space, I will demonstrate how the film's visual logic still shows us Atticus's blind spots based not only on his absence but also on his inability to "read" the situation.

What the visual logic of the film does not capture as fully, however, is Scout's broader vision. Ostensibly, and as many critics have argued, an integral element of the novel is Scout's moral education, especially through Atticus's teachings. Yet time and again, Scout provides the true moral compass of the novel, seeing past both Jem and Atticus—despite her own adoration of the men in her life—and raising questions they refuse to address. Unlike Jem or even Atticus, Scout is able to place the turbulent events of the novel—the trial of a black man accused of raping a white woman—in the broader cultural context of colonial exploitation and of slavery to expose the culpability of middle-class complacency, hypocrisy, and prejudice in a way that neither Jem nor Atticus fully acknowledges. Therefore, it is necessary to reexamine the novel in some depth, detailing the more expansive view of the southern rape complex that Scout provides as well as the pointed historical critique of Atticus in light of the defeat of the second Klan movement of the 1920s and the Scottsboro trial.

SCOUT'S "BROAD VIEW" OF HISTORY

Scout's role as narrator in the novel is noted for its dual nature: the "present" voice of Scout as a child between the ages of six through nine, when the events of the novel occur, and the mature voice of the adult Jean Louise reminiscing on the events of her childhood. The two voices are sometimes distinguished through the difference between the narrative past tense and the quoted dialogue in the present tense. But through the use of free indirect discourse, the child's voice is also at times incorporated into the narration. We might expect the more mature voice to provide the most progressive political viewpoint, but instead it is Scout, not the older narrator, Jean Louise, who raises the most pointed and potentially controversial questions and observations, as when she compares racial prejudice against African Americans in the United States to the persecution of the Jews in Nazi Germany.

There is, however, also a third "voice" that appears at the opening of the novel—Scout as an adolescent—who is "too old to settle" disputes with her brother through a fistfight and who has allowed "enough years to pass" so that she can look back on the events recounted in the novel. It is this third narrative voice—which has distance from the past but has not been fully incorporated into the adult world of southern womanhood—that is best able to take the "broad view of things."[17]

The opening of the novel sets up the difference in scope between Scout's and Jem's views of the origins of the events that led to Bob Ewell's attack on them. As the narrator explains: "I maintain that the Ewells started it all, but Jem, who was four years my senior, said it started long before that. He said it began the summer Dill came to us, when Dill first gave us the idea of making Boo Radley come out" (Lee 7). This difference between Jem's and Scout's initial concept of the origins of the "accident" is indicative of the two plotlines, which weave together (Boo's appearance and Tom Robinson's trial) and set up the identities of the two harmless "mockingbirds." Jem traces what he refers to euphemistically as the accident back to the appearance of Dill, whose fascination with Boo Radley helps to intertwine the children's lives and imaginations with that of Boo's. In turning the various accounts of Boo's life into a play that the three children perform over the summers, they inadvertently draw Boo into their world. Just as Boo is their only source of entertainment, they become his, and their porch becomes a stage where Boo watches the story of his life.[18] After playing the role of Boo in their amateur theatrics, Jem increasingly identifies with Boo and comes to the "startling revelation" that this identification was reciprocal, that Boo was "readin' [his] mind" when he sewed Jem's ripped pants and left them on the fence, knowing Jem would come looking for them (66). The accident for Jem is ultimately the story of Boo's coming to the rescue, not the story about the trial and racial discrimination. Jem's focus on Boo shows that he interprets the events leading up to Bob Ewell's assault from a personal perspective that does not go beyond the confines of the neighborhood: their "summertime boundaries (within calling distance of Calpurnia)" (7).

Adolescent Scout, on the other hand, situates the events squarely within the southern rape complex that the Ewells invoke to cover their own sins, when she maintains that the "Ewells [plural] started it," acknowledging both Mayella's and her father's role in the events. But looking further into the past, Scout places the story in the "broad view of things," beginning with Andrew Jackson's appropriation of the land on which her own ancestor, Simon Finch, built his plantation. Although her historical account of the origins of Finch's Landing is not as extensive as the origins of Jefferson, Mississippi, in Faulkner's protracted prologues in *Requiem for a Nun*—which detail the departure of the original Native American landowners—Scout, as narrator, succinctly embeds her story in a tale of colonial exploitation of native land and people and of the selectively self-serving use of religion to procure wealth through fraud and slavery. Her brief historical references are nodal points that encompass a variety of interrelated and controversial issues, but it takes a knowledgeable reader to understand their implications fully. Since the accident, adolescent Scout, unlike her eight-year-old counterpart, has learned enough to place the events in a larger context.

As adolescent Scout explains, Andrew Jackson was the original trigger of events: "If General Jackson hadn't run the Creeks up the creek, Simon Finch would never have paddled up the Alabama" (Lee 3). Jackson was able to run the Creeks "up the creek" and take their land only by betraying those Creeks who had fought with him in 1814 in the Battle of Horseshoe Bend against the British (and the "Red Stick" Upper Creeks, who sided with the British). When Jackson and his allies were victorious, he forced *all* Creeks to sign the Treaty of Fort Jackson, which ceded twenty-three million acres of land to the United States of America. This move opened up more land to slave-based plantations, like that of the fictional Finch's Landing, in what would be Alabama and Georgia, and ultimately led to the Indian Removal Act of 1830, which drove out Native Americans from the region on the infamous Trail of Tears. The act, which met with much resistance at the time, was supported by Jackson, who was by then president.

Scout implicates her own family in the history of exploitation through the story of her ancestor, Simon Finch, exposing how religious freedom was often an excuse for transatlantic and hemispheric expansionism and how religious hypocrisy and the rum trade facilitated the spread of slavery. Simon's purported reason for settling in Alabama was his need to practice Methodism, but as the narrator dryly insinuates, Simon's goals tend to be more monetary than religious. Simon was "irritated over the persecution of those who called themselves Methodist at the hands of their more liberal brethren, and as Simon called himself a Methodist, he worked his way across the Atlantic to Philadelphia, thence to Jamaica, thence to Mobile, and up the Saint Stephens."

The narrator is wonderfully adept at understated criticism, the ability to turn a fact into an insult or a critique. While her first reference to the persecution of those "who called themselves Methodist" is a neutral statement, in applying it to Simon, it suggests that he is a Methodist in name only, which is underscored in her characterization of his piety as "exceeded only by his stinginess" (Lee 8).

Scout's harshest criticisms are often subtle, but her irreverent views of her family history are often signaled by the use of slang, as we saw with *up the creek*. A case in point is the nature of Simon's wealth (his "pile" of money) and how he acquired it. Again, Simon uses his religion selectively, following only those strictures from John Wesley's "General Rules" that benefit him financially and ignoring those that directly go against his own practices. As the narrator explains by incorporating into the narrative Wesley's own language from the General Rules: "Mindful of John Wesley's strictures on the use of many words in buying and selling, Simon made a pile practicing medicine" (Lee 8). In the General Rules Wesley's first rule was to "do no harm, by avoiding evil of every kind," including the "use of many words in buying and selling" (Nausner 43–60).[19] It is easy to read over this statement or to dismiss it as a non sequitur: what does Wesley's directive against haggling and hawking of wares have to do with Simon's ability to acquire wealth? Furthermore, it is difficult to imagine how a backwoods doctor would make a pile of money, though significantly, Simon is not described as a doctor but as an itinerate "fur-trapping apothecary" (Lee 8). *Practicing medicine* thus appears to be a euphemism for selling patent medicines, which at this time were actually not patented. Although they promised to cure a variety of illnesses, their popularity was based in large part on the fact that often their main ingredient was alcohol, even though selling "spirituous liquors, or drinking them" was also prohibited in the General Rules.[20] When we combine this information with Simon's sojourn in Jamaica, an important stop for both the selling of rum and slaves, we can deduce Simon's "pile of money" came from keeping quiet about the alcoholic content of his medicine in order to sell it to "good" Christian people.

The narrator further undermines Simon's piety by again incorporating Wesley's own words in stating that Simon's pursuit of money had left him "unhappy lest he be tempted into doing what he knew was not for the glory of God, as the putting on of gold and costly apparel. So Simon, having forgotten his teacher's dictum on the possession of human chattels, bought three slaves and with their aid established a homestead on the banks of the Alabama River"

(Lee 8). Simon happily uses religion to justify his stinginess by avoiding buying expensive clothes and jewelry (presumably for his wife and daughters) while completely ignoring Wesley's passionate plea against slavery in his 1774 "Thoughts upon Slavery" and his active support of abolition, one of the most important and controversial aspects of Methodism at the time.

Scout thus actually provides the reader not just with the origins of the Finches but with the racist political origins of the nation and the South that set the stage for the southern rape complex and Tom Robinson's trial. This self-deprecating history also sets the stage for the equally understated critique of middle-class hypocrisy and elitism, which centers on the character of Aunt Alexandra. The narrator refutes Aunt Alexandra's later assertions of the Finches' superior family background before we even meet the character and also shows the "origins" of the religious hypocrisy characteristic of Aunt Alexandra's Women's African Missionary group, whose members bemoan the poverty of the Mruna tribe in Africa even as they condone the mistreatment of African Americans in their own community (Lee 264).[21] At the group's meeting the women accept the politics of the southern rape complex as they condemn Helen Robinson—not Mayella or Mr. Ewell—as well as Atticus (for taking Tom Robinson's case). Given the silent complacency or even overt obstructionism of many white churches (including Amasa Lee's belief that the Methodist Church should not be involved in civil rights politics), the novel's sendup of the cattiness and hypocrisy of the missionary group is an implicit critique of the stand on civil rights adopted by many white southern churches.

THE JURY IS OUT

While Aunt Alexandra is the more obvious source of narrow-mindedness, Atticus's own prejudices, while more muted, have even more dire consequences for his family and his client. The novel connects Atticus's inability to read Ewell to other events at the local and national level that more seriously undermine Atticus's judgment not only of other people but of the law. In chapter 23 Atticus's incorrect assessment of Bob Ewell is then followed by his historically "incorrect" analysis of the jury system. Atticus's inability to understand Ewell's danger is proved by the subsequent events in the novel, while his inability to defend and protect his client is proved by the extratextual events of the Scottsboro trial. In the novel, after Ewell has spit in Atticus's face and "told him he'd get him if it took the rest of his life" (Lee 247), Atticus assures the worried children, "We don't have anything to fear from Bob Ewell, he got it all out of his system that morning." Atticus begins his explanation to Jem with his characteristic advice, "See if you can stand in Bob Ewell's shoes a minute," and explains that Ewell has to have some kind of "comeback" and that he would "rather it be [against] me than that houseful of children out there" (249). So, while Atticus understands that Ewell would hurt children, his own sense of middle-class safety keeps him from believing that Ewell could harm *his* children.

Even though Atticus's attempts at empathetic understanding fail with Ewell, it appears that the rest of the town has no problem understanding his intentions and that they take his threats seriously. As Aunt Alexandra correctly surmises, "That man seems to have a permanent running grudge against everybody connected with the case." When someone (assumed to be Ewell) tries to break into Judge Taylor's home, the Judge goes back to reading in his study but with a shotgun on his lap. More important, when Ewell harasses Mrs. Robinson on her way to work, following her and softly "crooning foul words," her employer, Mr. Deeds, takes it very seriously and threatens to have Ewell put in jail for violating the "Ladies Law" (Lee 286), which states that "any person who, in the presence or hearing of any girl or woman, uses abusive, insulting, or obscene language must, on conviction, be fined not more than two hundred dollars, and may also be imprisoned in the county jail, or sentenced to hard labor for the county for not more than six months" (*Code of Alabama*). This incident is in some ways one of the most radical in the novel in that it legally designates Mrs. Robinson a "lady" and affords her the protection of the law against a white man who harasses her.[22]

After erroneously assuring the children that Ewell is harmless, Atticus follows this false assertion of safety with another: "that nothing would happen to Tom Robinson until the higher court reviewed his case, and that Tom had a good chance of going free, or at least of having a new trial" (Lee 250). These two pledges of safety are both proved wrong in the course of the novel, but the conversation that follows casts doubt on the success of Atticus's appeal, had Tom lived. Upon learning that Tom will "go to the chair" if he loses his appeal because rape is a capital offense in Alabama, Jem searches for a way to make the process more just. He poses three correctives to the current system, which prompts a discussion about rape laws, circumstantial evidence, and the jury system. Atticus refutes all three of Jem's suggestions, but Atticus's reasons for doing so reveal his own legal blind spots because they are not supported by history or by the appeals in the Scottsboro cases that were successfully argued before the Supreme Court during the time frame of the novel.

Jem's first suggestion that rape should not be a capital offense—so that it would not automatically call for the death penalty—has proven historically valid, and many states have changed the penalty not only because of its automatic use in interracial crimes but because of the difficulty of getting a conviction in intraracial cases when the death penalty is in play. Atticus rejects Jem's position out of hand and argues instead that rape cases should require one or two witnesses and not circumstantial evidence. As we saw in *Cape Fear,* and as a matter of simple common sense, a dominant element of most rapes is that they are carried out in seclusion, precisely to prevent witnesses. Atticus's requirement of eyewitnesses would make it almost impossible to win a rape case, but furthermore, it would not even have helped in Tom's case because Mr. Ewell testified that he saw that Tom was "ruttin' on my Mayella!" (Lee 196).

Jem's next suggestion is to do away with juries, but Atticus provides his own more "reasonable" solution: to change the law so that only judges are able to determine sentencing in a capital case.[23] Yet the events of the Scottsboro trial again prove Atticus wrong. In the first place judges already have the power to set aside jury verdicts because of insufficient evidence, which is what Judge James E. Horton did in the trial of Haywood Patterson, one of the Scottsboro defendants. Horton's reasoning is particularly relevant to Tom's case, and his statement was quoted in the 23 June 1933 issue of the *Mobile Register,* one of the newspapers that Atticus reportedly reads on a daily basis ("Retrial").[24] Horton focused on the evidence itself, claiming that "no defendant should be convicted in a prosecution for assault when the testimony of the prosecutrix bears evidence of unreliability" because of the lack of corroborating evidence in the face of conflicting testimony of the examining doctors.

Therefore, Judge Taylor, like Judge Horton, could have set aside the verdict in Tom's case without changing the law, but he chose not to. Atticus's assumption that judges would somehow be more impartial than juries and not subject to the same pressures or prejudices also is not supported by the historical events taking place in the early 1930s.[25] While Horton may have been immune to public pressure in making his judgment, he was not immune to politics and the backlash of the voters. Under pressure Chief Justice Anderson removed Horton from the case, and in the May 1934 primary Horton, who had run unopposed in 1928, lost the election (Carter 273).[26]

Finally, in this examination of the legal system, Jem questions the makeup of the jury and why "people like us and Miss Maudie" are not on juries, to which Atticus explains that women are not allowed to serve on juries. Although Scout is at first indignant, she and Jem both laugh at Atticus's quip that "I doubt if we'd ever get a complete case tried—the ladies'd be interrupting to ask questions" (Lee 252). In what sounds like the voice of the older Jean Louise, she acquiesces, "Perhaps our forefathers were wise" (253). Dean Shackelford argues that Atticus is being ironic, not sexist, when he says that women cannot serve on juries in order "to protect our frail ladies from sordid cases like Tom's" (111). While Atticus does not actually seem to believe that women are "frail," in making a joke of the idea, he nonetheless treats women's exclusion as something that need not be changed or even taken seriously. Although Aunt Alexandra is the most obvious enforcer of restrictions based on ladylike behavior, Atticus's dismissal of Miss Maudie's ability to serve on a jury, despite the fact that she is one of most consistently practical and level-headed characters, has a more pernicious ramification for Scout precisely because, although she is skeptical of her aunt, she respects her father's opinion. The mature narrative voice that agrees with the wisdom of her forefathers is a far cry from the voice of the adolescent Scout, who clearly saw her forefather as a hypocritical scoundrel concerning matters of race and gender: Simon Finch's willingness to ignore his own stated Methodist religious convictions against owning slaves in order to make money and his distrust (or worse) of his own daughters, whose bedrooms were situated so that the only way in or out was through their father's bedroom.[27]

Atticus's disputation on the jury system is especially striking compared to the actual legal debates surrounding the Scottsboro trial. At the very time that the character of Atticus myopically assumes that nothing can be done to protect black men from the prejudice of all-white juries, the landmark Supreme Court case *Patterson v. Alabama* went a step further than Judge Horton and ruled in favor of the Scottsboro defendant on the basis of the systematic exclusion of jury members based on their race. The novel therefore shows how deeply Jim Crow logic affects all the Finches'—even Jem's and Scout's—ability to imagine a legal solution to the southern rape complex and the automatic conviction of a black man charged with raping a white woman. Although much is made of Calpurnia's and her son Zebo's ability to read, Jem never thinks to ask why they are not selected for jury duty. Atticus maintains that "the one place a man ought to get a square deal is in a courtroom," no matter his color, but his anger shifts to "a low-grade white man who'll take advantage of a Negro's ignorance" (Lee 252). This subtle shift in Atticus's argument is especially problematic because it assumes that only "low-grade" whites do this but also that blacks are ignorant, an assumption that seems to support implicitly their being barred from jury duty. Just as the crime of rape obviously requires secrecy, the southern rape complex equally obviously requires white supremacy in the case of vigilante justice as well as in the cases that actually come to trial. An all-white jury is the key to conviction, regardless of the evidence, and the fact that this "problem" does not seem to occur to Atticus calls into question his ability to successfully appeal Tom's case.

In the discussion of the jury system Atticus assumes the role for which he is best known: a patient father explaining the need for justice. But nothing he advocates would actually bring about justice for his client. Rather than being uncharacteristic, this discussion demonstrates Atticus's conservative views, which, though they seem to clash with his image as a champion of justice, actually confirm what Atticus himself says. After the trial, when a classmate asks Scout if her father is a Radical, Atticus is amused and answers, "I'm about as Radical as Cotton Tom Heflin" (Lee 287). *Radical* in this context clearly refers to Atticus's willingness to defend a black man, which could be interpreted as a willingness to allow African Americans full rights as citizens or, as in the Scottsboro case, suggests an affiliation with the Communist Party. Although Atticus is obviously using Heflin as an extreme example, the comparison is especially problematic because of Heflin's support of the Klan, his efforts to disenfranchise African Americans in Alabama, and his open endorsement of lynching. Heflin perfectly sums up the southern rape complex: "Whenever a negro crosses this dead line between the white and negro races and lays his black hand on a white woman he deserves to die" (qtd. in Sundquist, "Blues" 78).[28] Heflin was also instrumental in having Judge Horton removed from the Scottsboro trial.[29] Again, calling up the language of the southern rape complex, Heflin in the pages of the *Montgomery Advertiser* (24 June 1933) blamed Horton's decision for "putting wicked thoughts in the minds of lawless Negro men and greatly increasing the danger to the white women of Alabama" (qtd. in Carter 272).

Atticus's reference to a Klan member who was also a U.S. senator from Alabama seems to fly in the face of his earlier assurance to Jem that the Klan has not existed since "way back about nineteen-twenty," that "it was a political organization more than anything," and that the "Ku Klux's gone" and will "never come back" (Lee 167). As noted earlier, Sundquist points to this statement as an instance in which Atticus directly lies to the children, but instead, it points to the complicated history of the Klan in Alabama in the 1920s. Being for or against the Klan in the 1920s and 1930s in Alabama was not the same as in the 1960s, during the third wave of Klan. The 1920s Klan members, and especial Heflin, were strongly linked to temperance, anti-immigration, and anti-Catholicism, unlike the 1950s and 1960s Klan, which was more directly a reaction to integration and the civil rights movement. But there was even a difference between the 1915–25 and 1926–29 Klan in Alabama (Feldman 121–26).

Through the early 1920s the Klan enjoyed wide support across Alabama, among the planter elite and industrialists (known as the Black Belt/Big Mule alliance) as well as among small farmers and the lower classes; at this time Black Belt planters favorably compared the Reconstruction Klan with the new Klan. While it is true that membership in the Klan plummeted by the time of the setting of the novel, as late as 1926, Klan members held some of the most important political offices in the state, and "Cotton" Tom Heflin was the most outspoken and most notorious Klan-affiliated politician. So, while Atticus is correct that the Klan was a political organization, it was still a terrorist group. But while it was fiercely against immigrant, blacks, and Catholics, it supported some progressive issues concerning public education, public health, highway construction, pro-labor legislation, and help for small farmers. In fact Alabama elites did not began a campaign against the Klan until the populist section of the Klan began to wield more political power and to push agricultural and labor agendas, such as abolishing the convict-lease program as a source of cheap labor, which went against Black Belt/Big Mule interests.

The anti-Klan proponents were as opposed to African American citizenship as were the Klan members themselves, but business interests in Alabama feared that the Klan's violence and Heflin's highly public prejudices, especially against Catholics, would inhibit new businesses from moving to the state. After 1926 Alabama experienced a strong anti-Klan campaign fueled by the editorials of Grover Cleveland Hall, who won a Pulitzer Prize for his work. According to Glenn Feldman, this was a politically calculated attack on the violence of the Klan as a way to derail its other political projects and its power in the state (121–26). The Big Mule/Black Belt alliance avoided attacking the Klan's populist agenda, which drew support from the common, voter and focused instead on its violence. Victor Hanson, who owned three Alabama papers, "advised his editors [including Hall] to attack the Klan indirectly by casting aspersions on the society's less defensible aspects: its violence, its mask, its secrecy, and the beating of women," hoping "to use the Klan's more unsavory aspects to embarrass the KKK politically" (Feldman 122).

Within the novel Atticus alludes to the contradictory relationship between anti-Klan sentiment and a belief in white supremacy. As Atticus points out, Maycomb's own editor, Underwood, who castigates his fellow citizens for killing Tom Robinson, an innocent cripple, also "despises Negroes, won't have one near him" (Lee 178). Underwood's editorial is indirectly linked to Grover Hall's anti-Klan editorials in the *Montgomery Advertiser;* the townspeople even seem to allude to Hall when they wonder if Underwood "was trying to write an editorial poetical enough to be reprinted in *The Montgomery Advertiser*" (275). Underwood's characterization of Robinson as a cripple invokes the case that Hall championed to bring down the Klan. Although Klan violence had been tolerated for years, the 1927 flogging of Jeff Calloway, a white mentally impaired orphan, brought about the trial of seven Klansman and swayed public opinion (Feldman 107). In his editorials Hall blamed Alabama's most prominent Klan-affiliated leaders—Governor Bibb Graves, U.S. senator Hugo Black, U.S. senator Tom Heflin, and Attorney General Charlie McCall—for the violence of its members, and other Alabama newspapers followed suit (108–09). Hall castigated Heflin as "a bully by nature, a mountebank by instinct, a Senator by choice . . . Thus this preposterous blob excites our pity if not our respect, and we leave him to his conscience in order that he may be entirely alone and meditate over the life of a charlatan whose personal interest and personal vanity are always of paramount concern to him" (qtd. in Greenhaw 51). Hall also invoked the fear of federal government interference, arguing: "Alabama should be allowed a free hand in working out this problem. It is an Alabama problem . . . the [Klan] evil should be . . . destroyed by the people on whom the responsibility principally rests . . . What really counts is the demonstration by the *State* of its power" (Feldman 135–36 [*Montgomery Advertiser* 10 Aug. 1927]). When three of the Klan defendants turned state's evidence, the state's case against the Klan succeeded, and the verdict signaled the end of the Klan in Alabama (Feldman 113–15).

The "end of the Klan," however, did not indicate greater justice for African Americans. The contradictory relationship of the anti-Klan movement of the 1920s and that of the 1960s is evident in the fact that though Hall denounced Klan violence in his 1927 editorials in the *Montgomery Advertiser,* in 1935 he also denounced the Supreme Court's ruling in the Scottsboro trial maintaining that the systematic exclusion of African Americans in Alabama juries was unconstitutional (Carter 327).[30] Thus, Hall's acceptance of all-white juries seems to mirror that of Atticus. While publicly the Klan was over, Klan-affiliated politicians still had influence in the state. McCall redeemed himself by vigorously prosecuting the Klan members in the Calloway case, and Graves, a staunch New Deal supporter, weathered the storm and in 1934 was the first two-term governor of Alabama. Heflin, however, remained unrepentant and continued to serve as a spokesman for Klan ideology by making racist and anti-Catholic speeches.[31] Even Heflin continued to exert power over state politics, as in his call for the removal of Judge Horton in the Scottsboro trial. Atticus may bear no resemblance to Cotton Tom Heflin, but Atticus's willingness to defend Tom Robinson, even as he upholds Jim Crow restrictions on the rights of African Americans to serve on juries, is totally compatible with anti-Klan politics. Although Atticus has given up his role as a planter to become a lawyer, his political point of view is still in line with this influential element of the elite planter class.

COTTON VERSUS PORK

Given the Depression-era plummet in cotton prices, Atticus's decision to go into law rather than cotton proved wise. Federal and state governments promoted strategies to combat falling cotton prices and to address soil erosion by restricting the planting of cotton and diversifying agricultural production. In Alabama diversification meant an increase in livestock production, and in Monroeville, the basis for the fictionalized Maycomb, this meant a push for greater hog production. While the surplus of hogs in the Corn Belt was subject to the federally ordered and devastating mass slaughter to try to raise pork prices, in Alabama many farmers were not raising enough pork even for personal consumption. As Walter Cunningham indicates over lunch at the Finches' home, he only eats meat when they can shoot squirrels and opossums, even though the Cunninghams farm their own land (despite their legal wrangle over property rights). In June 1937 the Alabama Extension Services (AES), "believing that livestock is essential to soil fertility, more efficient utilization of labor, and to sounder farm finances," began an education program for farmers to teach them how better to raise livestock ("Program Launched").[32] The AES spokesman was careful not to create a perceived slight to cotton growers, stating that "in promoting our livestock programs, we shall not in any sense discredit or depreciate cotton," but he also made it clear that the days of King Cotton were over: "That which we have had and now have, in the main, is inefficient in the use of labor, destructive in the use of soil, and unsound in financial practices (*Monroe Journal* 17 June 1937, 2).

On the night of her attack Scout is literally associated with the push for hog production as she wears a ham costume for the Halloween pageant celebrating Maycomb's agricultural products. Although the novel explains that the agricultural pageant is performed as an attempt to minimize Halloween vandalism (the type of youthful pranks that condemned Boo to a life of "house arrest"), its content is not arbitrarily chosen. The pageant that Scout participates in to celebrate Maycomb County agriculture is entitled (in the novel) "Ad Astra per Aspera"—from the mud to the stars, a message of economic improvement through agricultural production. Significantly, in the novel the only costumes mentioned in the Maycomb agricultural pageant are those associated with diversification—cows, butter beans, and peanuts—but there is no mention of cotton (Lee 289).[33] Cotton, in fact, is rarely mentioned in the novel, and when it is, it is typically in a negative light. Atticus and his brother both left Finch's Landing, and though Aunt Alexandra and her husband, Jimmy, remained on the plantation, Uncle Jimmy "spent most of his time lying in a hammock by the river wondering if the trot-lines were full" (5). Mr. Radley and his son both "buy cotton," which as Jem explains, is a "polite term for doing nothing" (10), and it was a cotton gin—the invention that made cotton production more profitable for planters, such as Simon Finch, and therefore paved the way for the overproduction of cotton as a cash crop and for the expansion of the slave trade (Walter Johnson 217–18)—that literally and symbolically maimed Tom when he was a boy, leaving his left arm useless. Despite his injury, Tom's main source of income still comes from picking cotton.

Scout's costume is particularly significant in relation to Monroeville, Alabama, which hosted Monroe County's annual Regional Hog Show and Festival. The 1939 Monroe County Hog Festival presents a similar hope for prosperity through diversification. In addition to a hog queen and the crowning of an actual hog, the festival features a parade in which the queen's float reads: "Our Hogs Are Pulling Us Out of a Rut," another message of hope through diversification.[34] Economic recovery through the promotion (educational program and research) of agricultural diversification on a voluntary basis, unlike the mandatory restrictions, which were ultimately declared unconstitutional, was a form of government assistance that even proud but poor farmers such as the Cunninghams—who "never took anything off of anybody," as Scout explains—could accept (Lee 26). Atticus's explanation in the novel of the Cunninghams' reluctance to accept assistance, that they don't want to "owe" anyone their vote, is a pointed critique of New Deal policies, in which assistance is allegedly tied directly to "buying" votes, a charge also made in *The Birth of a Nation* against the Freedman's Bureau. Both the Freedman's Bureau and the New Deal were federal programs that, however much they might benefit the citizens of the South, were feared as a sign of federal encroachment on states' rights.

If Scout's ham costume represents the potential for future prosperity, Bob Ewell, as her black-coded attacker, represents what threatens this hope, especially from the perspective of those who endorse segregation. Ewell embodies those aspects of the New Deal that opponents negatively associated with the ills of socialism and a free handout, which were often associated with African Americans. In the novel Ewell is characterized as the only man to be fired from a Works Progress Administration (WPA) job for laziness. This direct condemnation of Ewell also indirectly satirizes the WPA program by implicitly confirming the charge of laziness regarding its workers, which was so prevalent that the phrase *leaning on the shovel* became emblematic of WPA workers. Ewell, therefore, distinguishes himself as the laziest of lazy workers. He is also on welfare, a program more disparaged than the WPA, and it is while Ewell is picking up his welfare check that he makes threats against Atticus, ostensibly not for defending Tom Robinson but for allegedly getting Ewell fired from his WPA job.

Eric Sundquist maintains that Scout is a bystander, not a victim in the novel, and while this is true of her role at Tom Robinson's trial, Scout, like Mayella (and Helen Robinson in the novel), is a victim of Bob Ewell's vengeance. Although a "practical" reason is given in both film and novel for Scout's state of undress after Ewell's attack—in changing into her costume for the Halloween pageant, she loses her dress and shoes,[35] forcing her to walk barefoot and to wear the costume home—the image of Scout running home in only her slip (and the discovery of her dress at the scene of the attack in the novel) provides overtones of a sexual assault. If Flora's brother arrives too late to rescue her, Jem's presence does not guarantee safety from assault. Although Jem tries to fight off Ewell, he is no match for a grown man. Instead, what is needed is someone who is ever vigilant, a kinder, gentler presence that invokes both the Confederacy and the Klan. Boo literally embodies the Latin root of *vigilantism* as someone who keeps vigil overnight. It is only in the nighttime that he emerges to protect the children from his father (when he shoots at a "prowler") as well as their own (Jem does not want to be whipped) and from Ewell's own nighttime attack. Significantly, it is only after being a victim of violent crime that Scout condones Boo's vigilantism.

Scout's famous speech in which she uses the mockingbird analogy to justify falsifying Ewell's death, rather than being the zenith of her vision of justice—as this scene is typically understood—is her nadir, and as such it parallels her limited vision during the attack, as highlighted in the film sequence. Following the attack, Sheriff Tate discovers the body of Bob Ewell lying under the tree with a knife in his ribs; the sheriff subsequently decides to say that Bob Ewell fell on his own knife so as to spare Boo from being in the limelight with "his shy ways" and from being brought cakes by all the ladies of Maycomb. In accordance with the sheriff's decision, Scout discards the very legal and moral values that Atticus upholds, which have been lauded by critics and fans.

One of Atticus's most important qualities is that he is the same on the street as he is at home. Atticus takes the Robinson case out of a sense of duty to the law and due process because, as he tells his children, he could not expect them to listen to him if he did not; in other words, he would lose his authority as both a father and a lawyer, but Scout is asking him to treat the law differently when it hits closer to home. Atticus is persuaded to accede to Scout's earlier definition of *compromise:* "bending the law." What makes this decision even more problematic is that the reasons for such a tremendous shift in values are flimsy at best. Boo's actions would obviously be deemed justifiable homicide, and it is unlikely that his case would go to trial. Furthermore, while all the ladies might want to bring Boo cakes and put him in the "limelight," there is nothing in the history of the Radleys (who have perfected the art of living in seclusion) to suggest that they would allow anyone past the front porch. Nor is it clear that Boo wishes to remain a recluse; this state was after all imposed upon him, and he actually welcomes and encourages the children's interest in him. In both the film and novel Boo's form of vigilantism is valorized, but Boo himself, like the violence of the Klan, must be kept out of sight and therefore out of mind.

Boo's treatment under the law is not, however, the only thing at stake in this decision; there is also the question of Ewell's death. Although Scout's willingness to treat Ewell's death as an accident goes against her father's belief in enforcing the law equally, her willingness to condone Ewell's death outside the confines of the law is in fact in keeping with the state of exception Atticus cites concerning the Ewells. While Atticus is willing to extend the right to competent counsel—though not full citizenship—to Tom Robinson, a "humble, respectable Negro," he considers the Ewells to be bare life. Ewell can be killed with impunity because the Ewells are not subject to the same laws as everyone else, which includes respectable African Americans but presumably not non-respectable blacks or whites.

In the porch scene in which Atticus explains compromise to Scout, he also explains that Mr. Ewell is allowed to poach in order to feed his family. While Atticus bases this exception on the need to feed the Ewell children, he also accepts the idea that the Ewell children do not have to follow truancy laws. When Burris Ewell, who is as impervious to education as to soap and water, leaves school after only one day, Atticus maintains that no efforts should be made to enforce the Ewell children's attendance at school. The Ewells form an "exclusive society," and people "judiciously allowed them certain privileges by the simple method of becoming blind to some of the Ewells' activities," such as not attending school (Lee 34–35). The assertion that some people cannot be educated (or cleaned) is also a commentary on the efficacy of *Brown v. Board of Education,* suggesting that equal access to education is wasted on those who are inherently inferior. Even though Atticus's closing argument relegates a belief in the southern rape complex to people with the "caliber of mind" of the Ewells and suggests that Atticus's more sophisticated or knowledgeable neighbors do not believe such a "lie," he does not believe that the Ewells should be educated to improve the "caliber" of their minds. What Atticus explains, most tellingly in the novel, is that some people do not deserve an education, to vote, to serve on juries, or to be afforded due process.

The problem is not whether or not Atticus is a hero (he does act heroically in his attempt to stand up to the mob with only a book) but that he neither represents what progressive politics looked like in the past, nor does he serve as a model for progressive politics in the present or future. In many ways Atticus is a corrective to the abrasive style of Samuel Leibowitz and his alienation of the community through his condemnation of the jury as "lantern-jawed morons." Atticus, the antithesis of his northern counterpart, is a study in how to try a controversial case without insulting your neighbors or alienating the community. Although many of his neighbors condemn what he is doing, he nonetheless is elected unopposed to the state legislature even after the trial, although it might not have been the case had he won an appeal for Robinson. In the first Scottsboro trial, though the local lawyers lost the case so badly that they were declared incompetent counsel, the community was incensed that they nonetheless attempted to appeal the verdict. If Atticus is not a champion of racial equality, he is a model of the late 1920s anti-Klan movement: how to be nominally progressive in the South while maintaining segregation, preserving the power of the educated elite (who are best able to decide who deserves civil rights and who does not), keeping your friends, and getting reelected.

THE GRAY GHOST: READING AND SEEING TOM AND BOO

If the second Klan is labeled as lower-class ruffians—on par with Bob Ewell—Boo, like the anti-Klan movement of the 1920s, defeats those violent elements of the lower classes. By getting rid of Ewell, a welfare check–cashing, lazy WPA worker, Boo eliminates those aspects of the New Deal politics that threatened the status quo in Alabama. But Boo is not presented as part of the planter elite and industrialists who made up the anti-Klan movement; instead, his "ghostly" presence and his ability to arrive in the nick of time to save a young southern girl summon up a nostalgic image of the Reconstruction Klan. In the final pages of the novel Scout learns how to "read" Boo Radley, as a kinder, gentler version of the Klan, through an analogy with the "Gray Ghost" of a children's story. Listening to her father read Jem's copy of the book, Scout questions why he chose *The Gray Ghost,* and although Atticus sees no significance in the choice, Scout does. She explains that "Stoner's Boy (called the Gray Ghost because he wears a grey handkerchief to hide his identity) was falsely accused, but they could not catch him because they didn't know what he looked like (Lee 322): "When they finally saw him, why he hadn't done any of those things . . . Atticus, he was real nice." Atticus rejoins, "Most people are when you finally see them" (323). The implied analogy is that now that Scout has "seen" Boo, she knows that he is "real nice" and not the monster the children thought he was.

Associating Boo with the Gray Ghost renders him harmless, yet Boo has actually killed a man, however justified he may have been. But the correlation between Boo and the Gray Ghost goes beyond a children's book; the Gray

Ghost is also the nickname of the Confederate general John S. Mosby, famous for his nighttime raids against unsuspecting northern troops. The legend of the Gray Ghost would be familiar to southern children living in a time when there were still people who had lived through the Civil War. The legend was also still part of popular culture for the novel's contemporary readers, as the story of the Gray Ghost was turned into a syndicated television series in 1958–59. The image of the Gray Ghost is also relevant to the Klan, which saw itself as the ghost of Confederate soldiers rising up to put down African American citizenship. And it is the image of a ghost (white children putting a sheet over their heads to scare the black children) that inspires Ben Cameron in *The Birth of a Nation* to don white sheets and form the Klan.

Sundquist interprets Boo as a "displaced phantom of racial fear," which is "ultimately unmasked as the gentle, domesticated 'gray ghost' of harmonious integration," suggesting that the "racial hysteria" of the Klan "can be likewise unmasked, humiliated, and brought to justice once the South disposes of its childish fears." Rather than unmasking the Klan, however, Boo, as a nostalgic reminder of the Reconstruction Klan (in opposition to the second Klan of the 1920s), stays safely behind closed doors until he is needed. Furthermore, although Sundquist maintains that Boo is associated with "black superstition," which Sundquist uses as evidence for Boo's role as a "phantom of racial fear" ("Blues" 81), black superstition is actually what distances Boo from blackness and, instead, associates him further with the ghostly "power" of the Klan as depicted in *The Birth of a Nation*. As the narrator explains, "A Negro would not pass the Radley Place at night, he would cut across to the sidewalk opposite and whistle as he walked" (Lee 9), suggesting that Boo, like the white-hooded Klan, invokes fear in the heart of African Americans, forcing them to keep their distance. Yet given that Mr. Radley, later in the novel, freely admits to shooting at the trespasser whom he assumes is a "nigger," African Americans might have a more pragmatic, rather than merely superstitious, reason to fear crossing in front of the Radley home, just as African Americans had very real, not superstitious, reasons for fearing the Klan (61).

POINT OF VIEW: THROUGH BOO'S EYES

Instead of the "broad view of things" that Scout provides in the novel, the film takes us into a child's point of view with the opening credits, in which the camera gives us an overhead view of Scout opening her treasure box (in it are the gifts Boo gave the children) and then drawing a mockingbird as she hums to herself. As the theme music begins, an extreme close-up tracking shot of Scout's everyday treasures (including a marble, a whistle, and a crayon) takes us further into a child's world. The film proper begins with a camera consciousness that moves seamlessly from a moving shot looking up at the trees that then tilts down to show the town, as the narrative voice of the adult Jean Louise introduces Maycomb as a "tired old town." The camera picks up Walter Cunningham in his one-horse buggy and then dissolves into a long shot of Walter in front of the Finches' home, as Scout enters the shot by swinging in on a rope from off-screen. This opening sets up one of the first porch scenes in which we learn from Atticus about the Cunninghams' pride and that the crash hit the farmers hardest. As Rachel Watson argues, the film repeatedly uses the space of the porch as the "empathic register," the liminal space between public and private spaces that allows for sympathetic moral education through "the brokering of a compromise" and creates intimacy while maintaining distance and boundaries between whites and blacks (421). The next few scenes are all exterior shots that highlight the porch as the buffer between inside and outside, public and private: the introduction of Jem and his disappointment that his father is too old to play football for the Methodists; Dill (Charles Baker Harris), the new playmate staying next door with his Aunt Stephanie; the mysterious history of Boo Radley and the Radley place; and finally, another porch lesson from Atticus about how to get along with the crotchety Mrs. DuBose, who reportedly has a Confederate gun on her lap under her shawl.

The numerous shots of the porch manipulate off-screen space, suggesting but not revealing the interior, private space of the home. The Finch home is the only one the camera actually enters, but in the first interior shot the camera enters the house through a window and not the front door, creating a significant exception to the objective camera perspective of the porch scenes. This initial interior shot occurs after the porch encounter with Mrs. DuBose. As the children enter the Finch house with Atticus, the scene dissolves to a nighttime exterior shot in which Scout's window is framed in darkness. As the camera pulls in, we see—through the lace curtains—Scout in her bed reading a book out loud to Atticus (fig. 6.1). There is a straight cut from the exterior shot to an interior medium shot of Scout and Atticus, just as Scout stops reading and asks her father, "Does Boo Radley ever really look in my window at

FIG. 6.1. Looking into Scout's room through the lace curtains. *To Kill a Mockingbird* (1962).

night?" Thus, Scout draws attention to the off-screen space in the previous shot as she speculates on Boo's nocturnal peeping.

As Deleuze elucidates in *Cinema 1*, there are three types of movement in a film: the movement of the characters within the shot, the movement of the camera, and the movement between the shots created through editing—the movement of the cuts. Each framed shot creates its own closed system, which nonetheless communicates with other framed shots. In the cut from an external shot of the house shrouded in darkness to the bright interior shot of Scout's bedroom, the shot shifts in perspective from an objective (like the porch shots) to a subjective point of view of the ghostly, speculative presence of Boo Radley peeping in the window. But this connection is only made clear after we enter the room and hear Scout's question to her father. In an objective shot the viewer's gaze is aligned with a neutral perspective; the gaze is therefore disembodied, while the subjective point of view shots indicate the presence (or the possibility) of a reciprocal gaze. The camera consciousness therefore shifts into an embodied point of view shot, brought about not only by framing or camera movement but also through dialogue. This "shift" in point of view from objective to subjective implicates not only Boo but also the viewers themselves, as they are "caught" assuming Boo's voyeuristic gaze, looking in the window and eavesdropping on an intimate scene between father and daughter.

The "relative aspect" of the out-of-field refers to what is not seen but could be seen if the frame expands or the camera moves, but the "absolute aspect" refers to a "more disturbing presence" that is "neither seen nor understood, but is nevertheless perfectly present" and suggests a more "radical Elsewhere, outside homogenous space and time" (Deleuze, *Cinema 1* 16). Boo's "presence" in this shot hovers between the two aspects of the out-of-field; we never learn if he occupies the relative space that could be seen if only the camera moved to capture it, and because of that, he remains a more disturbing presence (which facilitates his association with the past).

On one level, and in keeping with the gothic overtones of the Radley legend, the camera work mimics that of the horror genre, in which the audience often views the unsuspecting victim through the eyes of the monster before learning who the monster really is. The monster's presence is typically signaled through the use of heavy breathing or ominous music, but in the exterior shot outside Scout's window, we hear only the night sounds of crickets, and when we cross inside the room, we hear only the dialogue between Scout and Atticus. Thus, the "monster" point of view, with its threatening and voyeuristic quality, is invoked and at the same time neutralized into a touching family scene. The audience is invited to reframe the shot once again and to shift back into an objective shot as we unobtrusively witness Scout and her father. The camera therefore literally and figuratively draws us in, allowing us to assume a neutral gaze even as we share the point of view of the peeping Boo.

This first interior scene establishes the warm relationship between Scout and Atticus, played with brilliant simplicity and charm by Mary Badham and Gregory Peck.[36] But this scene also introduces one of the many times in the film (and even more so in the novel) that Atticus's well-meaning sympathetic understanding is wrong and, like his other errors in sympathy, has deadly consequences in the future. Even as Boo appears to "see" Atticus and Scout, Atticus does not "see" Boo. Atticus admonishes Scout to "leave those poor people alone" and to "stop tormenting them." His intervention here is reasonable—of course, children should be taught not to "torment" their neighbors—but what Atticus cannot sympathetically imagine is that someone shut away from society since he was a teenager, with nothing to do and no one to talk to, might actually welcome the children's interest in him. While this event might seem trivial, it has profound ramifications for the children's safety.

We never know whether or not Boo was peeping in the window, but we do learn that he watches the children and tries to make contact with them indirectly through the gifts he leaves for them in the hollow of the tree. Their bond with Boo (and his nighttime vigil) is what allows him to save the children from Ewell, a father who is even meaner than Boo's own father (even though Jem describes Mr. Radley as the "meanest old man ever to draw breath"). The audience members therefore are visually primed to be sympathetic toward Boo and accept him as the children's savior because they (not Atticus) have perceptually "stood in his shoes" and looked from his point of view at this loving scene between father and daughter.

READING EWELL

On its own Atticus's inability to identify with Boo may seem a minor point, but it is part of a pattern in which Atticus misreads a person (Boo, Ewell) or situations (the possibility of a lynch mob, the efficacy of his closing speech to the jury) with dire ramifications for himself, his children, and his client.[37] While the "adult" voice of Jean Louise in the film and in the novel maintains that "there just didn't seem to be anything or anyone Atticus couldn't understand," the events of the novel especially, but also the film, demonstrate over and over that this is not true. It is precisely Atticus's white middle-class morality that makes him believe in the law, but it is also what makes him blind to much of what goes on around him and prevents him from understanding the real danger.

In the film Atticus assures Jem that there is "no need to be afraid of him [Ewell] . . . he's all bluff," but the camera's point of view and the editing tell a different story; they show us how and why Atticus does not understand Ewell's threat to the children and to Helen Robinson. If the ghostly point of view of Boo is not made monstrous in this first interior scene, the children's encounters with Bob Ewell, which Atticus does not see, follow many horror film conventions. Boo's proximity as a neighbor allows him to watch the children unseen, as a "friendly" ghost of the Finch neighborhood, but Ewell is a more frightening figure who haunts the Robinsons' neighborhood because of his proximity to the African American part of town. Ewell's abject status as white trash is literalized by his proximity to the town dump. The Robinsons live near the dump because of segregation, while for Ewell it suggests his unwillingness to work.

Ewell's position vis-à-vis the black neighborhood is also an indicator of the vulnerable position of the Robinsons. Both times Atticus brings the children with him in the car when he calls on the Robinsons, a drunken Mr. Ewell makes a threatening appearance. The first time, as Atticus approaches the

Robinsons' porch, only Helen and two of her young sons are present. David Robinson approaches the car, and in a two-shot Jem and David shyly wave at one another. (Another sign of the impact of segregation of schools as well as neighborhoods, this is the only time we see the Finch children interact with black children, who are invisible throughout most of the film.) Significantly, the racist Ewell, who emerges out of the dark, interrupts their tentative interracial encounter, just as many white southerners protested *Brown v. Board of Education*. As in the scene in *Cape Fear*, the car, not the porch, is the liminal space between public and private that provides the threatening lower-class man access to vulnerable children. Whereas Scout's question about Boo's peeping transforms an objective shot into a potential point of view, in this scene a medium close-up profile of Jem's worried face anticipates the eyeline match of Ewell's approach (in a shot similar to Nancy's recognition of Cady as he makes his way to her car in *Cape Fear*). The front windshield centers Ewell's face in an elongated rectangle framed in darkness, giving the appearance of a wide-screen format, thus magnifying his threat. (This rectangular frame also anticipates Scout's point of view through her costume, when Ewell makes good on his threats and actually attacks the children.) Unlike the quiet, nighttime sounds of insects as "we" look through the window at Scout in the earlier scene, when Ewell approaches the car and looks through the window at Scout asleep on the front seat, intense, suspenseful music begins (fig. 6.2). Furthermore, there is no point of view shot from Ewell's perspective, which would have mirrored the earlier point of view of the ghostly Boo through Scout's window. Instead, the camera looks through the window on the driver's side, where, moments earlier, Atticus stood as he got out of the car. This first frightening encounter with Ewell, therefore, links Atticus's absence to Ewell's menacing presence. In this shot Atticus is not there to witness the threat or to protect the children.

Ewell's status as a monster figure is reinforced further through lighting as he stumbles toward the car and his face is cast in bottom lighting, often called "Halloween lighting" because it creates strange shadows on the monster's face. In the next shot a musical stinger accompanies Ewell's snarling face, framed by the side window, as he suddenly puts his hand on the window and looks in at Jem. Although there is a pane of glass between them, it looks as if Ewell is reaching out to grab Jem, and the side lighting illuminates the whites of Ewell's eyes, leaving the rest of his face in shadow, extenuating his demonic

FIGS. 6.2–3. Bob Ewell appears when Atticus is absent from the shot. *To Kill a Mockingbird* (1962).

look (fig. 6.3). A reverse shot of Jem shows the shadow of Ewell's hand across his face; this shot again mirrors and yet distinguishes Boo from Ewell. In an earlier scene on the Radley porch, as Jem crouches down, Boo's shadow passes over, only to withdraw back into the darkness. Ewell's menace, however, is real, and in a shot/reverse shot with Atticus, who has returned to the car, Ewell hisses, "Nigger lover," before slouching off into the night.

After Atticus drives away, the shot of the Robinsons' porch—the same shot set up in which moments ago Atticus emerged from the house with Helen—contains only Helen and her son, who appear to be alone now that her husband is in jail. Again, Atticus's absence from the shot indicates danger. Therefore, while Atticus may be correct that Ewell will not actually hurt him, Helen is left in a much more precarious position, and because of the spatial distancing of segregation, Atticus will not be in calling distance if Ewell returns to harass her, as he was (this time) for his own children. This final point of view shot/reverse shot between Jem and Ewell, as Atticus drives away, makes the point clear. Jem, looking through and framed in the back window of the car, sees the drunken Ewell in the road outside the Robinson home, staggering with a bottle of whiskey and waving his fist. The audience and the children thus see what Atticus does not, that his words of comfort are based not on his understanding of other people but on his absence from the scene.

The threat to the entire Robinson family is underscored when Jem again accompanies Atticus to the Robinsons' cabin to inform them that Tom has been shot. As Atticus returns to the car in a series of shots/reverse shots, Ewell spits in his face and then flinches and takes a step back as if he is afraid of what Atticus will do. In a slow, deliberate act of palpable self-control, Atticus takes out his handkerchief, wipes the spit from his face, and throws the handkerchief on the ground before getting into the car. Ewell's fear of Atticus, a grown white man, is clearly shown but not his threat to the Robinsons. The scene ends with a medium close-up of Ewell backlit by the reflection of the headlights, while the Robinson family stands behind him on the porch. As the car backs up, the headlights literally highlight Ewell's menacing look. The Robinsons cannot simply drive home to safety, and while Helen is not alone this time, if the Robinson men defend themselves against Ewell, they face the same fate as Tom. As explained at trial, Tom cannot enter the yard, much less the porch, of a white family—no matter how low they are on the social ladder—without their permission. Even with Mayella's permission, Tom's entrance into the yard, past the porch and into the house places him in a deadly position. The Robinsons, on the other hand, could face grave reprisals (not just from Ewell but potentially from the white community) if they expel Ewell from their yard, especially because any physical reaction against Ewell could be interpreted as retaliation for his charges against Tom, which would remove the Robinsons from the category of "humble, respectable Negro[es]." The right to kill anyone trespassing on one's property, which Mr. Radley invokes when he shoots at the prowler and which plays such a crucial role in *The Executioners* (the novel that *Cape Fear* was based on), does not apply to the Robinsons. For the Robinsons the porch is not a liminal space between public and private, as it is for the Finches, because the Robinsons, like all the African Americans in Maycomb, cannot claim the right to private property that is afforded to a full-fledged citizen (or even the Ewells).

Ewell's highlighted, menacing image standing in front of in the Robinsons' house as Atticus drives away dissolves into a shot of Scout carrying her ham costume on the way to a Halloween pageant. The dissolve, which superimposes the long shot of Scout and the angry image of Ewell, therefore simultaneously presents Ewell as a threat to the Robinsons as well as to Scout.[38] Scout's papier-mâché ham outfit contributes to her role as victim by limiting her vision and her ability to run away, yet it is also emblematic of the New Deal initiatives in the South to combat soil erosion and to diversify agricultural production. The association between the belle-as-victim and the southern economy is a common trope of the southern rape complex, evident from the start in *The Birth of a Nation.* In that film the attack on Flora occurs after her scene of degradation as she tries to adorn her homespun dress using raw cotton to simulate ermine, and in *The Story of Temple Drake* and in *Sanctuary* (the movie) Temple, as a symbol of excess of the Roaring Twenties, is raped in the corncrib amid the corn shucks, the waste product of corn whiskey, an illegal alternative source of income for poor whites after the drop in cotton prices.

In *To Kill a Mockingbird* most of the action in Ewell's attack occurs around Scout, who is knocked to the ground and trapped by her costume, which pins her arms to her side and provides only a small rectangular opening for her eyes. The confinement of the costume coupled with her state of undress, therefore, make Scout more vulnerable, limiting her movement and her vision. The camerawork and editing of the scene create the subjective experience of the event as Scout recounts them later to Atticus. Although not a literal point of view shot through the opening in Scout's costume, what the viewer experiences is Scout's inability to see what is happening. The nighttime setting of the attack—the use of shadows, bodies, and editing—make the chase scene between Ewell and the children one of the most difficult to follow. The children's walk home from the Halloween pageant begins with the swelling, slightly melancholy music of the opening credits sequence. Aside from the footsteps Jem hears as they walk along, the first sign of real danger begins with a guttural yell as a shadow passes over a medium close-up of Jem and momentarily blacks out the screen. Through a series of rapid shots the viewer sees only fragments and blurred bodies for most of the attack. The only clear camera shots are a high angle medium long shot of Jem lying unconscious with his arm askew and the medium close-up of Scout's eyes framed by the costume as a struggle of hands takes place: first a shot of a dark, dirty hand

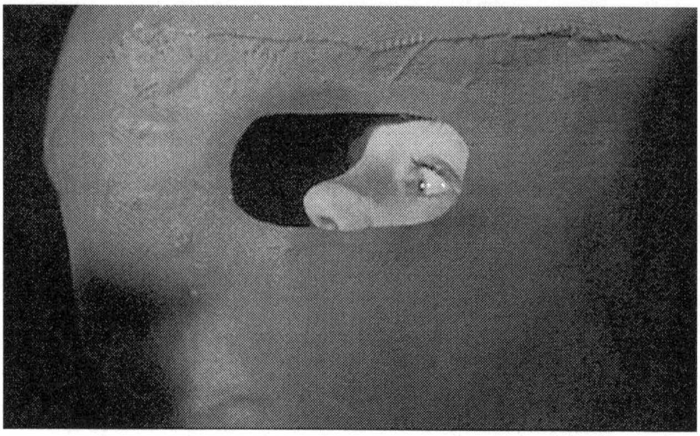

FIG. 6.4. Scout's limited vision of the struggle as seen through the opening in her pork costume. *To Kill a Mockingbird* (1962).

grabbing her costume, then another, much whiter hand pulling the first away. Although Ewell's skin color is more a product of hygiene than race, the color difference is nonetheless visually apparent. The stabbing of Ewell employs off-screen space, just as the ghostly presence of Boo did earlier but with an important difference. This time, through the use of off-screen sound, we hear rather than see Boo and Ewell, while visually there is a close-up of Scout's eyes framed by the opening in her costume as she tries to see from her limited vantage point (fig. 6.4). With Ewell's hand torn away from her, Scout is able to back out of her costume and run home but not before seeing Boo in the distance carrying Jem in his arms.

If the chase scene reconfigures elements of the southern rape complex, accentuating the way the violence limits the victim's vision, so does its aftermath. In the ending of the film Scout ostensibly learns to see Boo through his own eyes, but the visual logic of the shot belies this meaning. As Scout escorts Mr. Arthur (as she now refers to Boo, after her father properly introduces them) back to his home, the narrative voice of the mature Scout invokes Atticus's famous philosophy that you do not really know someone until you stand in their shoes and walk around in them, but rather than a point of view shot in which we see Scout "seeing" the world from Boo's perspective, the entire shot is presented from a high angle camera consciousness that literally looks down on Boo and Scout. The adult Scout in the voice-over then says, "Standing on the Radley porch was enough." This is a rather enigmatic statement that could mean that Scout was able to understand the loneliness of Boo's life from just standing on the desolate-looking porch, but it begs the question about why it is that Scout can understand Boo without really entering his world. Rachel Watson explains that this reticence to enter the house is characteristic of Adam Smith's *Theory of Moral Sentiments*, which she suggests is at the heart of Atticus's philosophy and in which it is "enough" that we sympathize with our neighbors while retaining a certain amount of distance as an "impartial spectator," the distance necessary to allow for the "harmony of society" and the proper workings of a capitalist system, which require an underclass of surplus labor (439–40).

In the film's end Boo's ghostly presence is further distanced and replaced with that of the absent mother; although Atticus is not reading *The Gray Ghost* to Scout in the film, we do return to the shot set up of the earlier scene of reading between Scout and Atticus. Once again, we look through the window and see Scout and Atticus sitting together. Even though this is the same voyeuristic gaze that invoked the ghostly presence of Boo in the earlier scene, this time the window is closed, and we do not enter the room. Boo is literally distanced from the scene because Scout has just escorted him home before returning to Atticus. The view through the window has therefore turned back into the safety of an objective shot; the viewer no longer "shares" Boo's gaze. In the first interior scene Boo's presence as the children's guardian is overlaid with that of the absent mother. As Scout plays with Atticus's watch and reads out the inscription from her mother—"to my beloved husband"—she learns that although it is customary for the son to inherit the father's watch, there is a pearl necklace and a ring that belonged to her mother that Scout will receive when she is older. In the novel the add-a-pearl necklace that Aunt Alexandra gives Scout is an unwelcome gift and a symbol of the "pink penitentiary" of ladylike behavior that Scout rebels against. In the film it is a token of love passed on to the daughter from her absent mother, and we could infer that Boo's absent presence in the scene mirrors that of the mother; he will retain the role of the children's "guardian angel" who "looks over" them, protecting them from harm.

The connection between Boo and Mrs. Finch is visually presented when we first see Boo. After he has killed Bob Ewell and brought the injured Jem home, he hides in the corner behind the door. When Scout tries to explain to Sheriff Tate who brought Jem home, she suddenly sees Boo in the corner and says, "Why there he is, Mr. Tate." Boo is revealed, looking ghostly pale and hugging the wall, but significantly, he shares the shot with a picture on the mantel of a young woman, presumably the children's mother (fig. 6.5). In

FIGS. 6.5–6. Boo, Scout, and the picture of the mother is replaced in the final shot with Atticus, Scout, and the image of the mother. *To Kill a Mockingbird* (1962).

the final shot of Scout and Atticus, purged of the "presence" of Boo, it is the mother's picture on the mantel that looks down on the pair, and the sanctity of the nuclear family is established. The past is now embodied by the image of the dead mother, rather than the ghostly Boo (fig. 6.6).

It is only in the final dissolve, after the camera pulls back from the window, that we finally see from Boo's perspective. As the credits roll, the final shot is shrouded in darkness but looks upon the Finch home from the perspective of the Radley porch. But this perspective, too, demonstrates the proper distance. All we can see from this vantage point is the light from Atticus's window (not Scout's). Boo, in his proper place, cannot actually know what goes on in the Finches' home. His view from the porch is not enough to be present in the Finches' lives, unless and until he is needed again to serve as a protector.

The emotional distance created by the "impartial subject" is also maintained in the film's use of aggregate point of view. Rachel Watson explains that the visual logic of the black-only balcony at the trial reflects the rhetorical weakness of white progressive politics because it creates an aggregate point of view of racial groups. This aggregate point of view allows Jem, Scout, and Dill (and white viewers) to identify with African Americans as a group without challenging racial difference or the role of segregation because "an assumed mystified homogeneity (or racial essentialism) constitutes the political ground of group identity, rather than the shared realities of their individual lives," which therefore undercuts Atticus's famous advice to stand in someone else's shoes or put on another person's skin (Watson, "View" 421).

In addition to the aggregate camera point of view of the black balcony that Watson discusses, the members of the balcony collectively rise as Atticus leaves the courtroom, which is one of the strongest signs in the film of Atticus's role as a champion of racial equality.[39] Although it is an individual, Reverend Sykes, who initiates the validation of Atticus's role as Tom's lawyer, the entire balcony, including Scout and Jem (at the reverend's insistence), stands in mute tribute. But there is an individual African American who is not part of this aggregate point of view, who does not participate in this ritual (because he has already been taken away), and who does not show the same level of appreciation. The film, unlike the novel, does not show us Atticus's blind spots about the jury system: that he does not seem to consider the absence of African Americans on the jury as grounds for appeal. Instead, it focuses on Tom Robinson's face and his lack of faith in Atticus to free him, in the courtroom or on appeal. When Tom leaves the courtroom after being found guilty, instead of gratitude, he simply stares blankly at Atticus and refuses even to acknowledge Atticus's optimism about their chances of an appeal.

Unlike the balcony members, who remain stoical throughout the trial, the close-up shots of Tom Robinson allow the audience to do what Atticus does not: sympathetically read and understand Tom's emotions. Adam Smith maintained that our sympathetic powers are such that as "impartial subjects" we can imagine the feelings of those who cannot express the appropriate emotional response. To illustrate his point, he refers to three examples: the madman, the dead, and the crying infant, but in these instances our ability to feel for the other person is based more on horror than on pity or compassion. We can imagine how terrible it would be to be insane ("by far the most dreadful" of the three) or to be deprived of life, or like the mother of the crying infant who "joins to its real helplessness," we can imagine our own "consciousness of that helplessness" and our own "terrors for the unknown consequences of its disorder" even though the infant experience "only the uneasiness of the present instant" (*Moral Sentiments* 1.1.1). Although Tom does not actually fit into any of these categories, as a black man in the South accused of raping a white woman, he is in a similar state of helplessness and terror, though unlike the baby, he understands the full implications of his situation, and even though he is able to testify, he is nevertheless an example of someone who cannot fully express his emotions verbally. Instead, he embodies them through his own affect at the trial, including crying during his testimony.

In her analysis of cinematic affect Eugenie Brinkema argues that "crying is structured like a language" because the meaning of corporeal affect is not obvious; it "commands a reading" within the context of any film (4). Although Brinkema does not discuss *To Kill a Mockingbird*, her analysis of cinematic tears is useful in "reading" Tom's reaction to the legal system. The first instance of Tom's crying occurs off-screen and is narrated by Dill as he looks through the window into the courtroom where Tom is being indicted for rape. As part of the child's perspective that dominates the first part of the film, Dill does not understand the context and therefore does not know how to read Tom's tears. Dill reports to Jem and Scout, as they boost him up to look through the window: "The colored man is crying. I wonder what he's got to cry about?" The second instance of Tom's tears occurs on the witness stand, and the context is all too clear; yet Tom does not cry throughout his entire testimony, only when Atticus questions him about Mayella's sexual advances. Although Tom, like the balcony members, has betrayed no emotion up to this point, when he is called to the stand, he looks repeatedly at Atticus with concern and/or dread (fig. 6.7). In order to win the case, or to have grounds for an appeal, there was no need to make Robinson tell the story of Mayella's sexual transgression. Atticus would only have to prove that Tom could not have choked Mayella with two hands or hit her with his left hand in order to leave the marks that are on the right side of her face. Instead, Atticus presses Tom to "tell the whole truth," that Mayella "jumped" on him and kissed him and told him to kiss her back. In the novel Atticus's reason for Tom's explicit testimony is made clear when Atticus says from the beginning, "That boy might go to the chair, but he's not going till the truth's told" (Lee 146). Maureen E. Markey interprets this line as demonstrating Atticus's "firm grasp of reality" (214), but Atticus's racist reference to Tom as "boy" at the very moment that he accepts

FIGS. 6.7–8. Tom's look of concern before his testimony turns to tears during the retelling of Mayella's advances. *To Kill a Mockingbird* (1962).

Tom's death is especially chilling and uncharacteristic of Atticus. The "truth," however, will not set Tom free. The close-ups of Tom's anguish as he cries on the stand, when relating his encounter with Mayella, suggests that he understands just how dangerous it is for him to disparage a white woman's honor, a point that Atticus, in his closing arguments, actually emphasizes by repeating the accusation that Mayella "tempted a Negro" (fig. 6.8). Smith asserts that in sharing their grief, the unfortunate actually find comfort in retelling their sorrows: "Their tears accordingly flow faster than before, and they are apt to abandon themselves" and "to take pleasure" in the sympathy of their listener. But Tom's tears are not a release because the jury's response indicates "the cruelest insult" that "can be offered to the unfortunate," which is "to make light of their calamity" or to "wear a serious [rather than sympathetic] countenance when they tell us their afflictions," and this even Smith regards as "real and gross inhumanity" (1.1.2).

Ultimately, the trial demonstrates not only the limits of empathetic understanding but that empathy itself is a matter of white privilege. In his cross-examination of Tom the district attorney also repeats a phrase, but it is even more damning than Tom's account of Mayella's conduct. To explain why he was willing to help Mayella with her chores, Tom, in an unguarded moment, says that he "felt right sorry" for her. Tom breaks off midsentence, realizing his mistake when someone off-screen scoffs. The DA seizes Tom's misstep and, turning toward the jury, says: "*You* felt sorry for *her*? *You* felt sorry for a *white* woman?" Tom cannot come onto the Ewells' porch or enter the house without fearing for his life, nor is he allowed to feel sorry for Mayella, despite her dire circumstances, having a shiftless father and seven siblings to look after.

In his closing arguments to the jury Atticus directly attacks the southern rape complex as a "time-honored code" that justifies the nullification of due process for African Americans based "on the assumption—the evil assumption—that *all* Negroes lie, that *all* Negroes are basically immoral beings, that *all* Negro men are not to be trusted around our women." This quotation represents the "commonsense" notion of Deleuze's power of the false, but even at this level Atticus himself employs the power of the false regarding the courts as the great levelers of society. The outcome of the trial disturbingly indicates that in this courtroom the power of the southern rape complex has more power to persuade (or coerce, as it is not clear that anyone believes the Ewells) than does the law.

If Atticus has trouble reading Tom's tears, he is equally incapable of empathizing with Tom as "madman" during his post-verdict escape, when he runs away "like a crazy person," despite the deputy's warning shot. The novelistic Atticus can at least imagine that Tom no longer had any faith in the justice system, but the filmic Atticus shakes his head in disbelief, repeating that they had "a good chance, more than a good chance," for an appeal. While it is left as a possibility that Tom committed suicide-by-cop in the novel (as Patrick Chura points out) Atticus does not question the explanation that Tom was shot while "trying to escape." Scout's uncontrollable shaking is triggered by her memory of the size of the prison yard, suggesting that she can put herself in Tom's shoes and therefore question the story that Tom ran the length of a football field and then scaled a fence with one hand before being shot seventeen times (7–8). In the film it is an unnamed deputy (not Sheriff Tate who is presented as an honorable man) who claims that he fired a warning shot first and then shot to wound but missed and "accidently" killed Tom. Both cases, therefore, allow for the distinct possibility that Tom was simply executed by those guarding him, again showing Atticus's naïveté when it comes to the safety of his client.

To Kill a Mockingbird not only dramatizes the limits of Adam Smith's *Theory of Moral Sentiments* regarding the "impartial subject"; it also demonstrates the limits of Smith's famous theory of the "invisible hand" of the marketplace. Even though *The Wealth of Nations* is often cited as the source of this term, Smith first uses it in *The Theory of Moral Sentiments*. The Depression, however, graphically demonstrates that Smith's belief in the "invisible hand," which will right all wrongs through the unimpeded process of competition (not federal oversight), has proven disastrous. Smith argues that fair prices and working conditions will prevail in a free market because consumers and workers can "vote" both with their pocketbooks and their feet. Many African Americans did "vote" with their feet during the Great Migration by leaving the South, but this did nothing to improve the wages or living conditions of blacks still living in the South. Smith's theory of moral sentiment assumes a similar "invisible hand" of sympathy that jibes with a kind of liberal laissez-faire morality that assumes that sympathy alone (not the National Guard or the government) can promote racial justice. Instead, Smith's theory justifies the "go slow" politics, which allows liberal whites to tolerate and even applaud the "baby steps" of gradualism that keeps the jury out longer than usual in Tom Robinson's case, rather than to experience fully and to fight against the tragedy of a man killed for no reason other than that he was black. Similarly, Boo Radley as the invisible hand of the Invisible Empire may have saved Jem and Scout, but his brand of social justice does nothing for Tom Robinson, who has already been killed under suspicious circumstances while in custody.

Gregory Peck as Sam in *Cape Fear* is willing to break the law and use violence (the hospital job) to attempt to rid himself of Cady, the dangerous lower-class white man. Gregory Peck as Atticus is too willing to believe in the equality of the law and in his own ability to reason with and/or understand the motives of the lower-class white man who actually threatens the safety of his client and his children. Ultimately, however, Atticus—at the insistence of the sheriff and with Scout's blessing—is willing to overlook the law and everything he has told the children to believe in, to accept extralegal violence, and to cover up the death of Bob Ewell, just so that the ladies of Maycomb will not bring Boo Radley too many cakes.

Coda

A Time to Kill and Post–Civil Rights Variations on the Southern Rape Complex

As a crucible of racial and gender politics, the southern rape complex is a dominant narrative that has shaped our very notion of southern violence both historically and culturally. Many of the cinematic features of the southern rape complex discussed in this study reappear in new forms in post–civil rights films, branching out to include new "threats" to southern white identity, threats that increasingly come from whites themselves. The southern rape complex as depicted in *The Birth of a Nation* displays a post–Civil War anxiety over the sexuality and identity of elite white southern males, which is related to their ambiguous status as a subjugated elite—a variation on Homi Bhabha's "not quite/not white" subaltern elite.[1] In subsequent variations of the complex, this "not quite/not white" male anxiety is often projected onto the lower-class white man. Therefore, the black-coded white man, featured in many of the films in this study, is a recurring variation on the southern rape complex, which continues after the civil rights movement in films such as *Deliverance* (1972), *Prince of Tides* (1991), and the remake of *Cape Fear* (1991).

Yet as in *To Kill a Mockingbird*, the black-coded white man increasingly represents not just a racist fear of blacks but also the fear of racism itself. The "redneck menace," as Allison Graham refers to him, localizes all of the most negative associations of the South—sexual violence and racial intolerance—in white lower-class southern males. Despite Griffith's (and Dixon's) attempts to solidify a definition of whiteness to maintain and justify white domination over blacks, class differences and economic interests disrupt any seamless definition. As the ending of *The Birth of a Nation* indicates, it is the marriage of northern and southern elites that establishes the city on a hill, not the interclass marriage of Griffith's *Swords and Hearts*. The poor, uneducated white male, precisely because he shares the economic situation of many poor blacks and is subject to the same negative stereotypes, is actually a greater threat to the myth of white superiority, the lynchpin of white political and economic domination.

Deliverance, adapted from James Dickey's novel of the same name, was one of the first feature films, and certainly the most graphic, to eschew the victimized belle as a surrogate for the white feminized (conquered) South in place of the male-on-male sexual assault that directly enacts the fear of elite white male emasculation that fuels the southern rape complex. Moreover, the threat to white masculinity is not embodied by the black perpetrator but by the worst stereotypes of the redneck white southern male. *Deliverance* was also one of the first films to position the southern suburbanite, not the northern "carpetbagger," as the interloping opportunist who defiles the land and its resources for his own gain. As Lewis, the group's leader, played by Burt Reynolds, explains in a voice-over at the beginning of the film (while we see the bulldozing of the land to make way for the dam as a source of electricity and recreation), "You push a little more power into Atlanta, a little more air conditioners for your smug little suburb and . . . they're gonna rape this whole landscape . . . just about the last wild, untamed, unpolluted, unfucked-up river in the South." The hillbillies, who are dispossessed of their homes to provide more power as well as a respite from the city for the urban South, exemplify both an extreme version of the ecological lost cause and the most potent threat to white southern elite masculinity.

The "hillbillies" of *Deliverance* are undeniably threatening, yet they seem to have no desire to venture outside of their own world. It is, after all, the Atlantans who enter uncharted waters as a form of recreation. In *Prince of Tides,* on the other hand, the lower-class menace cannot be contained. Multiple family members (mother, sister, and younger brother) are raped by three white escaped convicts. As convicts, they have been found guilty and confined to prison, but this does not prevent them from violating the white home and family. While the older brother kills all three rapists, it is the mother's desire to keep the rapes a secret to maintain her family honor that exacerbates the trauma of the attack: the older son kills himself, and the victimized son and daughter are emotionally damaged. As the remaining son, now a grown man, tells the story of his family's enforced silence, he links it to the concept of southern family honor and mockingly finishes his story by singing, "And that's what I like about the South." The lower-class mother's social climbing desires prove to be more destructive than the convicts. She reaches her goal by marrying Old Money, after divorcing her poor husband, but at the price of destroying her own family. As in many of Griffith's early Civil War films, family honor is a corrosive charade.

Almost thirty years after the original *Cape Fear*, in Martin Scorsese's 1991 remake, Max Cady is no longer a black coded white man because his status as white redneck menace is much more threatening and is the source of his almost superhuman power. Cady, played by Robert De Niro, is a meaner, stronger, smarter, more demented, and virtually indestructible incarnation of the 1962 Cady. In rejecting his status as a "white trash piece of shit," Cady actually confirms it and demonstrates why he is so threatening: "I'm better than you all! I can out-learn you. I can out-read you. I can out-think you. And I can out-philosophize you. And I'm gonna outlast you. You think a couple whacks to my guts is gonna get me down? It's gonna take a hell of a lot more than that, Counselor, to prove you're better than me!" But this Cady is also a religious fundamentalist who sees himself as the scourge of God and who credits his Pentecostal background as the source of his superhuman tolerance to pain: "Granddaddy used to handle snakes in church, Granny drank strychnine. I guess you could say I had a leg up, genetically speaking." Screenwriter Wesley Strick explained it very directly when he said he created the revised Cady as "a monster of the South" that was terrifying to him as a "New York Jew" (*The Making of Cape Fear*). If stop-and-frisk policies and stand your ground laws, both of which disproportionally target African American men, indicate that white America is still very much afraid of black men and teenagers (especially if they are wearing hoodies, as in the Trayvon Martin case, and whether or not they are armed), Hollywood increasingly localized and dramatized such fears in the lower-class white racist.

While many of the black-coded white men were still strangers, some films, such as *Fried Green Tomatoes* (1991), *Forrest Gump* (1994), and *Bastard Out of Carolina* (1997), reverse the image of the rapist as outsider, placing him within the home as husband, father, or stepfather. The examination of intraracial incest and domestic violence in the South depicts the threat located within the white home and therefore serves as a critique of the prominence of the southern rape complex in the American cultural imagination. In the domestic setting, sexual violence enacts a blatant form of control over women's bodies, but it also extends to economic and social control over women. *The Color*

Purple (1985) reexamines the black male rapist within the confines of the black family, and although bell hooks admonished Alice Walker for playing into the stereotype of the black male rapist, both the novel and the film allowed for Mister's redemption (though not that of her stepfather) by breaking the generational chain of male domination that included physical abuse as a means to control women.

Post–civil rights films such as *Daughters of the Dust* (1991), *Kill the Girls* (1996), *Beloved* (1998), *Django Unchained* (2012), and *12 Years a Slave* (2013) have increasingly made "morally legible" the abuse of African American women at the hands of white men, depicting the impact of this violence not only for the women attacked but also for their families and the communities.[2] *Daughters of the Dust* is unique among the adaptations discussed in this study as it was first a film and then adapted into a novel. It also is significant in examining the place of children of rape within the family. The triangulated relationship of the southern rape complex involves the victim, alleged perpetrator, and the self-appointed executioners, but by including the unborn child, *Daughters of the Dust* reconfigures this triangle to include the mother, her husband, and her child. What connects the three is not strictly biology (as the husband may or may not be the father) but, instead, the African ancestors, a more expansive category that creates a tie between Eli and his unborn daughter. The actual rape is never visualized, and although we are told he is white, we do not see the rapist. Eula Peazant withholds this information from her husband, Eli, not to protect the rapist but to prevent Eli from acting out the vigilante justice associated with the complex. Yet because the purpose of the southern rape complex is to define African Americans as bare life, Eli cannot invoke the state of exception that the complex supports; if he tries to do so, he will in turn be subject to white vigilante violence. Fittingly, the unborn child narrates the story of her parents' struggle and her father's doubts about his parentage. Her spirit suggests another form of middle passage, as she comes from the ancestors across the ocean to the United States, but if she originated in the past, her impact on the future is indicated in her relationship to modern technology. The unborn child is an interesting counterpoint to the baby in *Touch of Evil*, which is held up to distract Susan so that the Grandi nephew can take a seemingly incriminating picture of Susan with Pancho, "a souvenir with a million kisses." The unborn child, on the other hand, is invisible to the characters in the film, yet as the photographer takes the family portrait, when he looks through the camera lens, he detects her presence. Like the time-image, the unborn child embodies the past, present, and future as well as the actual and the virtual. For Eula, Eli, and the unborn child to become a family, Eli must relinquish the past event and the dictates of the southern rape complex that demand vengeance for his wife's rape and embrace his kinship with the child. Instead of violence, he combats the vigilante violence he rejects and joins an antilynching association.

Kiss the Girls, based on James Patterson's Alex Cross novel of the same name, is another film that rejects the lower-class, black-coded white man as rapist and instead implicates the white southern gentleman and the white law officer. While *Beloved, Django Unchained,* and *12 Years a Slave* return to the past to indict the sexualized violence of slavery, *Kiss the Girls* is set in the present. The white rapist is presented as a vestige of the abuses of slaveholders, as he keeps his victims in the basement of a former plantation house that burned down years earlier, while the African American psychologist Dr. Cross is the hero. Dr. Cross attempts to rescue his niece, who, unbeknownst to him, has been kidnapped by the southern white detective who is working on the investigation. The detective, who calls himself "Cassanova" and speaks with a refined southern accent, has paired up with another serial killer who calls himself the "gentleman caller," a southern term for suitor. Dr. Cross, along with the niece's African American boyfriend, and a white southern woman doctor, who has escaped from Cassanova, use their knowledge of psychology, history, and medicine, respectively, to locate the former plantation and rescue the other women (black and white) being held as sex slaves by Cassanova. Thus, the film revises the southern rape complex, and the very characters who typically are the victims in that narrative (the black man and the white southern woman) pursue and eventually kill the characters who are usually depicted as the hero (the white southern gentleman and the white law officer).

As an example of another variation of the post–civil rights reinvention of the southern rape complex and its relationship to the judicial system, I will conclude with a brief analysis of *A Time to Kill* (1996), based on John Grisham's novel. The film employs many of the variations of the southern rape complex under discussion in this study (the white lawyer as hero and the redneck as villain) but differs significantly in that it includes the white-on-black attack of a young girl. Directed by Joel Schumacher, *A Time to Kill* reimages both *The Birth of a Nation* and *To Kill a Mockingbird* by reversing the race, but not the logic, of the southern rape complex. *A Time to Kill* depicts the brutal rape of a young black girl and positions the white trash rapists (and the Klan, which supports them) as the true evil, while leaving in place the justification of vigilante justice, even in the courtroom. *A Time to Kill* is nevertheless relevant to the study of white anxiety surrounding racial violence because, even though the father's revenge against the white men who attacked his daughter is central to the plot, the film, like *To Kill a Mockingbird*, still privileges the negative effects the subsequent trial has on his white lawyer, Jake Brigance, and on his family and friends.

Schumacher's depiction of the film's bestial white rapists owes more to Dixon than to Griffith, as it combines elements of Dixon's black gang rape in *The Clansman* and the attack on young Flora in *The Leopard's Spots*. In the first scenes of the film we are introduced to the white rapists, the reprehensible and irredeemable villains of the film. The film makes clear from the start that the white trash villains are responsible for destroying the bucolic tranquillity of the rural South. As with films set in the South, the contemporary setting of the film still employs markers of a nostalgic past. The opening shot, for example, is of an expansive green field surrounded by trees with a dirt road (one of the most ubiquitous icons of the rural South) next to it. The tranquillity of the scene is highlighted as the ominous country-twinged music of the opening credits cuts out and we are left only with silence, which is destroyed by the entrance of a bright yellow "souped-up" pickup truck, which we hear before we see. Unlike the beat-up red pickup truck, which is another marker of the southern past, the garish yellow truck signals the presence not just of rural poverty and the past but of white trash. We hear the yells and laughter of the two men in the truck before we see them, but their status as racist rednecks is signaled from the start in a series of shaky handheld close-ups that focus on a Confederate flag decal, a skull head ring, drug paraphernalia, a cropped T-shirt exposing a protruding belly, mullet haircuts, and then a shot of the two men drinking whiskey and smoking a joint as they race through the countryside. The chaotic depiction of the two men (referred to throughout the film as "boys," "animals," "hyenas," and "monsters") and the noise of the scene is then crosscut with a low-key medium close-up of fresh green corn. Framed in light, a young black girl, Tanya Hailey, reaches for an ear of corn as she shops for groceries at the all-black grocery store, which despite the presence of refrigerated display cases, is also a nostalgic image of a quiet (though segregated) rural past, complete with a group of black men sitting on the porch with fishing rods in their hands. Rather than disturbing this scene, as in the case of the white racists, Tanya reinforces a sense of innocence and calm, which is shattered as she leaves the store when the same white men enter, knocking over merchandise and disrupting the peace. The crosscutting between the two scenes sets up the contrast between black innocence and white depravity that collides in the brutal rape of Tanya.

When Tanya's father, Carl Lee Hailey, shoots the two suspects in cold blood on the courthouse stairs, the film shifts into a courtroom drama. As in *To Kill a Mockingbird,* the white lawyer Jake Brigance is defending a black man in the face of an all-white jury. But unlike Tom Robinson, Carl Lee is guilty, and unlike Atticus, Jake wins the case for his client, appealing not to the jury's duty to uphold the law (as Atticus says, "For God's sake, do your duty") but to their own racial prejudice. Jake, therefore, is asking the all-white jury in the South to do what they did repeatedly in the past, to acquit a premeditated murderer based on the state of exception supported by the southern rape complex: the difference is that class is substituted for race.

A Time to Kill also reimagines the relationship between the white lawyer and his black client depicted in *To Kill a Mockingbird.* Jake is not appointed by the court, as is Atticus, and Carl Lee takes control of his own defense from the beginning: he comes to Jake before the murders to ask if Jake would represent him if anything happened, he negotiates with outside groups to raise funds, and he tells Jake what questions to ask in court as well as what Jake must do to get him acquitted. Like *To Kill a Mockingbird, A Time to Kill* has echoes of the Scottsboro trial, especially with regards to the struggle between the NAACP and the International Labor Defense (established by the Communist Party), over who would defend the accused. Although the NAACP accused the ILD of wanting to martyr the Scottsboro defendants for propaganda purposes, the ILD hired Samuel Leibowitz, who, though not a Communist, had an excellent record in capital cases. After his own problems with the ILD, including its attempt to bribe a witness, Leibowitz broke with the group and attempted to secure permission to serve as defense counsel, as did the ILD. The defendants and their families were pulled in both directions, with each side accusing the other of colluding with the "Alabama lynchers." From October to November 1934 the defendants changed counsel five times (Carter 310–19). In the end the defendants decided on separate counsel: Leibowitz continued as Norris's defense counsel under the American Scottsboro Committee, while Patterson remained with the ILD (330–35).

In *A Time to Kill* it is the NAACP that hires a New York Jewish lawyer, Norman Reinfeld, whose policy of handling only capital murder cases has earned his team the nickname the "Death Squad." Just as the NAACP suggested that the Communist Party wanted to lose the Scottsboro case for publicity purposes (to highlight racial intolerance in the United States), Jake asks Reinfeld, "How many of these cases were you supposed to lose?" The film thus signals that it is not "politically correct" in its willingness to vilify the NAACP and that Jake is not a "bleeding heart liberal," as he states emphatically that he is *for* the death penalty. While Leibowitz took the lead in negotiating the coalition that eventually became the Scottsboro Defense Committee,[3] it is Carl Lee who orchestrates the meeting with the NAACP and invites Jake, though neither party understands at first what Carl Lee is planning. Carl Lee has learned from his wife that the Reverend Agee of the local Baptist church raised two thousand dollars from the congregation, with the promise that the money was going to support the Haileys. When Reverend Agee, who the viewer knows is getting an "administrative fee" from the NAACP, shows up claiming that the money is for the NAACP, which has also raised five thousand dollars toward the defense, Carl Lee threatens to expose him if he does not give all the money to the Hailey family. Carl Lee then uses Jake's knowledge of law—that it is illegal to solicit clients—to secure the money to pay Jake for his defense. The NAACP therefore is depicted as a group of manipulative outsiders who cynically take the case for political reasons. After the meeting, when they are back in the jail, Jake is impressed with Carl Lee's maneuvering and boasts, "We make a pretty good team," but Carl Lee rejects this characterization. In the earlier jail scene of Jake and Carl Lee conferring, they were both on the inside of the cell, but in this scene the bars separate them, as Carl Lee points out when he replies: "We ain't no team. You on the outside, I'm on the inside."

A Time to Kill revises *To Kill a Mockingbird* by allowing the black defendant to teach the white lawyer how to make a convincing closing argument to an all-white jury. The night before the closing arguments, when Jake advises Carl Lee to take a deal because "there are no more points of law" to make, Carl Lee explains why he chose Jake over Reinfeld and the NAACP, why he considers Jake "his secret weapon." Jake is shocked to learn that Carl Lee did not chose him because he is a "liberal lawyer" but because he's "one of the bad guys."

As Carl Lee goes on to explain: "You don't mean to be but you are. It's how you were raised. You think just like them [the all-white jury]. That's why you gotta convince them that I'm innocent." Carl Lee's directive to Jake points out the problems with Atticus's summation to the jury. In *A Time to Kill* the DA's remarks to the jury echo those of Atticus as he tells them to do their duty according to the law and to have the courage to find Carl Lee guilty, but he is no more successful than Atticus. Although Atticus's most famous dictum on empathy to his children is to be able to stand in someone else's shoes, at key moments, including the closing argument, his inability to identify with the jury (to speak *to* them rather than *at* them) is crucial. As Scout explains in the novel, Atticus talks to everyone the same way, and although his children are used to this and know that they can ask him to explain what he means, the jury cannot. Furthermore, although Atticus rejects the logic of the "time honored code" of the southern rape complex, he also invokes the white anxiety surrounding it when he repeats that Mayella "tempted a Negro. Not an old uncle, but a strong, young black man."

Atticus's final summation is characteristic of the problem with his defense throughout the trial. In putting Tom on the stand, Atticus duplicates the double bind Tom found himself in with Mayella, in which he had either to physically push away a white woman or put himself in the dangerous position of kissing her. Because we never see Tom and Atticus discussing the case, it is possible that Tom is indeed a "humble" Negro who did not object to Atticus's strategy of putting him on the stand to describe a white woman making a pass at him, but Tom's painful reaction to narrating the event suggests that he realizes the equally dangerous position in which Atticus has placed him. In his closing arguments, Atticus need only state that he does not know who beat and raped Mayella but that it could not have been Tom. By resting his defense on the fact that Mayella "tempted a Negro," Atticus in effect forces the jury to come to her defense or to admit the larger proposition that white women are attracted to black men, which violates the very premise of the southern rape complex—that any contact between a black man and a white woman is rape.

Jake is Carl Lee's secret weapon because he can identify with the jury's own racism, something Atticus could not do. Jake took the case and stayed on because, as he confesses to his wife, he did not call the sheriff as she advised when Carl Lee came to him before the murders: precisely because he wanted them dead for what they did, and he would do the same if it were his daughter.

FIG. C.1. Tonya's point of view during the rape. *A Time to Kill* (1996).

Therefore, Jake's strategy is to try to appeal not to the jury's intellect but to their most basic emotions. He has to make them want to see the "boys" dead too. Jake enacts Gilles Deleuze's famous phrase that the "brain is a screen" as he tells the jury to close their eyes so that they can "see" the story that he is about to tell them, thus creating a kind of voice-over narration to their own mental pictures. As affect is registered through the body, close-ups of the jurors, some with tears running down their faces, register the horror and pity they feel as Jake graphically describes what the two men did to Tanya, adding details that the audience did not see in the earlier rape scenes.

The rape scene is unusual in that it employs a point of view shot from Tanya's perspective intercut with close-ups of her hand and feet as she is tied up, raped, hanged, and then thrown into a truck. Rather than using a close-up of Tanya's face to invoke fear, as is typical in a rape scene, the viewer is forced to watch the rapists and to see the world through Tanya's eyes, not as an "impartial" spectator (fig. C.1). Jake's retelling is horrific in its own right, but because the audience has already viewed the rape through Tanya's eyes (in which the close-ups of killers, not the little girl, invoke disgust, not pity), when Jake asks the jury "Can you see her?" the audience is asked to see the event again, this time as a spectator. Jake's question thus facilitates the audience's ability both to identify and to sympathize with the victim. But Jake's final instruction to the jury, "Now imagine she's white," forces the white jury (and perhaps the white audience as well) to completely reimagine the narrative and also presumably to have an even stronger affective response, one that would make them want to kill "those boys."

A Time to Kill suggests the disturbing conclusion that true sympathy is still limited by race and that the southern rape complex still elicits an irrational emotional response that condones cold-blooded murder and the acquittal of a guilty man, as long as the murder victims are conceived of as "animals." Despite the differences in the two films, the end of *A Time to Kill* is in keeping with that of *To Kill a Mockingbird;* ultimately, it is up to the middle-class white citizens to decide when the law should and should not be upheld, and this decision is based on their ability to identify with the perpetrator. Of course, the heinous nature of the act should provoke a visceral response, but as we saw in the beginning, the two men were deemed animals, and therefore bare life, before the attack occurred. *A Time to Kill* brings us full circle back to *The Birth of a Nation* and the cinematic power of the southern rape complex, which, as long as it invokes a strong response from the audience (viewers/readers), will continue to be a staple of American culture, even if in an altered form.

NOTES

INTRODUCTION

1. My work benefits from the developing interest in and analysis of southern film, including Allison Graham, *Framing the South: Hollywood, Television, and Race during the Civil Rights;* George M. Fredrickson, "A Man but Not a Brother: Abraham Lincoln and Racial Equality," *Struggle* (2001); Jane M. Gaines, *Fire and Desire: Mixed-Race Movies in the Silent Era* (2001); Linda Williams, *Playing the Race Card: Melodramas of Black and White from Uncle Tom to O. J. Simpson* (2002); Tara McPherson, *Reconstructing Dixie: Race, Gender, and Nostalgia in the Imagined South* (2003); Riché Richardson, *Black Masculinity and the U.S. South* (2007); and Andrew Leiter, *Southerners on Film: Essays on Hollywood Portrayals since the 1970s* (2011). This burgeoning interest is reflected in the first collection of essays on southern film in thirty years, *American Cinema and the Southern Imaginary,* which I edited with Kathryn McKee (2011), and the media volume of *The New Encyclopedia of Southern Culture,* edited by Allison Graham and Sharon Monteith (2011). Because the southern rape complex is so pervasive in southern cinema, all of these studies incorporate elements of the complex, and they therefore provide a significant context for my work.

2. The southern rape complex draws on earlier uses of racialized rape in the colonization of the United States. Focusing on California, Antonia I. Castañeda maintains that eighteenth-century Spanish captivity narratives used stories of the rape of white women by Native American men as a justification for violence against Native Americans and the seizing of their lands for white settlement. Such narratives were also popular in New England and wherever whites sought to colonize new territory.

3. In her analysis of the "rhetoric of rape" Sabine Sielke compares the processes of identity formation that are based on "both the assignment and the subordination of difference" with the "refiguration" that is the central paradigm of the "rhetoric of rape": the "rhetoric of rape is one of many discourses by which such differences are being ascribed, victims and violators othered, set off, while the subject who assigns difference remains unmarked and unlimited in his or her possibilities" (5). Although Sielke argues that those who assign difference through rape are unmarked, the southern rape complex both limited and marked not only victims and violators but also its main proponents and, more broadly, the culture that has read and/or watched it for over one hundred years. The cinematic apparatus adds an additional dimension to the rhetoric of rape by tapping into the spectacular uses of sexualized violence against African Americans as a form of coercion around which the southern rape complex is organized. These cinematic images continue to focus the lens through which we visualize and process the southern rape complex.

4. For the past several decades there has been a strong feminist and sociological interest in

issues of rape, but more recently critics have turned to literary and cinematic representations of rape; see, e.g., by Sielke; Tanner; Cuklanz; Patterson; Projansky; Horeck; and Shaw.

5. Sarah Projansky details a history of rape narratives in American films beginning in 1903, arguing for the ubiquity and versatility of the narratives and their functions (26–65). She includes a section on how these narratives are used to solidify various forms of racial and ethnic identity to construct a U.S. identity "by linking the national identity to a whiteness distanced from rape" (51), concluding that "the overwhelming majority of rape films sublimate race by depicting rape as something that happens between white women and white men who are not aware of themselves as racialized" (248n59). In the southern context, however, rape is frequently racialized, even in depictions of white-on-white rape.

6. For an excellent description of the literary legacy of the southern rape complex and its relation to the southern woman, see Seidel, *Southern Belle* 14.

7. As Daniel Bernardi explains, "Griffith's articulations of style and of race are involved in the same cinematic and discursive processes; pragmatically, they co-constitute the filmmaker's narrative system" ("Voice" 104). For the most comprehensive history of *The Birth of a Nation*, see Stokes. See also Schickel. While many white Americans chose to see *The Birth of a Nation* as an unproblematic representation of the historical truth of white superiority, the National Association for the Advancement of Colored People (NAACP) and the black press condemned the film for its racism and sought to prevent it from being shown. For an extensive discussion of the black press's response to *The Birth of a Nation*, see Everett.

8. For studies on lynching, see Harris; Brundage; Wiegman; Gunning, *Race;* Cardyn; Wallace; Pfeifer, *Rough Justice;* Goldsby; Rosen; Amy Louise Wood, *Lynching;* Feimster; and Pfeifer, *Roots.* More recent work has questioned the geographical assumptions associated with lynching in the United States: Pfeifer, *Lynching;* and Carrigan and Waldrep. For work on miscegenation, see Hodes; Gaines; and Courtney.

9. Writing in 1971, C. Vann Woodward stated that "no other book on Southern history rivals Cash's in influence among laymen and few among professional historians," and Richard H. King maintains that it "still compels even when it cannot persuade" (146). On the fiftieth anniversary of its publication in 1991, a reappraisal of *The Mind of the South* was the focus of the annual Porter L. Fortune Symposium on Southern History, and Alfred A. Knopf published an anniversary edition, which punctuated fifty years of continually being in print (Eagles ix).

10. Although, as Sommerville documents, slaves were not necessarily lynched as a form of punishment for sexual assault, lynching was already employed as a terrorist tactic to stifle antislavery campaigns. From 1836–56, according to the abolitionist newspaper *Liberator,* three hundred white abolitionists were lynched (White 91). Furthermore, Sharon Block demonstrates in her analysis in *Rape and Sexual Power in Early America* that rape laws still helped to enforce white male domination and solidify racial and gender hierarchies, which fed into narratives of Africans as bestial.

11. In analyzing Oscar Micheaux's *Within Our Gates,* Jane M. Gaines points out that in the overdetermined nature of lynching, "it is not the taboo sexual thought that is repressed; it is the economic motive" (167).

12. Accordingly, the literary author was often accorded greater weight than the director in fidelity criticism. With the rise of *auteur* theory and the French New Wave, directors were given

greater weight as the source of creativity and, when they used literary source material, tended to choose lesser-know pulp fiction in order to create their own style and not to be eclipsed by the author (DeBona 25–29).

13. Murray, *Adaptation Industry* 9. For a detailed analysis of Faulkner's relationship to mass culture, including film, see Peter Lurie's *Vision's Immanence.*

14. As Sarah Gleeson-White points out in her analysis of sound in William Faulkner's film treatment of "Sutter's Gold" and in *Absalom! Absalom!* film scholarship has too often privileged the visual over the auditory.

15. For a discussion of the film, see Gaines 52–56.

16. Surprisingly, Maurice does not discuss *The Birth of a Nation* in any detail and refers to it only briefly as overshadowing the role of race in *The Cheat,* which also came out in 1915.

17. Robert Burgoyne credits *The Birth of a Nation* as an early example of how historical films "have served as vehicles of artistic ambition and as catalysts of public debate" that can "awaken a powerful sense of national belonging or a probing sense of national self-scrutiny" (1, 2).

18. Joel Williamson in *The Crucible of Race* maintains that by 1915, coinciding with the release of *Birth,* white elites had "effectively completed" their attempt to achieve a "cultural system that put black people firmly to one side and tied the mass of white people tightly to the white elite. The final crusade for whiteness produced, among many other things, all-white factories, all-white one-party politics, compulsory public school for every white child, public health campaigns that favored whites, segregation, a rage against miscegenation, and the relatively total divorce of white religion, language, and music from black" (513). By the 1930s the disfranchisement and segregation of blacks in the South was virtually complete, and "the white electorate, itself greatly reduced, was super-satisfied with its world. The exclusion of blacks from politics was not even thought about; it was accepted simply as the natural order of things" (248).

19. The lawyer as southern hero will reemerge in the 1990s in films such as *Mississippi Burning* (1988), *Ghosts of Mississippi* (1996), and *A Time to Kill* (1996), although in these retrospective visions of civil rights, the lawyer/lawman is victorious.

20. Focusing on silent film, Gaines's work on mixed-race cinema in *Fire and Desire* addresses key elements of the southern rape complex and includes outstanding readings of *The Birth of a Nation.* Gaines's work is particularly useful because she employs Deleuze and Guattari's theories from *Anti-Oedipus* and *A Thousand Plateaus,* but she does not include Deleuze's cinematic concepts from *Cinema 1* and *Cinema 2,* which are crucial to my work, nor does she move beyond silent film. Marco Abel's *Violent Affect: Literature, Cinema, and Critique after Representation* (2007) brings together affect theory and violence using Gilles Deleuze's theories, but oddly enough, he does not integrate Deleuze's specifically cinematic work in *Cinema 1* and *Cinema 2,* nor does he investigate southern film. Laura Marks's *Skin of the Film* (2000) is an excellent application of Deleuze's film theory for what she terms "intercultural films," which includes important southern-based films such as *Daughters of the Dust* (2000). Marks's work also takes up Deleuze's cinema theory to elucidate an embodied understanding of film that stresses the role of affect and sensation.

21. Deleuze was heavily influenced by *auteur* theory, as put forth by Cahiers du Cinéma, and his cinema books have been criticized as elitist; however, as Patricia Pisters has demonstrated, his concepts are equally applicable to popular culture, not just "art" films, and therefore applicable to any of the films in this study (Pisters 8, 9).

22. Again, drawing on Bergson, Deleuze understands the perceived image as a bifurcation or forking of time. In order to create memory, a virtual image of the past-present is created alongside an actualized image of the present. In the affection-image, perception registers as a sensation or affect that forms a wider and wider circuit with other virtual images from the past that relate to the image. When the gap or interval of the affection-image has been filled with the actual image and its virtual past, this leads to the action-image, or response in the form of physical action, thought, or emotion. The virtual image expands outward into the past, is contracted into the actual present, and extends into the becoming of the future. In films associated with the time-image, however, this gap cannot be readily filled when the characters and/or audience responds to "pure visual or sounds images" that do not lead to action but instead create a suspension or release of time. The characters become "seers" rather than "doers."

23. The prime figure of the falsifying narrative is the forger because he is in a constant state of becoming, in which there can be no single or absolute truth. This leads beyond good and evil, and the forger is a figure that defies any narrative that attempts to contain him or her. Ultimately, for Deleuze the power of the false is a productive power of becoming, especially for the artist, but he also recognizes in the chain of forgers the connection between the good or truthful man who can never stop lying and the man who lies to enforce his own truth. The connection between these men, as in *Touch of Evil*, is based on betrayal that implicates all parties. As Deleuze explains, the "falsifying narrative . . . shatters the system of judgment because the power of the false (not error or doubt) affects the investigator and witness as much as the person presumed guilty" (*Cinema 2* 133).

24. Deleuze does not discuss "assemblage" in the cinema books; however, critics such as Pisters and Rizzo have clearly demonstrated its applicability to Deleuzian film analysis.

25. These images of hysteria and fear mirror the fear and panic of a Confederate deserter fleeing the battle that unsettle Griffith's earlier Civil War films, especially two of his 1910 films, *The Honor of His Family* and *The House with Closed Shutters*.

26. Certainly, the "dark ravisher" was a cinematic staple in films made famous by Rudolph Valentino in *The Sheik* (George Melford 1921) and *The Son of the Sheik* (George Fitzmaurice 1926) and in the swashbuckling adventure films of swarthy pirates kidnapping wealthy, noblewomen—which also drew on the titillation of the southern rape complex—but these films avoid a direct comparison to American racial politics by employing exotic locales.

27. Dixon only hints at this with Flora—Ben Cameron's little sister who is accosted by Gus—when she puts herself in danger, but for the most innocent of reasons. Against her brother's orders, she goes alone to fetch water and then lingers in the woods to watch the antics of a squirrel, which makes her vulnerable to Gus's advances.

CHAPTER 1. Confederate Abjection in D. W. Griffith's Early Civil War Films and Thomas Dixon's *Clansman*

1. Jack Temple Kirby discusses all three of these early Civil War films yet still maintains that one of the main messages of Griffith's Civil War films is "Dixie as a superior breeding ground for physical courage" (10). Melvyn Stokes (68) and Robert Lang (29) register the importance of Griffith's eleven Biograph films about the Civil War in establishing elements of *The Birth of a*

Nation, such as the use of northern and southern families, battle scenes, and the loyal slave, but do not discuss the problem of southern cowardice. Robert Jackson is the exception to this trend, and he examines the cowardice of Confederate soldiers in *His Family's Honor* and *House with Closed Shutters,* but he emphasizes the courage and honor of the female characters as a precursor to the importance of southern female honor in *The Birth of a Nation* (36–38).

2. Griffith also uses Stoneman as an "enemy" of the South and Lincoln as its "friend." In an intertitle Stoneman also refers to the South as "conquered provinces," but Stoneman does not use the same extensive language of abjection in describing the Confederacy.

3. There are some contemporary accounts that suggest that there was an intertitle and accompanying image of "Lincoln's" plan for colonization of African Americans in Liberia, but if it existed, it was cut (perhaps to stem the criticisms especially from African American critics of the film) and does not appear in the later extant versions of *Birth.* The film thus gestures to, but does not go as far in scope as, Dixon's *Clansman.*

4. The Civil War film was a popular genre between 1909 to 1915, in part because of the renewed interest in war brought about by the fiftieth anniversary of the Civil War. See Gunning, "House" 142; and Chadwick 39–54.

5. From 1911 onward Civil War films started to focus on the Confederate version of the war. See Bowser 178; Ehrlick, 77–78; and Stokes 181–82.

6. The southern rape complex was entrenched in southern politics during the period in which *The Clansman* was published. In North Carolina, the book's setting, even politicians who opposed lynching, such as Governor Charles Aycock, refused to interfere in lynchings that were justified on the basis of a sexual assault on a white woman by a black man (Clegg 77–78).

7. Ironically, earlier in *The Leopard's Spots* Dixon has the white supremacist Rev. John Durham make a similar statement implying that the "old constitution, made by a slave-holding aristocracy," for which the Old South fought, runs counter to "the resistless movement of humanity from the idea of local sovereignty toward nationalism, centralization, solidarity" (332). Scott Romine asserts that even as Dixon romanticizes and praises the Old South, he looks past it to an "all-conquering Saxon" empire (193).

8. For an extensive study of the role and rituals of death during the American Civil War, see Faust, esp. ch. 7, "Accounting: "Our Obligations to the Dead."

9. As Melvyn Stokes points out, Lincoln's "apotheosis" did not emerge until two decades after his death. John Nicolay and John Hay's biography of Lincoln presents him as "an ideal hero and semi-mythical" figure. *The Birth of a Nation,* therefore, relies upon as well as promotes the turn-of-the-century idealization of Lincoln (187).

10. While over one thousand African Americans settled in Liberia in 1866–67, emigration was increasing unpopular in the face of black suffrage, and rather than looking for homes in Africa, many African Americans in 1867 campaigned for the confiscation and redistribution of white-owned lands (Foner, *Reconstruction* 290). For a discussion of the history of African American resistance to colonization, see Forbes.

11. For a discussion of Lincoln's complicated position on colonization, see Fredrickson.

12. For a discussion of the corruption and mismanagement that resulted in the failed attempt at colonization as well as Lincoln's own culpability, see Lockett.

13. Even as late as 1910, William P. Pickett advocated colonization as the solution to the "Negro" problem, using Lincoln's speeches as support.

14. In addition to directing ten Civil War films, Griffith also supervised one and served as producer on three others (Chadwick 44).

15. See Jackson 38–43.

16. For a discussion of *The Honor of His Family, The House with Closed Shutters,* and *Hearts and Swords,* see Courtney 44–46.

17. See Elizabeth Young on cross-dressing in the Civil War (149–94).

18. In one version of the film, when Agnes reaches the battlefield, the horse bolts, but in the version at the Museum of Modern Art there is a direct cut to Agnes approaching the battlefield.

19. Young places the stories and cartoons lampooning Davis's cross-dressing in the context of a cross-dressing female Confederate soldier Loreta Velazquez, arguing that Velazquez's "cross-dressing implicitly literalizes and extends the transvestite terms of [Davis's] humiliation as they had been developed in 'Belle of Richmond' imagery" (183).

20. The southern belle is at best an ambivalent figure in Griffith's pre-*Birth* films, and at times she is a negative character. She threatens to emasculate the southern aristocrat, either by taking over his role through cross-dressing or by preventing him from performing his duties, enticing him away from his post.

21. Critics have often attempted to differentiate between Dixon's and Griffith's motivations for bringing *Birth* to the screen, between Dixon's virulent racism and Griffith's desire to exonerate his father's postwar failure. Ultimately, both motivations are racist in their implications. My aim in this essay is not to minimize Griffith's own racism. In *Birth* and in his early Civil War films he clearly presents the apologist's view of slavery, which depicts slaves as happy in their state and loyal and loving toward their masters.

22. Michael Rogin interprets *Birth* as Griffith's solution to his own psychological oedipal conflicts. The movie honors the father (Griffith's own father was a Confederate officer in the Civil War) yet replaces him with the heroic son. This move is especially important in light of the early Civil War films in which the southern son is seen as not only defeated but cowardly. Although I find it problematic to attempt to psychoanalyze an individual based on his creative work, I find many of Rogin's insights extremely compelling, especially if we look at the cultural work performed by Griffith's films rather than trying to analyze Griffith himself.

23. Before *The Birth of a Nation, The Leopard's Spots,* and *The Clansman* were converted by Dixon into a successful play, which included the conflation of Flora and Marion. The scene in the cellar and the chase sequence with Gus, Flora, and Ben are Griffith's additions. This type of scene is very characteristic of Griffith's style; he often created a sense of the home, typically a place of security, as a claustrophobic scene of entrapment with crosscuts to the danger that confronts the home, in this case the black troops.

24. In the *Judith of Bethulia* Judith, a Jewish widow played by Blanche Sweet, uses her sexuality to infiltrate the enemy camp, where she entices Holofernes and then cuts off his head with his own sword as he lies in a drunken stupor. In *The Avenging Conscience* Blanche Sweet again plays the female lead, although instead of being a strong woman, she is a "passive sexual target of oedipal rivalry"; however, she is still a threat because "as the subject, object, and eliciter [*sic*] of desire,

Sweet as Annabel disempowers both herself and the two male protagonists. Their collective disturbance generates madness and parricide" (Rogin 264). In what turns out to be merely a guilty nightmare, the nephew (also played by Henry Walthall) kills his uncle because he refused to allow the two lovers to marry. Walthall, who is tracked down by the police detective and trapped in an isolated cabin, prepares to hang himself, while Annabel, out of guilt, jumps to her death.

25. Sylvester Russell, columnist for the *Chicago Defender,* maintained that the presence of mulattoes in Dixon's work would backfire because it showed the "Southerner's hatred of the sins of his own father" (qtd. in Everett 67).

26. Although Griffith never directly said so, Dixon's stated mission in *Birth* was to make whites equate any form of racial equality with interracial marriage. The unstated assumption set forth in *Birth* is that all forms of interracial marriage constitute rape. Both Griffith and Dixon stress that it is intermarriage between black and white, not between white North and South, that is the real threat (Lang 12).

27. In *The Leopard's Spots* Flora is the young daughter of a lower-class Confederate veteran. She is abducted, raped, and left for dead, while her assailant is burned alive.

28. At the war's end many southern states established Black Codes, which required African Americans to have written proof of employment and prevented anyone from offering work to an African American already under contract (Foner, *Reconstruction* 198–99). The Black Codes were abolished under Radical Reconstruction, but the end of Reconstruction brought back laws, especially vagrancy laws and "antienticement" laws, that were enforced primarily to control black labor (587–98).

29. While Wilson resisted bailing out cotton farmers, he was able to show his support and sympathy for the South symbolically through the White House showing of *Birth.* The film is ostensibly presented as antiwar through the epilogue, in which the god of war is defeated by Christ, the Prince of Peace; however, the film's attempt to reunite white America through a shared sympathy for the defeated South was just the kind of political propaganda that could help to rally the southern states in support of a war in which Americans fought together against an external foe. It was also the kind of propaganda that in 1915 helped to revive the Klan, which saw not only blacks but also immigrants as a threat to the "American" way of life.

CHAPTER 2. Taking the South Out of the Southern Rape Complex in *The Story of Temple Drake*

1. In 1933 the furor over the release of *The Story of Temple Drake* helped to strengthen the Production Code—Hollywood's self-imposed code of censorship—and its enforcement under Joe Breen, who in turn prevented the movie's rerelease (Doherty 114–18; Vasey 124–25; Miller 76–78; Vieira 148–50). The film was not shown again until 1958. It is still associated with the pre-Code period and was shown in 1999 as part of a pre-Code film festival. As recently as July 2005, it was shown in New York at the Film Forum. For a detailed discussion of the Hayes Office's involvement in *The Story of Temple Drake,* see Binggeli.

2. D. Matthew Ramsey discusses the advertisements for *The Story of Temple Drake* that prominently link Faulkner's name to the film and even directly connect the film to *Sanctuary,* despite Breen's order not to use the name of the novel (20).

3. The legacy of *The Birth of a Nation* is particularly salient for films such as *The Story of Temple Drake* because *The Birth of the Nation* is also the birth of Hollywood appropriations of the South and southern literature. Although Griffith did not have the Hayes Office to deal with, he too had the problem of how to adapt for the screen a graphic rape scene and lynching, as depicted in Thomas Dixon's *Clansman*. He had to take into account the sensibility of his audience, judging how far he could go in horrifying his (white) viewers without losing their sympathy.

4. In a letter to the editor on 15 February 1931, appearing within days of the publication of *Sanctuary*, Faulkner writes, "Lynching is an American trait" (Polk and McMillen 5). To explain the motivation behind lynching, Faulkner refers indirectly to the "southern rape complex," explaining that the crime "in compensation of which lynching occurs," is "Sacredness of womanhood . . . Not a thing, but a reaction" (qtd. in Polk and McMillen 5). Unlike *Sanctuary*, which presents a white perpetrator, in his letter to the Memphis paper Faulkner assumes a black male perpetrator and a white "America" that instigates the lynching. Although Faulkner qualifies his comments to the paper—saying, "No balanced man can, I believe, hold any moral brief for lynching"—he does seem to regard lynching as inevitable and as a fairly effective means to bring about justice. In closing his letter, he again maintains, "I hold no brief for lynching," but at the same time he equates the "justice" served by both mobs and juries: "There is one curious thing about mobs. Like our juries, they have a way of being right" (6). Faulkner's comments were in response to an earlier letter written to the paper by W. H. James of Starkville, Mississippi, a black man who wrote in appreciation of the work of the antilynching movement led by Mrs. J. Morgan Spense, a southern white women. James's letter (his appreciation of the white woman's attempt to protect black men from lynching) becomes the mediation through which the white man (Faulkner) addresses the white woman, putting her back into the position of object of the debate (the symbolic center of lynching) rather than as an independent southerner working for political change. In other words, the letter, like the southern rape complex, is a way for a white man to address the conduct of both black men and white women.

5. Cotton that was selling for eighteen cents per pound in 1929 was less than six cents in 1933 (Wolters 9).

6. As Jacquelyn Dowd Hall argues, the implied punishment for those who violated the taboos included white southern women (333–40): "A woman who had just been raped, or who had been apprehended in a clandestine interracial affair, or whose male relatives were pretending that she had been raped, stood on display before the whole community. Here was the quintessential Woman as victim: polluted, 'ruined' for life, the object of fantasy and secret contempt" (335).

7. F. Scott Fitzgerald's *Great Gatsby* (1926) highlights the role of cars as showy symbols of new money and bootleg gin as the source of Gatsby's wealth.

8. Critics have also been rather hard on Temple and seem to accept Ruby's characterization. Kathryn Lee Seidel suggests that Temple's hysterical reactions at the plantation reflect a narcissistic attempt to attract attention to herself at all costs (*Southern Belle* 106).

9. The image of a cat would later be employed in *The Women* (1939) to condemn gossipers who threaten the marriage of the "good woman," but in the case of *The Women* there is a clear distinction between the meddling women (who also get their comeuppance) and the good woman who gets her husband back.

10. Earlier in *The Sound and the Fury* (1929), Faulkner explicitly racializes the "wanton" belle, Caddy. Even though Caddy is still living at home, her promiscuous behavior threatens the reputation of the Compson family. Quentin thinks of it in racial terms as he asks, "*Why won't you bring him to the house, Caddy? Why must you do like nigger women do in the pasture the ditch the dark woods hot hidden furious in the dark woods?*" (113–14). Thanks to Jay Watson for pointing out this connection between Caddy and Temple.

11. For a recent discussion of Popeye's ambiguous racial representation, see Guttman 15–34; and Duvall 131–47. Doreen Fowler suggests that the "bootleggers and prostitutes in *Sanctuary* function as substitutes for a nearly invisible black community. Quite possibly without conscious awareness, Faulkner racializes the men and women of Frenchman's Bend" (422). While the black community is significantly missing from *Sanctuary* and Popeye is clearly coded as "black," not all the characters at Frenchman's Bend are associated with "blackness." The hillbilly, white trash bootlegger is a stereotype associated with southern whites and not with blacks. Visually, the old man lifting the jug is an image that continued in popular culture with Al Capp's *Dogpatch,* the TV series *The Real McCoys,* and even *The Beverly Hillbillies,* just as the idiot Tommy represents the same stereotype of the inbreeding hillbilly banjo player in *Deliverance.*

12. Jerry Williamson traces the hillbilly back to George Washington Harris's Sut Lovingood, "a tall lanky east Tennessee ridgerunner," "short on manners, intimate with dirt and ignorant of 'progress'" (33). The hillbilly, according to Williamson, "gives the horse-laugh to middle-class respectability. He's absurdly and delightfully free" (4). The hillbilly "drinks hard liquor . . . He's theatrically lazy but remains virile. He nearly always possesses the wherewithal for physical violence—especially involving dogs and guns . . . He reminds us symbolically of filth, of disgusting bodily functions. Why else is he so frequently pictured with outhouses?" (2–3).

13. The mass media, including the tabloids and the movies, helped to promote the image of the glamorized gangster (Rosow 113–18).

14. Skal maintains that the European setting is a thinly veiled America, but *The Story of Temple Drake* brings the horror film to America (37–61).

15. Universal Studios pioneered the horror film in the 1930s with its release of *Frankenstein* and *Dracula,* but Paramount, which produced *The Story of Temple Drake,* responded with its own horror hit, *Dr. Jekyll and Mr. Hyde,* for which Struss was the cinematographer.

16. For a discussion of the importance of staircases in German Expressionist films, see Eisner 131.

17. I would like to thank Judith L. Sensibar for alerting me to the reference to Mex in the storyboard.

18. The moment in the novel when Benbow most identifies with Temple as rape victim is directly linked to his own incestuous desire for his stepdaughter, Little Belle. As Sabine Sielke maintains, "We repeatedly find Benbow in one particular position: bent over a watery surface or looking directly into a mirror from which the object of his incestuous desire stares back at him" (99).

CHAPTER 3. Believing in Mammy: *Sanctuary,* the Movie

1. In October 1933 Faulkner wrote to Harrison Smith: "I have another bee now, and a good title, I think: *Requiem for a Nun.* It will be about a nigger woman. It will be a little on the esoteric

side, like *As I Lay Dying*" (Blotner, *Faulkner* 75). Although the publisher would announce in March 1934 that the *Requiem for a Nun* would be postponed, two early drafts were found, dated 17 December 1933, that link the story to *Sanctuary.* One draft begins with the description of the jail, as does *Requiem for a Nun,* and the other uses elements from *Sanctuary* that link both to the lynching of a black man in Oxford when Faulkner was eleven years old (Polk 238–43).

2. Faulkner, *Sanctuary* 47. For a more extensive reading of the gender and racial implications of "that black man," see Duvall 131–47.

3. Faulkner, *Sanctuary* 289.

4. See also Morrison, "*Requiem's* Ruins."

5. For a discussion of abjection and black male rape during slavery, see Scott 126–52. Kristeva's theory of abjection has been used productively to explain the contradictions inherent in national identity, especially in terms of race and ethnicity. See Duck 93–95, 108–14; Romine, "Darkness Visible."

6. See also Roberts 3–15. For a discussion of violence against black women during Presidential Reconstruction in Texas, see Kosary 55–78.

7. From the perspective of African American women, Corrie Claiborne argues that Kristeva's notion of abjection as the first step toward becoming a subject—because "to be an abject is to be on the verge of becoming"—does not hold true for African American women, who have historically been cast as abject on the verge of becoming an object for dominant white Western culture. "It is the move to challenge the definition, to separate black women from this abject history and propose a counter-history that opens up the space for black female presence" (32).

8. Maeve McCusker, in her analysis of early Creole novels, examines the vilification of the black mother: "These women have necessarily to be shown to be repulsive, filthy, and morally hideous in old age in order to counteract the fascination they provoke, and to embody a phantasized repellent to the disavowed desires of the white male" (75).

9. As Margaret Mitchell writes at the end of *Gone with the Wind:* "Suddenly [Scarlett] wanted Mammy desperately, as she had wanted her when she was a little girl, wanted the broad bosom on which to lay her head, the gnarled black hand on her hair. Mammy, the last link with the old days" (1024). For a detailed discussion of the role of the mammy in popular culture from the 1820s to 1935, see Wallace-Sanders.

10. See Welling; and Wallace-Sanders 118–32.

11. For an excellent discussion not only of how mammy enforces the rules but of how these rules have been incorporated into modern popular culture, see Richardson "Mammy's Mules."

12. On the early mammy figure in minstrelsy, see Toll 79–80; for a detailed history of the postbellum mammy, see McElya.

13. Referring to a 12 May 1923 article in the *Chicago Defender,* McElya explains, "The figure of the mammy stood at the place where affection for her and sexual violence met and became indistinguishable from each other" (161).

14. Using contemporary comparative data, Michael Johnson argues that infant mortality among slaves was often caused by sudden infant death syndrome, which may have been aggravated by the poor diet and strenuous labor of pregnant slave women.

15. As we have seen, just as the mammy is credited with and/or blamed for maintaining the

very hierarchies of race, class, and gender in the Old South that excluded her from the role of lady, Nancy is also credited with or blamed for preserving the rotting Gowan family.

16. Temple maintains that the failure to be listened to is what creates "arsonists and rapists and murderers and thieves and the rest of the anti-social enemies" (138). If we apply this logic to the early events of Temple's life, it oddly suggests that if only Popeye had had someone to listen to him, he would not be a rapist and murderer.

17. For a good discussion of the different readings of Gavin's role, see Ladd. Kelly Lynch Reames suggests that the power Gavin achieves in his role as confessor makes his motives suspect (34).

18. For a discussion of *scientia sexualis,* see Foucault 54–73. As Reames suggests, "Gavin wants to force sex into discourse" (34). Watson also notes the convergence of "forensic, religious, and psychoanalytic motifs" in act 2, but he sees Gavin as playing a positive role in helping Temple to acknowledge and take responsibility for her past (*Forensic Fictions* 190–207).

19. As Foucault explains, confessional discourse comes from "an obligatory act of speech which, under some imperious compulsion, breaks the bonds of discretion or forgetfulness"; however, "the agency of domination does not reside in the one who speaks . . . but in the one who questions and is not supposed to know" (62). Reames suggests that the power Gavin achieves in his role as confessor makes his motives suspect (34).

20. In "That Evening Sun" Nancy was already on her way to jail when she saw the banker and began yelling at him, but in *Requiem for a Nun* Temple indicates that Nancy is put in jail because of her encounter with the banker.

21. Although we cannot assume consistency of characters and events across all of Faulkner's works, he does have Temple specifically mention Nancy's history as portrayed in "That Evening Sun."

22. The story was first published in March 1931 in the *Mercury* as "That Evening Sun Go Down." Faulkner was persuaded by the editor H. L. Mencken to change the name "Jesus" to "Jubah," but in subsequent printings it was restored to the original. For a discussion of the different versions of the story, see Manglaviti 649–54.

23. Any attempt to assess Nancy's motives, however, is based on speculation because the laconic Nancy never directly addresses her motives; it is the other characters and the critics who fill in the blanks. In many ways Nancy and Temple have traded places. In *Sanctuary* we view Temple almost completely from the outside, being given very little understanding of how she feels and thinks beyond a description of how she physically reacts to what is happening to her and her final hallucinatory monologue about the rape. Characters and critics again have to fill in the blank, either condemning her or sympathizing with her. In *Requiem for a Nun* Temple—though perhaps not voluntarily—tells us all about what she is thinking, even if much of her dialogue is an attempt to evade the topic, and though Gavin also fills in many of the details, it is Nancy who remains an enigma.

24. Temple traces the origins of her sin back to her decision to "go to a baseball game" eight years ago and her decision to slip off the train. Tellingly, however, even as Temple accepts blame, she undermines it. Admittedly, she violates a cardinal rule of conduct for a belle when she leaves the train unchaperoned, but as the origin of sin, it is one of her most innocuous acts. As mentioned earlier, she never accounts for her real crime of condemning an innocent man to death, or in this case a fate worse than death.

25. Richard C. Moreland also sees Nancy's act as repetition of her past trauma, but he interprets it in a more positive light as her attempt to fight back and to mourn for her own lost child "by challenging Temple to 'fight back' for another child Nancy has come to love—Bucky" (236).

26. The jail scene in *Sanctuary* (the movie) is reminiscent of another filmic adaptation of Faulkner's work, the 1947 *Intruder in the Dust,* a film in which Faulkner also dealt with lynching. In the jail scene in the movie version of *Intruder*—whose script Faulkner helped to edit—there is a shot of Chick and Lucas Beauchamp as they talk through the jail cell's door. (Faulkner wrote to Bennett Cerf concerning the filmic version of *Intruder in the Dust,* "I rewrote, re-arranged, the dialogue in the jail cell sequences" [qtd. in Blotner, *Faulkner* 502]). The shot symbolizes their cooperation at the same time it establishes their separation: both pairs of hands cling to the bars that separate them (black from white and free from imprisoned). Then, in a tight two shot in which the characters literally see eye to eye, the lattice of the jail door between them creates a kind of iris shot of Lucas's eye as he explains to Chick what he must do to free Lucas from the charges and also from the lynch mob. Lucas and Chick must work together to see that justice is done, but they still must work outside the segregated system that, like lawyer Stevens, cannot imagine Lucas's innocence.

27. Deleuze maintains that an extreme close-up of only part of the face or body, or even an object (such as hands or a bar), can exhibit facticity (*Cinema 1* 97).

CHAPTER 4. The Power of the False in *Touch of Evil*

1. In addition to the novel *Badge of Evil,* Paul Monash wrote a screenplay dated 24 July 1956 for Universal Studios. John C. Stubbs asserts that Welles used both sources for his own screenplay, dated 5 February 1957, because he incorporated elements of the novel not included in the Monash adaptation and also included elements of the Monash screenplay not included in the novel (20). Welles places the film in Los Robles and augments the racial tension by changing Holt to Vargas, a Mexican official, the Grandi family into a Mexican drug cartel, Quinlan into a racist cop, and Shayon into Sanchez. For a detailed discussion of the differences between the three versions, see Stubbs, "Evolution."

2. For a discussion of the elements of the movement-image, see the introduction.

3. There are now three versions of *Touch of Evil:* the 1958 theatrical version (95 mins.), which was reedited by the studio while Welles was out of the country and includes extra scenes not directed by Welles; the longer pre-studio version (110 mins.), discovered in 1975, which includes some of the material that was cut in the studio version; and the 1998 version, which was reedited using Welles's fifty-eight-page memo to the studio, in which he explains in details what he was trying to achieve and why the changes should be restored to his original version. I am using the 1998 version, as it follows most closely Welles's suggestions for revision in his memo to the studio. Unless otherwise noted, all quotations are directly from the 1998 version of *Touch of Evil.* For a discussion of the differences between the 1958 and 1975 versions, see Belton.

4. For Heath the other characters symbolize various extreme responses to desire in the form of the fetish or hysteria or through what Heath deems a kind of gender confusion or ultimately annihilation.

5. Nericcio identifies Los Robles as on the U.S. side of the border, but as you watch the film, it is difficult to ascertain which side of the border Los Robles is on.

6. In Lacan's theory of the mirror stage of Imaginary identification, the child narcissistically misrecognizes the m/other/mirror image as his or her own intact body, in much the same way as a fetish serves as a mask for what is lacking (the mother's penis in the case of the fetish, the intact body in the case of identification). But this very misrecognition/mask implies the recognition of the lack that it necessitates and opens up the fear of the Other, whose face threatens to show through the screen, therefore creating both pleasure/mastery and anxiety/aggression.

7. As Homi Bhabha explains: "As a form of splitting and multiple belief, the stereotype requires, for its successful signification, a continual and repetitive chain of other stereotypes. The process by which the metaphoric 'masking' is inscribed on a lack which must then be concealed gives the stereotype both its fixity and its phantasmatic quality" (110–11).

8. Donald Pease addresses these issues in his analysis of *Touch of Evil*, but Pease argues that Bhabha's analysis is too ahistorical to accomplish these goals.

9. As John C. Stubbs explains, this dialogue was in the novel but not the Monash screenplay, indicating that Welles put it back into his version (22).

10. This reference to a shoe actually begins by repeating the first five words of the nursery rhyme about shoes: "There was an old woman who lived in a shoe" (Jack).

11. Furthermore, the white control of "black" representation is reinforced in the plot of the film in which the white "scalawags" incite the otherwise docile former slaves to violence.

12. Heston's inability to speak Spanish has even become part of pop culture. In the movie *Man in the Chair* (2007) Christopher Plummer's character, who used to work in Hollywood, yells at the screen during a revival screening of *Touch of Evil*, mocking Heston's performance as a Mexican and his inability to speak Spanish.

13. Pease argues that Sanchez, because he worked on Linnekar's construction project in Mexico, is a migrant worker. But nothing in the film indicates that Sanchez worked in Mexico. Pease also maintains that "Susan, who has become a criminal suspect released into his [Vargas's] protective custody, has becomes the personification of the emergency powers of the state" (99), but Susan is no longer a suspect.

14. The plot of the movement-image, unlike the time-image, facilitates clichés, which are then solidified into generic features of the western, screwball comedy, romance, or film noir. *Touch of Evil* has been called a classic film noir (Stubbs 19), and Welles demonstrates his mastery of film noir techniques, settings, subject matter, and characters: in his use of black and white chiaroscuro; seedy bars, strip joints, hotels, and back alleys; violent murders, betrayals, and corruption; and dangerous dames, crooked cops, and loyal but disillusioned sidekicks. But Welles gives the noir style his own signature with his inclusion of sequence shots, depth of focus, distorting wide-angle lens, and soviet montage.

15. In the novel, of course, Shayon and Tara are not guilty. In the Monash screenplay Shayon (though not Mexican) is guilty. The confession takes place off-screen as well, and when Chief Gould relays the news, he explains: "Shayon just confessed. Linneker's daughter—it was her idea" (Stubbs 24) (note that the spelling of *Linneker* in the novel becomes *Linnekar* in the film). In the film there is no mention of Marcia, only that Sanchez confessed.

16. Menzies is the only one to offer a logical motive when he states that Sanchez was afraid that Mr. Linnekar would change the will, but this is stated in one of the many instances of the characters' talking over each other, and this line of reasoning is never mentioned again.

17. Critics often make the comparison between Susan and Zita, the stripper, as examples of dangerous female sexuality; however, Zita is also the one in danger because of her relationship to Linnekar.

18. The forger of becoming "makes the direct time-image visible; he provokes undecidable alternatives and inexplicable differences between the true and the false, and thereby imposes a power of the false as adequate to time, in contrast to any form of the true which would control time" (Deleuze, *Cinema 2* 132).

19. But the string of forgers need not be limited to a single film: Deleuze sees a pattern of forgers across Welles's film oeuvre, especially in his film adaptations of Shakespeare's *Macbeth* and *Henry IV*. (Deleuze uses Robin Woods's insights about Welles's Shakespearean adaptations in his discussion of the role of the forger in Welles's work.)

20. This breakdown of the system of justice is most obviously seen in *Mr. Arkadin* (1955), in which the title character is an amnesiac detective hired to kill all the people from his own past who could identify him; in the "infinite sham of justice" in *The Trial* (1962), based on the Kafka story; and especially in *F for Fake* (1973), a fake documentary about a fake biography of a forger, in which Welles as narrator appears in the guise of a conjuror.

21. For a discussion of Welles's memo to Universal, see Welles and Rosenbaum. For a detailed account of the difference between released version and preview version, see Belton.

22. This scene references other absent mothers; just before this, as Susan and Vargas come down the stairs, Vargas, in an act of double consciousness, views his world as a reflection of the face of Susan's mother: "I can just imagine your mother's face if she could see our honeymoon hotel." Perhaps more problematically, Vargas's own mother is never mentioned, and we do not know how she will view having an Anglo daughter-in-law. Another important missing mother is Mrs. Linnekar, who is never mentioned either, though the disdain in Marcia's voice when she mentions not being acquainted with her father's girlfriends could indicate a more personal motive for Linnekar's murder: that Marcia was punishing her father for his treatment of her mother.

CHAPTER 5. "A Man Like that Doesn't Deserve Civil Rights": Systemic Violence in *Cape Fear*

1. The justification for lynching in the South, as put forth in *The Birth of a Nation* and *The Clansman,* was that the end of slavery also abolished the master-slave relationship that was necessary to "control" blacks and that national laws (as martial law) during Reconstruction did not protect its white citizens, particularly its white women.

2. For a comparison of *To Kill a Mockingbird* and *Cape Fear,* see Graham 160–64.

3. While the affection-image produces pure affect in any-space-whatever, which is then actualized in the action-image as modes of behavior in a determined milieu, the impulse-image comprises elementary impulses from an originary world (*Cinema 1* 121).

4. Mitchum played a similar character in *Night of the Hunter,* an itinerate "preacher" who moved from town to town marrying widows and then killing them. Robert De Niro drew from

Mitchum's performance in both *Cape Fear* and *Night of the Hunter* for his own version of Cady.

5. Two years after *Cape Fear* came out, Charles Fenster was arrested three times for vagrancy in New York City. Although he was acquitted on all three charges, he appealed his case, and in 1967 the New York Court of Appeals declared the state's vagrancy laws unconstitutional. The court ruled that vagrancy "in no way impinges on the rights of others," concluding that "the New York vagrancy statue overreaches the proper limitations of the police power and violates the requirements of due process of Law" (Murtagh 51, 52).

6. Ultimately, however, MacCannell limits the power of patriarchy to the unconscious, not the law: "That a Max Cady can and does erupt from within modern society as a brutal, self-appointed enforcer of male mastery over women prompts us to realize that archaic patriarchal Law persists—in the unconscious: in Cady's and that of his female victim" (60). Here MacCannell comes dangerously close to blaming the victim. Even though MacCannell acknowledges the rape shield laws that will begin in the 1970s, in defining democratic, modern law as based on freedom, the thrust of her argument accepts the film's basic premise that the law is helpless to save Diane: Cady "forces us to recognize that family 'law' retains enormous power over modern subjective life" because "Cady has not fundamentally transgressed the psychical law that grants a primal Father ultimate power over the girl's unconscious and programs her reaction in moments of fear . . . She remains very much a subject of the power and prestige of a (legally outmoded) patriarchal order" (59–60). But even modern laws are not based solely on freedoms; in the 1960s modern law is very capable of limiting freedoms, particularly for African Americans.

7. In Greek mythology tritons used their horn as harbingers for the gods, to calm or disturb the ocean or to frighten enemies. We can interpret the tritons as either "warning" the town of the danger Cady represents or as characteristic of Cady himself.

8. Frances M. Nevins documents how difficult it was to prove "rape" under Georgia law, suggesting that Cady's attempt to blackmail Peggy into having sex with him might still have been construed as consent in the absence of signs of physical abuse. Verbal refusal was not enough to support lack of consent: "In order that the offense might constitute rape, she must have resisted with all her power and kept up that resistance as long as she had strength" (Nevins 642).

CHAPTER 6. "Blind Spots": The Visual Logic and Historical Context of *To Kill a Mockingbird*

1. Other important films dealt with rape trials (*Anatomy of a Murder* [1959]) and lynching (the film adaptation of Faulkner's *Intruder in the Dust* [1949]), but none dealt directly with the trial of an innocent black man accused of raping a white woman.

2. President George W. Bush cited Atticus's number one status when he awarded Harper Lee the Presidential Medal of Freedom in 2008. *To Kill a Mockingbird* may also have such a lasting impact, in part because the novel is still regularly taught in middle and high school, to such an extent that teaching the novel has become a filmic trope of the American classroom: films that focus on the classroom setting, such as *Bad Teacher* or *Freedom Writers*, routinely feature *To Kill a Mockingbird* as the topic of class discussion.

3. Mary McDonagh Murphy in *Scout, Atticus, and Boo,* interviewed prominent people about how the book had impacted their lives. As R. Barton Palmer asserts, not until 2007 was there a

collection of essays that dealt with Lee's literary career. For an overview of early critical reception, see Palmer 239–56. Recent collections of essays on *To Kill a Mockingbird* include Myer; Petry; and Bloom. For a discussion of the impact of *To Kill a Mockingbird* on the law, see Engar 66–80. As Engar explains, *To Kill a Mockingbird* has been the subject of countless discussions in legal journals and book, most of which have upheld Atticus as a paragon of legal and ethical virtue. Even those who recognize his failings still hold him up as a role model because of his integrity and dedication. A notable exception is Steven Lubet, who maintains that Atticus resorts to the "she wanted it" defense in his depiction of Mayella as the sexual aggressor and uses her status as a lower-class woman to question her morality (1345–48, 1362). Lubet nevertheless maintains that Atticus provides a "moral archetype" of the lawyer (1340).

4. For a discussion of this shift, see Metress. In his own defense Monroe Freedman rejects the notion of "presentism" and takes Atticus to task for his complacent acceptance of Jim Crow segregation as both a lawyer and a member of the state legislature: "the terrorizing of the Levy family [that Atticus dismisses as evidence of the danger of the Klan presence in Maycomb], the attempted lynching of Tom Robinson, and the apartheid that Atticus Finch practiced every day of his life—those things are wrong today, and they were wrong in Maycomb, Alabama, in the 1930s" (477).

5. Charles J. Shields, Lee's biographer, describes Amasa Coleman as a centrist Democrat, "an advocate of States' rights, and a fiscal conservative" whose two special interests were "finance and morality" (66). In 1935 (which coincides with the time of the novel) Lee voted for compulsory sterilization for "those suffering from perversions, constitutional psychopathic personalities or marked departures from normal mentality," which would include a "sexual pervert, Sadist, homosexualist, Masochist, Sodomist, or any other grave form of sexual perversion"; at the same time, Lee voted to ban voluntary sterilization as a means of birth control (67).

6. I am not suggesting that Lee herself was a civil rights activist, only that the novel presents a historical critique that demonstrates Atticus's own legal blind spots in terms of racial equality and the law. Although she supported Martin Luther King Jr., she rejected the actions of the Freedom Riders as inciting violence and seeking publicity (Shields 223).

7. Jennifer Murray's article "More than One Way to (Mis)Read a *Mockingbird*" points out that critics have too often filled in "the disturbing blanks, smooth[ed] over contradictions, or simply [misread] the text," which includes ignoring Atticus's moments of naïveté (76, 87). See also Gladwell 57–65. Gladwell compares Atticus's racial politics to that of James "Big Jim" Folsom, governor of Alabama, who, like the pro-Klan populists, was against the Big Mules. Although Folsom was more liberal in his dealings with African Americans (he worked toward enfranchising blacks, proposed equal pay for black and white teachers, and commuted the sentences of blacks when he considered the jury verdict unfair), he was not a civil rights activist and still believed in the superiority of whites (57–58). But Gladwell assumes that Lee's and Atticus's views are the same and that therefore the novel only inadvertently presents a critique of Atticus.

8. Patrick Chura provided one of the earliest treatments of the historical present of the novel's publication, including the importance of *Brown v. Board of Education* and the Emmett Till trial of 1955.

9. For a discussion of how the Scottsboro trial helped to redefine rape in American culture, see Estelle Freedman's chapter "Scottsboro and Its Legacies," in *Redefining Rape*.

10. Monroe Freedman takes issue with Atticus's characterization, given the 1915 lynching of Leo Frank, during whose trial crowds outside yelled, "Hang the Jew." Freedman maintains that Levy would certainly be aware of this case and fear for his own life (473–75).

11. This is one of the moments in which the fictional Atticus diverges from Mr. Lee, who actually confronted a group of one hundred Klansmen marching in Monroeville before the 1934 elections. Lee was said to have threatened to give them "a drubbing in one of his editorials." After the exchange with Lee, although the group did not disband, they did agree to drop their "militant pose and walked the rest of the way like pedestrians" (Shields 57).

12. Not all the early criticism of *To Kill a Mockingbird* was positive; a notable exception is the *New Yorker* critic Brendan Gill, who describes the moral of the film to be that "while ignorant rednecks mustn't take the law into their own hands, it's all right for *nice* people to do so" (qtd. in Shields 227).

13. The novel shows its readers how to love and even admire Atticus, as a father, friend, and lawyer, even though he is wrong about important historical and political issues, and the novel shows us over and over just how wrong he is. Atticus sums up this very position when he admonishes the children that Mrs. Dubose, even though she is an overt racist, is courageous because she fights to overcome her morphine addiction before she dies (Lee 128). Atticus explains, in reference to the "war" they will fight against racial prejudice: "It's different this time . . . This time we aren't fighting the Yankees, we're fighting our friends. But remember this, no matter how bitter things get, they're still our friends and this is still our home" (87).

14. Barton Palmer maintains that "after the film's release it became quite impossible to separate Peck from the role. In a sense he had become Atticus" (196).

15. Producer Alan J. Pakula teamed up with director Robert Mulligan and Brentwood Productions, formed by Gregory Peck, and Lee's own company, Atticus Productions, to produce the film for Universal Studios (Shields 202; Palmer 118). Foote wanted Atticus's closing argument to represent his limitations as a man who wrestled with his own prejudice, not a "noble man" who talks down to those less enlightened (Palmer 228). After the first showing of the film, Peck wrote a memo to his agent, George Chasin, and to Universal executive Mel Tucker complaining that Atticus was not edited to maximize his dramatic effect, that he did not get enough screen time, and that the focus too often was on the child actors who could not carry the scene (Palmer 204–07).

16. Charles J. Shields maintains that Hollywood "heightened the intensity of the novel's social criticism" (205–06), although the critique of Atticus is more muted in the film, as are the important references to key historical events; nonetheless, the historical setting of the film still invokes many of these events.

17. Jennifer Murray asserts that Scout, "moving from six to nine years of age does not undergo radical transformation, does not move from childhood to adolescence" and that only Jem moves from childhood to adolescence (80), but even looking back on the events of the novel, Jem's vision remains limited and personal, unlike Scout's broader view of things.

18. At various times he oversteps his role as audience when he leaves gifts for the children in the hollow tree, sews Jem's pants and leaves them waiting for him, and brings Scout a blanket as she stands shivering in the snow watching Miss Maudie's house burn down.

19. For an analysis of Wesley's "General Rules," see Nausner 43–60.

20. For a discussion of the role of rum as currency in the slave trade, see Blue.

21. Despite her crucial role in the novel as an indictment of white middle-class racism, Aunt Alexandra is completely missing from the film, and we are given no hint about the family background of the Finches beyond the nuclear family nor any history of the slave trade in Alabama or the removal of Native Americans. In her absence the responsibility for racism falls exclusively on the lower and working classes: the Ewells and rural farmers. This localization of racism in the lower classes is a trend that recurs in films throughout the civil rights period and beyond.

22. It is also a similarity to Boo that, like the others, actually indicates their differences. Boo is also charged under the Ladies' Law for disturbing the peace by locking the deputy in the courthouse outhouse because the deputy said that the teen cursed so loudly that "some lady must have heard them" (Lee 11). A charge that is comical in relation to Boo is menacing in the case of Ewell.

23. When Jem holds Atticus accountable as a state legislator and demands that he change the law, Atticus states only that it is not so easy.

24. Horton sidestepped the defense's claim of "mob sentiment" at the trial as well as the "alleged exclusion of negroes from jury service" (the reason that the Supreme Court would use to revoke the verdict of the third trial).

25. Although after Horton's June 1933 decision some state newspapers such as the *Birmingham Post* supported him, declaring that he showed that "political considerations mean nothing to him whatever," by October public sentiment had shifted (Carter 270–71).

26. A new trial began in November, presided over by Judge William Washington Callahan.

27. Atticus in this moment deviates most strongly from Amasa Lee, upon whom the character is based. If Atticus could not seriously consider women participating in the legal system, Mr. Lee, on the other hand, encouraged both his daughters to go into law, and while Harper decided against it (even though the novel indicates her continued interest in the workings of the law), her sister, Alice, was one of the first female lawyers in Monroeville and was a partner in her father's firm. Not only a trailblazer in the law, Alice, unlike her forefathers and her father, also tackled religious racial discrimination and helped to integrate the Methodist Church, despite her father's initial belief that the church should not comment on issues of civil rights (Shields 126).

28. Although Sundquist states that the novel "is a confirmation of the hoary defense of lynching offered in the United States Senate by Alabama's J. Thomas Heflin" (*Strangers* 174), it is only in a footnote that he mentions Atticus's reference to Heflin, which he dismisses as a "joke" (567).

29. Specifically regarding the Scottsboro trial, Heflin sent a wire to Attorney General Knight concurring with the "keen resentment that you feel over the strange and annoying action of Judge Horton" and offering his help in unseating Horton from the trial. Heflin asserted that "this dallying about with the Scottsboro rapists is a humiliating insult to the white race in Alabama and the very worst thing that could happen to the law-abiding Negroes of this state" (Carter 271).

30. Furthermore, many of the trials that resulted from the anti-flogging campaign, which involved the flogging of African American victims, were either dismissed or the defendants were acquitted by all-white juries; two of the Klansman convicted of the flogging of Jeff Calloway had their convictions overturned by the state supreme court in 1929 (Feldman 158, 216).

31. In the 1928 presidential campaign he supported Republican Herbert Hoover over the Democratic candidate, Al Smith, because Smith was a Catholic. In light of Heflin's vitriolic attacks on Smith, the Alabama Democratic Party expelled Heflin, refusing to let him run in the Democratic primary for reelection; as an independent candidate, Heflin was defeated by John H. Bankhead II. FDR apparently did not hold a grudge, however, and Heflin was appointed special representative to the Federal Housing Administration.

32. Only a month later the *Monroe Journal* announced that the federal government would fund a major regional livestock research laboratory at Auburn as a result of the Bankhead Bill that was passed in 1936 ("New Livestock Laboratory Will Be Constructed Soon"). John H. Bankhead II, the U.S. senator from Alabama and a New Deal Democrat who defeated Heflin, represented the drive for diversification in Alabama. Bankhead supported the Agricultural Adjustment Act of 1933, which provided subsidies for cotton farmers who limited the number of acres they planted in hopes of raising prices, but when such voluntary limits did not result in an overall drop in production, he was willing to create mandatory limits on the actual amount of cotton produced and cosponsored the Bankhead Cotton Control Act of 1934 (which was later repealed) with his brother William, a U.S. representative from Alabamians. The measure was still an attempt to raise cotton prices, but many conservative Alabamians were opposed to this type of federal intervention characteristic of the New Deal ("John Hollis Bankhead II").

33. Even before the Depression, the boll weevil infestation that decimated the cotton crop had caused Alabama farmers to begin diversifying. Enterprise, Alabama, actually erected a statue to the boll weevil precisely because it precipitated crop diversification, thus inadvertently preparing farmers for the economic turmoil to come.

34. Monroe County's efforts to increase pork proved successful; a 1948 article on the Monroeville Hog Festival in the *Tuscaloosa News* reports that hog production is "approaching a million dollar business in Monroe County alont [*sic*] with prospects for steady growth" (17 October 1948, 28, col. 1–2). If Maycomb, like Monroeville, was putting its faith in pork in 1933–35, the time frame of the novel, the million-dollar pork industry of 1948 was nowhere in sight, and it would take World War II and the increased need for pork to feed the troops, including the pork-based Spam used in K-rations, to raise pork prices.

35. In the novel she wears her costume home because she is embarrassed that she fell asleep during the pageant and missed her cue to go onstage.

36. Atticus and Scout's relationship is the antithesis of Mayella and Bob Ewell's relationship, which includes physical abuse and, as the novel hints, perhaps incest as well. In Tom's account of the events, Mayella told him she wanted to be kissed by a man because what her father did to her did not count, leaving unclear just what it was her father did to her. In *Fearful Symmetry* (1998), a documentary on the making of *To Kill a Mockingbird*, Collin Wilcox Paxton, who played Mayella, said that she played the character as a victim of incest. For a discussion of incest in *To Kill a Mockingbird* and a detailed historical account of the prosecution of incest, in which an adult daughter could be considered a coconspirator for consenting, as well as a detailed history of the disposition of rape trials depending on the race of the victim and perpetrator, see Halpern 768–70 and 772–76.

37. "Being Atticus Finch: The Professional Role of Empathy in 'To Kill a Mockingbird'" ac-

knowledges Atticus's lack of empathy for Bob Ewell, or rather, Atticus's "well-meaning but blinkered attempts at empathy (which indeed may not be empathy at all, so much as paternalistic pity)" (1687). The article goes on, however, to commend Atticus's professional ritual of empathy (his dispassionate but polite demeanor) as a form of empathy that is appropriate for a lawyer: "ritualized empathy makes a personal emotion professional, and vice versa" (1702). See also Pryal 174–89; and Wood, "Bending the Law" 81–97.

38. This transition between scenes reinforces an earlier dissolve that links Ewell's menace to the children. The first time we see Ewell, just after Tom has been indicted, he angrily confronts Atticus about taking Tom's case and accepting "his word agin' ourn." From a medium two shot of Ewell and Atticus, as Atticus walks out of the shot, the camera slowly pulls into a medium close-up of Ewell yelling after Atticus: "What kind of man are you? You've got children of your own." Ewell's angry visage slowly dissolves to a nighttime shot of Scout and Jem on their front porch. In this way the audience, even before the children's first encounter with Ewell, is visually cued to his threat to the children. The nighttime shot of the children introduces the scene in which they try to look in the window of the Radley house to get a glimpse of Boo. This scene, therefore, is "bookended" by the references to Ewell and Mr. Radley, two of the worst fathers in the film, both of whom are a danger to their own children as well as to Scout and Jem. The real danger in the scene is not from Boo, as the children think, but from Mr. Radley, who shoots at what he claims is a prowler.

39. As Ann Engar explains, this scene is one often quoted by lawyers as a demonstration of the respect Atticus commands as a lawyer (67).

CODA: *A Time to Kill* and Post–Civil Rights Variations on the Southern Rape Complex

1. Scott Romine gives an excellent and nuanced account of the applications and limitations of postcolonial theory in relation to Dixon's *Leopard's Spots* and Thomas Nelson Page's *Red Rock: A Chronicle of Reconstruction* (1898). Romine makes clear that the application of postcolonial theory to the South necessitates a nuanced understanding of colonizer and colonized, victor and vanquished—one that can account for the same group occupying and/or appropriating both positions in relation to different populations.

2. *The Klansman* (1974) was an early post–civil rights film that depicts the gang rape of a black women by white men, but the film still focused on the white hero and his stand against the Klan. For an excellent comparison of *The Birth of a Nation* and *The Klansman*, see Richardson, *Black Masculinity* (23–72).

3. The ASC later merged with the ACLU, ILD, and NAACP to form the Scottsboro Defense Committee (Carter 335).

WORKS CITED

Abel, Marco. *Violent Affect: Literature, Cinema, and Critique after Representation*. Lincoln: U of Nebraska P, 2007. Print.

"AFI's 10 Top 10." *AFI.com*. American Film Institute, 2008. Web. 8 Apr. 2013.

"AFI's 100 Years . . . 100 Heroes & Villains." *AFI.com*. American Film Institute, 2003. Web. 8 Apr. 2013.

Agamben, Giorgio. *Homo Sacer: Sovereign Power and Bare Life*. Trans. Daniel Heller-Roazen. Stanford: Stanford UP, 1998. Print.

———. *State of Exception*. Trans. Kevin Attell. Chicago: U of Chicago P, 2005. Print.

Allen, James, ed. *Without Sanctuary: Lynching Photography in America*. Santa Fe: Twin Palms, 2000. Print.

Anatomy of a Murder. Dir. Otto Preminger. 1959. Sony, 2000. DVD.

Arnold, Edwin T., and Dawn Trouard. *Reading Faulkner: Sanctuary*. Jackson: UP of Mississippi, 1996. Print.

Atkinson, Ted. *Faulkner and the Great Depression: Aesthetics, Ideology, and Cultural Politics*. Athens: U of Georgia P, 2006. Print.

Bad Teacher. Dir. Jake Kasdan. Columbia, 2011. DVD.

Barker, Deborah, and Kathryn B. McKee, eds. *American Cinema and the Southern Imaginary*. Athens: U of Georgia P, 2011. Print.

The Battle. Dir. D. W. Griffith. 1911. *The Birth of a Nation and the Civil War Films of D. W. Griffith*. Kino Intl., 2002. DVD.

"Being Atticus Finch: The Professional Role of Empathy in *To Kill a Mockingbird*." *Harvard Law Review Association* 117.5 (Mar. 2004): 1682–702. One Search. Web. 3 Jan. 2006.

Beloved. Dir. Jonathan Demme. Touchstone, 1999. DVD.

Belton, John. "A New Map of the Labyrinth: The Unretouched *Touch of Evil*." *Movietone News* 47 (21 Jan. 1976): 1–9. Academic Search Premier. Web. 8 Nov. 2010.

Bernardi, Daniel, ed. *The Birth of Whiteness: Race and the Emergence of U.S. Cinema*. New Brunswick: Rutgers UP, 1996. Print.

———. "The Voice of Whiteness: D. W. Griffith's Biograph Films (1908–1913)." *The Birth of Whiteness: Race and the Emergence of U.S. Cinema*. New Brunswick: Rutgers UP, 1996. 103–28. Print.

The Beverly Hillbillies. 1962–71. *Beverly Hillbillies: The Ultimate Collection.* MPI, 2005. DVD.

Bhabha, Homi. *Location of Culture.* New York: Routledge, 1994. Print.

Binggeli, Elizabeth. "Worse than Bad: *Sanctuary,* the Hayes Office, and the Genre of Abjection." *Arizona Quarterly* 65.3 (Fall 2009): 87–116. One Search. Web. 10 June 2012.

The Birth of a Nation *and the Civil War Films of D. W. Griffith.* Dir. D. W. Griffith. Kino Intl., 2002. DVD.

Block, Sharon. *Rape and Sexual Power in Early America.* Chapel Hill: U of North Carolina P, 2006. Print.

Bloom, Harold, ed. *Harper Lee's* To Kill a Mockingbird. Updated ed. New York: Chelsea-Infobase, 2007. Print. Bloom's Modern Critical Interpretations.

Blotner, Joseph. *Faulkner: A Biography: One-Volume Edition.* Jackson: UP of Mississippi, 2005. Print.

Blue, Anthony Dias. *The Complete Book of Spirits: A Guide to Their History, Production, and Enjoyment.* New York: HarperCollins, 2004. Print.

Brinkema, Eugenie. *The Forms of Affects.* Durham: Duke UP, 2014. Print.

Broken Blossoms: or, The Yellow Man and the Girl. Dir. D. W. Griffith. 1919. *Griffith Masterworks.* Kino, 2002. DVD.

Brundage, W. Fitzhugh. *Lynching in the New South.* Urbana: U of Illinois P, 1993. Print.

"Buffalo Soldiers at Huachuca: Villa's Raid on Columbus, New Mexico." *Huachuca Illustrated.* 1993. Web. 7 Feb. 2013.

Cape Fear. Dir. J. Lee Thompson. Universal, 1962. DVD. *Cape Fear.* Dir. Martin Scorsese. Universal, 1991. DVD.

Cape Fear. Dir. Martin Scorsese. Universal, 1991. DVD.

Cardyn, Lisa. "Sexualized Racism/Gendered Violence: Outraging the Body Politic in the Reconstruction South." *Michigan Law Review* 100 (Feb. 2002): 675–867. Academic Search Premier. Web. 8 Nov. 2009.

Carrigan, William D., and Christopher Waldrep, eds. *Swift to Wrath: Lynching in Global Historical Perspective.* Charlottesville: U of Virginia P, 2013. Print.

Carter, Dan T. *Scottsboro: A Tragedy of the American South.* Rev. ed. Baton Rouge: Louisiana State UP, 2007. Print.

Cash, W. J. *The Mind of the South.* 1941. New York: Vintage, 1991. Print.

Castañeda, Antonia I. "Sexual Violence in the Politics and Policies of Conquest: Amerindian Women and the Spanish Conquest of Alta California." *Building with Our Hands: New Directions in Chicana Studies.* Ed. Adela de la Torre and Beatriz M. Pesquera. Berkeley: U of California P, 1993. 15–33. Print.

Chadwick, Bruce. *The Reel Civil War: Mythmaking in American Film.* New York: Vintage, 2002. Print.

The Cheat. Dir. Cecil B. DeMille. 1915. *Manslaughter and The Cheat.* Kino, 2002. DVD.

Chesnutt, Charles. *The Marrow of Tradition.* Boston: IndyPublish, 2005. Print.

Chura, Patrick. "Prolepsis and Anachronism: Emmett Till and the Historicity of *To Kill a Mockingbird.*" *Harper Lee's* To Kill a Mockingbird. Ed. Harold Bloom. Updated ed. New York: Chelsea-Infobase, 2007. 115–40. Print. Bloom's Modern Critical Interpretations.

Claiborne, Corrie. "Leaving Abjection: Where 'Black' Meets Theory." *Colorizing Literary Theory.* Spec. issue of *Modern Language Studies* 26.4 (Fall 1996): 27–36. JSTOR. Web. 8 May 2013.

Clegg, Claude A., III. *Troubled Ground: A Tale of Murder, Lynching, and Reckoning in the New South.* Urbana: U of Illinois P, 2010. Print.

The Code of Alabama, vol. 3: *Criminal.* Nashville: Compant, 1907. Web. 4 July 2013.

Courtney, Susan. *Hollywood Fantasies of Miscegenation: Spectacular Narratives of Gender and Race, 1903–1967.* Princeton: Princeton UP, 2004. Print.

Cuklanz, Lisa M. *Rape on Prime Time: Television, Masculinity, and Sexual Violence.* Philadelphia: U of Pennsylvania P, 2000. Print.

Daughters of the Dust. Dir. Julie Dash. Kino, 2000. DVD.

Davis, Angela. *Women, Race, and Class.* New York: Vintage, 1983. Print.

DeBona, Guerric. *Film Adaptation in the Hollywood Era.* Urbana: U of Illinois P, 2010. Print.

Degenfelder, E. Pauline. "The Four Faces of Temple Drake: Faulkner's *Sanctuary, Requiem for a Nun,* and the Two Film Adaptations." *American Quarterly* 28.5 (1997): 544–60. JSTOR. Web. 4 April 2007.

Deleuze, Gilles. *Cinema 1: The Movement-Image.* Trans. Hugh Tomlinson and Barbara Habberjam. Minneapolis: U of Minnesota P, 1986. Print.

———. *Cinema 2: The Time-Image.* Trans. Hugh Tomlinson and Robert Galeta. Minneapolis: U of Minnesota P, 1986. Print.

Deleuze, Gilles, and Félix Guattari. *A Thousand Plateaus: Capitalism and Schizophrenia.* Trans. Brian Massumi. Minneapolis: U of Minnesota P, 1987. Print.

Deliverance. Dir. John Boorman. 1972. Warner, 2007. DVD.

Denning, Michael. *The Cultural Front: The Laboring of American Culture in the Twentieth Century.* New York: Verso, 1996. Print.

Dixon, Thomas, Jr. *The Clansman.* New York: Doubleday, 1905. Print.

———. *The Leopard's Spots: A Romance of the White Man's Burden.* 1865–77. New York: Doubleday, 1902. Print.

———. *The Sins of the Father: A Romance of the South.* 1912. Lexington: UP of Kentucky, 2004. Print.

Django Unchained. Dir. Quentin Tarantino. 2012. Weinstein, 2013. DVD.

Douglass, Frederick. *The Life and Writings of Frederick Douglass.* Vol. 4. Ed. Philip S. Foner. New York: International, 1995.

Dracula. Dir. Tod Browning. 1931. Universal, 2014. DVD. Print.

Dr. Jekyll and Mr. Hyde. Dir. Rouben Mamoulian. 1931. *Dr. Jekyll and Mr. Hyde Double Feature*. Warner, 2004. DVD.

Duck, Leigh Anne. *The Nation's Region: Southern Modernism, Segregation, and U.S. Nationalism*. Athens: U of Georgia P, 2006. Print.

Dunning, William A. *Essays on the Civil War and Reconstruction and Related Topics*. New York: Macmillian, 1898. Print.

Duvall, John. "Faulkner's Black Sexuality." *Faulkner's Sexualities: Faulkner and Yoknapatawpha, 2007*. Ed. Annette Trefzer and Ann J. Abadie. Jackson: UP of Mississippi, 2010. 131–47. Print.

Dyer, Richard. "Into the Light: The Whiteness of the South in *The Birth of a Nation*." *Dixie Debates: Perspectives on Southern Culture*. Ed. Helen Taylor and Richard King. New York: New York UP, 1996. 165–76. Print.

Eagles, Charles W., ed. *The Mind of the South: Fifty Years Later*. Jackson: U of Mississippi P, 1992. Print.

Eisner, Lotte H. *The Haunted Screen: Expressionism in the German Cinema and the Influence of Max Reinhardt*. Berkeley: U of California P, 1969. Print.

Engar, Ann. "*To Kill a Mockingbird:* Fifty Years of Influence on the Legal Profession." *Harper Lee's* To Kill a Mockingbird: *New Essays*. Ed. Michael J. Myer. Plymouth: Scarecrow, 2010. 66–80. Print.

Epps, Michael. "Raising Minstrelsy: Humour, Satire and the Stereotype in *The Birth of a Nation* and *Bamboozled*." *Canadian Review of American Studies* 33.1 (2003): 18–35. Print.

Everett, Anna. *Returning the Gaze: A Genealogy of Black Film Criticism, 1909–1949*. Durham: Duke UP, 2001. Print.

Falkner, W. C. *The Little Brick Church*. 1882. Upper Saddle River, NJ: Literature, 1970. Print.

Faulkner, William. "Dry September." *Collected Stories of William Faulkner*. New York: Random, 1950. 169–83. Print.

———. *Requiem for a Nun*. New York: Vintage, 1975. Print.

———. *Sanctuary, 1931: The Corrected Text*. New York: Vintage, 1993. Print.

———. *The Sound and the Fury, 1929: The Corrected Text*. New York: Random, 1987. Print.

———. "That Evening Sun." *Collected Stories of William Faulkner*. New York: Random, 1950. 289–309. Print.

———. "There Was a Queen." *Collected Stories of William Faulkner*. New York: Random, 1950. 727–44. Print.

Faust, Drew Gilpin. *This Republic of Suffering: Death and the Civil War*. New York: Knopf, 2008. Print.

Fearful Symmetry: The Making of To Kill a Mockingbird. Dir. Charles Kiselyak. Universal, 1998. DVD.

Feimster, Crystal Nicole. *Southern Horrors: Women and the Politics of Rape and Lynching.* Cambridge: Harvard UP, 2009. Print.

Feldman, Glenn. *Politics, Society, and the Klan in Alabama, 1915–1949.* Tuscaloosa: U of Alabama P, 1999. Print.

Fitzgerald, F. Scott. *The Great Gatsby.* 1925. New York: Macmillan, 1988. Print.

Foner, Eric. *The Fiery Trial: Abraham Lincoln and American Slavery.* New York: Norton, 2011. Print.

———. *Reconstruction: America's Unfinished Revolution, 1863–1877.* New York: Perennial, 1989. Print.

Forbes, Ella. "African-American Resistance to Colonization." *Journal of Black Studies* 21.2 (Dec. 1990): 210–23. JSTOR. Web. 8 Nov. 2012.

Foucault, Michel. *The History of Sexuality,* vol. 1: *An Introduction.* Trans. Robert Hurley. New York: Vintage, 1980. Print.

Fredrickson, George M. "A Man but Not a Brother: Abraham Lincoln and Racial Equality." *Journal of Southern History* 41.1 (Feb. 1975): 39–58. JSTOR. Web. 9 Nov. 2006.

Freedman, Estelle B. *Redefining Rape: Sexual Violence in the Era of Suffrage and Segregation.* Cambridge: Harvard UP, 2013. Print.

Freedman, Monroe H. "Atticus Finch—Right and Wrong." *Alabama Law Review* 45.2 (Winter 1994): 473–82. *LexisNexis Academic.* Web. 6 Nov. 2013.

Freedom Writers. Dir. Richard LaGravenese. Warner, 2007. DVD.

French, Warren. *The South and Film.* Jackson: U of Mississippi P, 1981. Print.

Gaines, Jane M. *Fire and Desire: Mixed-Race Movies in the Silent Era.* Chicago: U of Chicago P, 2001. Print.

Geraghty, Christine. *Now a Major Motion Picture: Film Adaptation of Literature and Drama.* Lanham, MD: Rowman & Littlefield, 2008. Print.

Ghosts of Mississippi. Dir. Rob Reiner. 1996. Turner, 2010. DVD.

Gitter, Dean. Backnotes on *Odetta Sings Ballads and Blues.* Tradition Recordings. 1956. http://ftpmirror.your.org/pub/wikimedia/images/wikipedia/en/9/91/Odetta_Sings_Ballads_and_Blues_-_original_back_cover.jpg Web. 7 July 2010.

Gladwell, Malcolm. "The Courthouse Ring: Atticus Finch and the Limits of Southern Liberalism." *Harper Lee's* To Kill a Mockingbird: *New Essays.* Ed. Michael J. Myer. Plymouth: Scarecrow, 2010. 57–65. Print.

Gleeson-White, Sarah. "Auditory Exposures: Faulkner, Eisenstein, and Film Sound." *PMLA* 128.1 (Jan. 2013): 87–100. Print.

Goldsby, Jacqueline. *A Spectacular Secret: Lynching in American Life and Literature.* Chicago: U of Chicago P, 2006. Print.

Gone with the Wind. Dir. Victor Fleming. MGM, 2000. DVD.

Graham, Allison. *Framing the South: Hollywood, Television, and Race during the Civil Rights Struggle.* Baltimore: Johns Hopkins UP, 2001. Print.

Grantham, Dewey W. *The South in Modern America: A Region at Odds.* 1994. Fayetteville: U of Arkansas P, 2001. Print.

Greenhaw, Wayne. *Fighting the Devil in Dixie: How Civil Rights Activists Took on the Ku Klux Klan in Alabama.* Chicago: Chicago Review, 2011. Print.

Gunning, Sandra. *Race, Rape, and Lynching: The Red Record of American Literature, 1890–1912.* New York: Oxford UP, 1996. Print.

Gunning, Tom. "The House with Closed Shutters." No. 277. *The Griffith Project.* Ed. Paolo Cherchi-Usai. Vol. 4. London: British Film Institute, 2000. 141–46. Print.

Guttman, Sondra. "Who's Afraid of the Corncob Man? Masculinity, Race, and Labor in the Preface to *Sanctuary.*" *Faulkner Journal* 15.1–2 (1999–2000): 15–34. Print.

Hall, Jacqueline Dowd. "'The Mind That Burns in Each Body': Women, Rape, and Racial Violence." *Powers of Desire: The Politics of Sexuality.* Ed. Ann Snitow, Christine Stansell, and Sharon Thompson. New York: Monthly Rev., 1983. 328–49. Print.

Halpern, Iris. "Rape, Incest, and Harper Lee's *To Kill a Mockingbird:* On Alabama's Legal Construction of Gender and Sexuality in the Context of Racial Subordination." *Columbia Journal of Gender and Law* 18.3 (2009): 743–806. One Search. Web. 6 Sept. 2012.

Harris, Trudier. *Exorcising Blackness: Historical and Literary Lynching and Burning Rituals.* Bloomington: Indiana UP, 1984. Print.

Harvith, Susan, and John Harvith. *Karl Struss: Man with a Camera.* Lansing, MI: Henry, 1976. Print.

Hearts and Swords. Dir. D. W. Griffith. 1911. The Birth of a Nation *and the Civil War Films of D. W. Griffith.* Kino Intl., 2002. DVD.

Heath, Stephen. "Film and System: Terms of Analysis, 1." *Screen* 16.1 (Spring 1975): 7–77. Print.

———. "Film and System: Terms of Analysis, 2." *Screen* 16.2 (Summer 1975): 91–113. Print.

His Trust. Dir. D. W. Griffith. 1911. The Birth of a Nation *and the Civil War Films of D. W. Griffith.* Kino Intl., 2002. DVD.

His Trust Fulfilled. Dir. D. W. Griffith. 1911. The Birth of a Nation *and the Civil War Films of D. W. Griffith.* Kino Intl., 2002. DVD.

Hodes, Martha. *White Women, Black Men: Illicit Sex in the Nineteenth-Century South.* New Haven: Yale UP, 1997. Print.

The Honor of His Family. Dir. D. W. Griffith. 1910. The Birth of a Nation *and the Civil War Films of D. W. Griffith.* Kino Intl., 2002. DVD.

hooks, bell. "Writing the Subject: Reading *The Color Purple.*" *Reading Back, Reading Feminist.* Ed. Henry Louis Gates Jr. New York: Meridian Books, 1990. 454–70. Print.

Horeck, Tanya. *Public Rape: Representing Violation in Fiction and Film.* London: Routledge, 2003. Print.

The House with Closed Shutters. Dir. D. W. Griffith. 1910. The Birth of a Nation *and the Civil War Films of D. W. Griffith.* Kino Intl., 2002. DVD.

Hutcheon, Linda. *A Theory of Adaptation.* New York: Routledge, 2006. Print.

In the Border States. Dir. D. W. Griffith. 1910. The Birth of a Nation *and the Civil War Films of D. W. Griffith.* Kino Intl., 2002. DVD.

In Old Kentucky. Dir. D. W. Griffith. 1909. The Birth of a Nation *and the Civil War Films of D. W. Griffith.* Kino Intl., 2002. DVD.

Intruder in the Dust. Dir. Clarence Brown. MGM, 1949. DVD.

Jackson, Robert. "The Celluloid War before *The Birth:* Race and History in Early American Film." *American Cinema and the Southern Imaginary.* Ed. Deborah E. Barker and Kathryn McKee. Athens: U of Georgia P, 2011. Print.

Jack, Albert. *Pop Goes the Weasel: The Secret Meanings of Nursery Rhymes.* New York: Penguin, 2009. eBook.

Jacobs, Harriet. *Incidents in the Life of a Slave Girl.* New York: Harcourt Brace Jovanovich, 1973. Print.

Jesionowski, Joyce E. *Thinking in Pictures: Dramatic Structure in D. W. Griffith's Biograph Films.* Berkeley: U of California P, 1987. Print.

Jet 21 Apr. 1960. Johnson Publication 17. Front page. Microfilm.

"John Hollis Bankhead II." *The Encyclopedia of Alabama.* Auburn U. Web. 10 Sept. 2013.

Johnson, Michael P. "Smothered Slave Infants: Were Slave Mothers at Fault?" *Journal of Southern History* 4.4 (Nov. 1981): 493–520. Academic Search Premier. Web. 4 June 2009.

Johnson, Walter. *River of Dark Dreams: Slavery and Empire in the Cotton Kingdom.* Cambridge: Belknap-Harvard UP, 2013. Print.

Judith of Bethulia. Dir. D. W. Griffith. 1914. *D. W. Griffith Classics: Judith of Bethulia, Transformation of Mike.* Alpha, 2012. DVD.

Katznelson, Ira. *Fear Itself: The New Deal and the Origins of Our Times.* New York: Liveright, 2013. Print.

Kawin, Bruce F. *Faulkner and Film.* New York: Ungar, 1977. Print.

King, Richard H. *A Southern Renaissance: The Cultural Awakening of the American South, 1930–1955.* New York: Oxford UP, 1980. Print.

Kirby, Jack T. *Media-Made Dixie: The South in the American Imagination.* Baton Rouge: Louisiana State UP, 1978. Print.

Kiss the Girls. Dir. Gary Felder. Warner, 1998. DVD.

The Klansman. Dir. Terence Young. Paramount, 1974. DVD.

Kosary, Rebecca A. "To Degrade and Control: White Violence and the Maintenance of Racial and Gender Boundaries in Reconstruction Texas, 1865–1868." Diss. Texas A&M U, 2006. Print.

Kristeva, Julia. *Powers of Horror: An Essay on Abjection*. Trans. Leon S. Roudiez. New York: Columbia UP, 1982. Print.

Krueger, E. M. "*Touch of Evil:* Style Expressing Content." *Cinema Journal* 12.1 (Fall 1972): 57–63. Academic Search Premier. Web. 7 Sept. 2007.

Lacan, Jacques. *Écrits: A Selection*. Trans. Alan Sheridan. New York: Norton, 1997. Print.

Ladd, Barbara. "'Philosophers and Other Gynecologists': Women and the Polity in *Requiem for a Nun*." *Mississippi Quarterly* 52.3 (1999): 483–502. Print.

The Lady from Shanghai. Dir. Orson Welles. 1947. Columbia, 2000. DVD.

Lang, Robert, ed. *The Birth of a Nation*. New Brunswick: Rutgers UP, 1994. Print.

Lee, Harper. *To Kill a Mockingbird*. New York: Perennial-Harper, 2001. Print.

Leiter, Andrew, ed. *Southerners on Film: Essays on Hollywood Portrayals since the 1970s*. Jefferson, NC: McFarland, 2011. Print.

Lenning, Arthur. "Myth and Fact: The Reception of *The Birth of a Nation*." *Film History* 16.2 (2004): 117–41. Print.

Lévi-Strauss, Claude. *The Elementary Structures of Kinship*. Trans. James Harle Bell and John Richard von Strumer. Boston: Beacon, 1969. Print.

Lockett, James D. "Abraham Lincoln and Colonization: An Episode That Ends in Tragedy at L'Ile a Vache, Haiti, 1863–64." *Journal of Black Studies* 21.4 (Jan. 1991): 428–44. *JSTOR*. Web. 9 July 2013.

The Long, Hot Summer. Dir. Martin Ritt. 1958. Fox, 2003. DVD.

Lubet, Steven. "Reconstructing Atticus Finch." *Michigan Law Review* 97.6 (May 1999): 1339–62. *LexisNexis Academic*. Web. 9 Apr. 2011.

Lurie, Peter. *Vision's Immanence: Faulkner, Film, and the Popular Imagination*. Baltimore: Johns Hopkins UP, 2004. Print.

MacCannell, Juliet Flower. "Between the Two *Fears*." *Lacan and Contemporary Film*. Ed. Todd McGowan and Sheila Kunkle. New York: Other, 2004. 47–82. Print.

MacDonald, John D. *Cape Fear: A Novel (Formerly Titled* The Executioners). New York: Mass Market, 2006. Print.

Making of Cape Fear, *The*. Dir. Laurent Bouzereau. Universal, 2001. DVD.

"Mammoth Hog Show Planned for Southern Alabama Area." *Tuscaloosa News*. 17 Oct. 1948: 28. Historical Newspapers Online. Web. 7 June 2013.

Manglaviti, Leo M. J. "Faulkner's 'That Evening Sun' and Mencken's 'Best Editorial Judgment.'" *American Literature* 43.4 (Jan. 1972): 649–54. Print.

Man in the Chair. Dir. Michael Schroeder. 2007. IFC, 2007. DVD.

Markey, Maureen. "Natural Law, Positive Law, and Conflicting Social Norms in Harper Lee's *To Kill a Mockingbird*." *North Carolina Central Law Review* 32.162 (2009–10): 162–213. HeinOnline. Web. 9 Sept. 2011.

Marks, Laura. *The Skin of the Film: Intercultural Cinema, Embodiment, and the Senses.* Durham: Duke UP, 2000. Print.

Masterson, Whit [Robert Wade and William Miller]. *Badge of Evil.* 1956. New York: Carroll, 1992. Print.

Maurice, Alice. *The Cinema and Its Shadow: Race and Technology in Early Cinema.* Minneapolis: U of Minnesota P, 2013. Print.

Mbembe, Achille. "Necropolitics." *Foucault in an Age of Terror: Essays on Biopolitics and the Defense of Society.* Ed. Stephen Morton and Stephen Bygrave. New York: Palgrave, 2008. 152–82. Print.

McCusker, Maeve. "Figuring Abjection: The Slave Mother in the Early Creole Novel." *French Studies* 67.1 (2013): 61–75. Print.

McElya, Micki. *Clinging to Mammy: The Faithful Slave in Twentieth-Century America.* Cambridge: Harvard UP, 2007. Print.

McPherson, Tara. *Reconstructing Dixie: Race, Gender, and Nostalgia in the Imagined South.* Durham: Duke UP, 2003. Print.

Merritt, Russell. "D. W. Griffith's The *Birth of a Nation:* Going after Little Sister." *Close Viewings: An Anthology of New Film Criticism.* Ed. Peter Lehman. Tallahassee: Florida State UP, 1990. 215–37. Print.

Metress, Christopher. "The Rise and Fall of Atticus Finch." *Harper Lee's* To Kill a Mockingbird. Ed. Harold Bloom. Updated ed. Chelsea-Infobase, 2007. 141–48. Print. Bloom's Modern Critical Interpretations.

Metz, Christian. *The Imaginary Signifier.* Bloomington: Indiana UP, 1986. Print.

Michaels, Walter Benn. *Our America: Nativism, Modernism and Pluralism.* Durham: Duke UP, 1995. Print.

Mississippi Burning. Dir. Alan Parker. 1988. Fox, 2001. DVD.

Mitchell, Margaret. *Gone with the Wind.* New York: Scribner, 2007. Print.

Moreland, Richard. *Faulkner and Modernism: Rereading and Rewriting.* Madison: U of Wisconsin P, 1990. Print.

Morrison, Spencer. "*Requiem's* Ruins: Unmaking and Making in Cold War Faulkner." *American Literature* 85.2 (2013): 303–31. Print.

Morrison, Toni. *Beloved.* New York: Vintage, 1987. Print.

Mr. Arkadin. Dir. Orson Welles. 1955. *The Complete Mr. Arkadin.* Criterion, 2006. DVD.

Murray, Jennifer. "More than One Way to (Mis)Read a *Mockingbird.*" *Southern Literary Journal* 43.1 (Fall 2010): 75–91. Print.

Murray, Simone. *The Adaptation Industry: The Cultural Economy of Contemporary Literary Adaptation.* New York: Routledge, 2013. Print.

Murtagh, John M. "Status Offenses and Due Process of Law." *Fordham Law Review* 36.1 (1967): 51–58. Academic Search Premier. Web. 10 Mar. 2013.

"Music: Baby in the Cradle." *Time* 5 Dec. 1960. Academic Search Premier. Web. 7 July 2010.

Myer, Michael J., ed. *Harper Lee's* To Kill a Mockingbird: *New Essays*. Plymouth: Scarecrow, 2010. Print.

Nausner, Helmut. "The Meaning of Wesley's General Rules, an Interpretation." *Asbury Theological Journal* 44.2 (Fall 1989): 43–60. Academic Search Premier. Web. 11 Oct. 2012.

Nericcio, William Anthony. *Tex[t]-Mex: Seductive Hallucinations of the "Mexican" in America*. Austin: U of Texas P, 2007. Print.

Nevins, Francis M. "Cape Fear Dead Ahead: Transforming a Thrice-Told Tale of Lawyers and Law." *Legal Studies Forum* 24.3–4 (2000): 611–44. HeinOnline. Web. 10 Mar. 2014.

"New Livestock Laboratory Will Be Constructed Soon." *Monroe Journal* 8 July 1937. Microfilm.

Nicolay, John G., and John Hay. *Abraham Lincoln: A History*. Ed. Paul M. Angle. Chicago: U of Chicago P, 1966. Print.

Nosferatu. Dir. F. W. Murnau. 1922. *German Horror Classics*. Kino, 2004. DVD.

O'Brien, Michael. "A Private Passion: W. J. Cash." *Rethinking the South: Essays in Intellectual History*. Baltimore: Johns Hopkins UP, 1988. Print.

Olds, Madelin Joan. "The Rape Complex in the Postbellum South." *Black Women in American*. Ed. Kim Marie Vaz. London: Sage, 1995. 179–205. Print.

Oliver, Kelly, and Benigno Trigo. *Noir Anxiety*. Minneapolis: U of Minnesota P, 2002. Print.

Omi, Michael, and Howard Winant. *Racial Formation in the United States: From the 1960's to the 1990's*. 2nd ed. New York: Routledge, 1994. Print.

Palmer, R. Barton. *Harper Lee's* To Kill a Mockingbird: *The Relationship between Text and Film. Screen Adaptations*. London: Methuen, 2008. Print.

Patterson, Laura S. "Ellipsis, Ritual, and 'Real Time': Rethinking the Rape Complex in Southern Novels." *Mississippi Quarterly* 54.1 (2000–01): 37–58. Print.

Payne, Arthur Frank. "Temple Drake Mirror for All Women Now, Psychologist Declares." The Story of Temple Drake *Press Book*. Hollywood: Paramount Pictures, 1933. Print.

Pearson, Roberta E. *Eloquent Gestures: The Transformation of Performance Style in the Griffith Biograph Films*. Berkeley: U of California P, 1992. Print.

Pease, Donald. "Borderline Justice/States of Emergency: Orson Welles' *Touch of Evil*." *CR: New Centennial Review* 1.1 (Spring 2001): 75–105. Academic Search Premier. Web. 11 Dec. 2012.

Petry, Alice. *On Harper Lee: Essays and Reflections*. Knoxville: U of Tennessee P, 2007. Print.

Pfeifer, Michael J., ed. *Lynching beyond Dixie: American Mob Violence Outside the South*. Urbana: U of Illinois P, 2013. Print.

———. *The Roots of Rough Justice: Origins of American Lynching*. Urbana: U of Illinois P, 2011. Print.

Phillips, Gene D. *Fiction, Film, and Faulkner: The Art of Adaptation*. Knoxville: U of Tennessee P, 1988. Print.

Pickett, William P. *The Negro Problem: Abraham Lincoln's Solution*. New York: Putnam's, 1909. Print.

Pisters, Patricia. *The Matrix of Visual Culture: Working with Deleuze in Film Theory*. Stanford: Stanford UP, 2003. Print.

Polk, Noel. *Faulkner's* Requiem for a Nun: *A Critical Study*. Bloomington: Indiana UP, 1981. Print.

Polk, Noel, and Neil McMillen. "Faulkner on Lynching." *Faulkner Journal* 8.1 (1992): 3–14. Academic Search Premier. Web. 4 July 2004.

Prince of Tides. Dir. Barbara Streisand. 1991. Sony, 2001. DVD.

"Program Launched for Increasing Livestock." *Monroe Journal* 17 June 1933. Microfilm.

Projansky, Sarah. *Watching Rape: Film and Television in Postfeminist Culture*. New York: New York UP, 2001. Print.

Pryal, Katie Rose Guest. "Walking in Another's Skin: Failure of Empathy in *To Kill a Mockingbird*." *Harper Lee's* To Kill a Mockingbird: *New Essays*. Ed. Michael J. Myer. Plymouth: Scarecrow, 2010. 174–89. Print.

Ramsey, D. Matthew. "'Lifting the Fog': Faulkner's Reputation and *The Story of Temple Drake*." *Faulkner Journal* 16.1–2 (2000–01): 7–33. Print.

The Real McCoys. 1957–63. Inception, 2012. DVD.

Reames, Kelly Lynch. "'All That Matters Is That I Wrote the Letters': Dis-course, Discipline, and Difference in *Requiem for a Nun*." *Faulkner Journal* 14.1 (1998): 31–52. Print.

Rear Window. 1954. Dir. Alfred Hitchcock. Universal, 2012. DVD.

"Retrial Given in Assault Case." *Mobile Register* 23 June 1933. Microfilm.

Richardson, Riché. *Black Masculinity and the U.S. South: From Uncle Tom to Gangsta*. Athens: U of Georgia P, 2007. Print.

———. "Mammy's 'Mules' and the Rules of Marriage in *Gone with the Wind*." *American Cinema and the Southern Imaginary*. Ed. Deborah Barker and Kathryn B. McKee. Athens: U of Georgia P, 2011. 52–78. Print.

Rizzo, Teresa. *Deleuze and Film: A Feminist Introduction*. New York: Continuum Intl., 2012. Print.

Roberts, Dorothy. *Killing the Black Body: Race, Reproduction, and the Meaning of Liberty*. New York: Vintage-Random, 1997. Print.

Rogin, Michael. "'The Sword Became a Flashing Vision': D. W. Griffith's *The Birth of a Nation*." *The Birth of a Nation*. Ed. Robert Lang. New Brunswick: Rutgers UP, 1994. 250–93. Print.

Romine, Scott. "Darkness Visible: Race and Pollution in Southwestern Humor." *The Humor of the Old South*. Ed. Thomas Inge and Edward J. Piacentino. Lexington: UP of Kentucky. 2001. 72–83. Print.

———. "Things Fall Apart: The Postcolonial Condition of *Red Rock* and *The Leopard's Spots*." *Look Away! The U.S. South in New World Studies*. Ed. Jon Smith and Deborah Cohn. Durham: Duke UP, 2004. 175–200. Print.

Rosen, Hannah. *Terror in the Heart of Freedom: Citizenship, Sexual Violence, and the Meaning of Race in the Postemancipation South*. Chapel Hill: U of North Carolina P, 2008. Print.

Rosow, Eugene. *Born to Lose: The Gangster Film in America*. New York: Oxford UP, 1978. Print.

Sanctuary. Dir. Tony Richardson. Fox, 1961. Film.

Schickel, Richard. *D. W. Griffith: An American Life*. New York: Simon, 1984. Print.

Scott, Darieck. *Extravagant Abjection: Blackness, Power, and Sexuality in the African American Literary Imagination*. New York: New York UP, 2010. Print.

Seidel, Kathryn Lee. *The Southern Belle in the American Novel*. Tampa: U of South Florida P, 1985. Print.

Shackelford, Dean. "The Female Voice in *To Kill a Mockingbird*: Narrative Strategies in Film and Novel." *Mississippi Quarterly* 50.1 (Winter 1996–97): 101–13. Academic Search Premier. Web. 12 Nov. 2006.

Shadoian, Jack. *Dreams and Dead Ends: The American Gangster Film*. 2nd ed. Oxford: Oxford UP, 2003. Print.

Shaw, Denise R. *The Rape Narrative in the American South: A Psychoanalytical Examination of Sexual Violence and the Melancholic Internalization of Loss in the Modern Southern Novel*. Lewiston: Mellen, 2007. Print.

The Sheik. Dir. George Melford. 1921. *The Sheik: The Son of the Sheik, Special Edition*. Image, 2002. DVD.

Shields, Charles J. *Mockingbird: A Portrait of Harper Lee*. New York: Griffin–St. Martin's 2006. Print.

Sielke, Sabine. *Reading Rape: The Rhetoric of Sexual Violence in American Literature and Culture, 1790–1990*. Princeton: Princeton UP, 2002. Print.

Silber, Nina. *The Romance of Reunion: Northerners and the South, 1865–1900*. Chapel Hill: North Carolina P, 1997. Print.

Silverman, Joan L. "*The Birth of a Nation*: Prohibition and Propaganda." *The South in Film*. Ed. Warren French. Jackson: UP of Mississippi, 1981. 23–30. Print.

Simmon, Scott. "*The Honor of His Family*." No. 229. *The Griffith Project*. Ed. Paolo Cherchi Usai. Vol. 3. London: British Film Institute, 1999. 167–70. Print.

Skal, David J. *The Monster Show: A Cultural History of Horror*. 1993. New York: Faber, 2001. Print.

Smith, Adam. *The Theory of Moral Sentiments.* Ed. Knud Haakonssen. Cambridge: Cambridge UP, 2002. Print.

———. *The Wealth of Nations.* Ed. Edwin Cannan. New York: Modern Lib., 1937. Print.

Sommerville, Diane Miller. *Rape and Race in the Nineteenth-Century South.* Chapel Hill: U of North Carolina P, 2004. Print.

———. "The Rape Myth in the Old South Reconsidered." *Journal of Southern History* 61 (August 1995): 481–518. Academic Search Premier. Web. 10 Oct. 2006.

Stanfield, Peter. "An Excursion into the Lower Depths: Hollywood, Urban Primitivism, and *St. Louis Blues,* 1929–1937." *Cinema Journal* 41.2 (2002): 84–108. Academic Search Premier. Web. 13 Sept. 2004.

Stokes, Melvyn. *D. W. Griffith's* The Birth of a Nation: *A History of the Most Controversial Motion Picture of All Time.* Oxford: Oxford UP, 2008. Print.

The Story of Temple Drake. Dir. Stephen Roberts. Paramount, 1933. DVD.

The Story of Temple Drake Press Book. Paramount, 1933. Print.

Stubbs, John. "The Evolution of Orson Welles's *Touch of Evil* from Novel to Film." *Cinema Journal* 24.2 (Winter 1985): 19–39. Academic Search Premier. Web. 11 Nov. 2005.

Sundquist, Eric. "Black Skin, Yellow Star; or, Blues for Atticus Finch." *Strangers in the Land: Blacks, Jews, Post-Holocaust America.* Cambridge: Belknap, 2008. Print.

———. "Blues for Atticus Finch: Scottsboro, *Brown,* and Harper Lee." *The South as an American Problem.* Ed. Larry J. Griffin and Don H. Doyle. Athens: U of Georgia P, 1995. 181–209. Print.

———. *Strangers in the Land: Blacks, Jews, Post-Holocaust America.* Cambridge: Belknap, 2008. Print.

Sutter's Gold. Dir. James Cruze. Universal, 1936. Film

Tanner, Laura E. *Intimate Violence: Reading Rape and Torture in Twentieth-Century Fiction.* Bloomington: Indiana UP, 1994. Print.

A Time to Kill. Dir. Joel Schumacher. 1996. Warner, 2009. DVD.

To Kill a Mockingbird. Dir. Robert Mulligan. 1963. Universal, 2012. DVD.

Toll, Robert C. *Blackening Up: The Minstrel Show in Nineteenth-Century America.* New York: Oxford UP, 1974. Print.

Touch of Evil: 50th Anniversary Edition. 1958. Dir. Orson Welles. Universal, 2008. DVD.

The Trial. Dir. Orson Welles. 1962. *The Orson Welles Collection.* Passport, 2006. DVD.

12 Years a Slave. Dir. Steve McQueen. 2013. Fox, 2014. DVD.

"Video of White Supremacist Learning He Is 14 Percent Black May Be the Best Thing Ever." *Huffington Post.* Web. 12 Nov. 2013.

Vizzard, Jack. *See No Evil: Life Inside a Hollywood Censor.* New York: Simon, 1970. Print.

Walker, Alice. "One Child of One's Own." *In Search of Our Mother's Gardens.* New York: Harcourt, 1983. Print.

Wallace, Michele Faith. "The Good Lynching and *The Birth of a Nation:* Discourses and

Aesthetics of Jim Crow." *Cinema Journal* 43.1 (2003): 85–104. Academic Search Premier. Web. 3 May 2007.

Wallace-Sanders, Kimberly. *Mammy: A Century of Race, Gender, and Southern Memory.* Ann Arbor: U of Michigan P, 2009. Print.

Watson, Jay. "Dangerous Return: The Narratives of Jurisgenesis in Faulkner's *Requiem for a Nun.*" *Modern Fiction Studies* 60.1 (Spring 2014): 108–37. Print.

———. *Forensic Fictions: The Lawyer Figure in Faulkner.* Athens: U of Georgia P, 1993. Print.

Watson, Rachel. "The View from the Porch: Race and the Limits of Empathy in the Film *To Kill a Mockingbird.*" *Mississippi Quarterly* 63.3 (Summer 2010): 417–41. Print.

Webb, James R. *Cape Fear: Revised Final Screenplay.* 27 Mar. 1961. Print.

Weiner, Tim. "Odetta, Voice of Civil Rights Movement, Dies at 77." *New York Times* 3 Dec. 2008. Web. 7 July 2010.

Weisenburger, Steven. "Faulkner in Baghdad, Bush in Hadleyburg: Race, Nation, and Sovereign Violence." *American Literary History* 18.4 (2006): 739–71. Academic Search Premier. Web. 3 Aug. 2008.

Welles, Orson, and Jonathan Rosenbaum. "Touch of Evil: Orson Welles' Memo to Universal." *Film Quarterly* 46.1 (1992): 2–11. *MLA International Bibliography.* Web. 5 Jan. 2013.

Welling, Bart H. "In Praise of the Black Mother: An Unpublished Faulkner Letter on 'Mammy' Caroline Barr." *Georgia Review* 55.3 (September 2001): 536–42. Print.

Wells, Ida B. *On Lynching: Southern Horrors.* Amherst: Humanity Books, 2002. Print.

Wesley, Charles H. "Lincoln's Plan for Colonizing the Emancipated Negroes." *Journal of Negro History* 4.1 (Jan, 1919): 7–21. *JSTOR.* Web. 3 June 2013.

Wesley, John. *The Nature, Design, and General Rules of the Methodist Societies Established by the Revered John Wesley.* London: Story, 1800. *Eighteenth Century Collections Online.* Web. 17 Aug. 2014.

———. *Thoughts upon Slavery.* London: Hawes, 1774. *Eighteenth Century Collections Online.* Web. 17 Aug. 2014.

What Happened in the Tunnel. Dir. Edwin S. Porter. Edison, 1903. Film.

White, Mimi. "The Birth of a Nation: History as Pretext." *The Birth of a Nation: D. W. Griffith, Director.* Ed. Robert Lang. Rutgers: Rutgers UP, 1994. 214–24. Print.

Wiegman. Robyn. *American Anatomies: Theorizing Race and Gender.* Durham: Duke UP, 1995. Print.

Williams, Linda. *Playing the Race Card: Melodramas of Black and White from Uncle Tom to O. J. Simpson.* Princeton: Princeton UP, 2001. Print.

Williamson, J. W. *Hillbillyland: What the Movies Did to the Mountains and What the Mountains Did to the Movies.* Chapel Hill: U or North Carolina P, 1995. Print.

Williamson, Joel. *The Crucible of Race: Black and White Race Relations in the American South since Emancipation.* New York: Oxford UP, 1984. Print.

———. "How Black Was Rhett Butler?" *The Evolution of Southern Culture.* Ed. Numan Bartley. Athens: U of Georgia P, 1988. Print.

———. *William Faulkner and Southern History.* Oxford: Oxford UP, 1993. Print.

Within Our Gates. Dir. Oscar Micheaux. 1920. Alpha, 2012. DVD.

Wollen, Peter. "Foreign Relations Welles and Touch of Evil." *Sight and Sound* 6.10 (1996): 21–23. *International Index to Performing Arts Full Text.* Web. 21 Dec. 2012.

Wolters, Raymond. *Negroes and the Great Depression: The Problem of Economic Recovery.* Westport: Greenwood, 1970. Print.

The Women. Dir. George Cukor. 1939. Warner, 2005. DVD.

Wood, Amy Louise. *Lynching and Spectacle: Witnessing Racial Violence in America, 1890–1940.* Chapel Hill: U of North Carolina P, 2009. Print.

Wood, Gerald. "From *The Clansman* and *Birth of a Nation* to *Gone with the Wind:* The Loss of American Innocence." *Recasting:* Gone with the Wind *in American Culture.* Ed. Darden Asbury Pyron. Miami: UP of Florida, 1983. 123–36. Print.

Wood, Jeffrey B. "Bending the Law: the Search for Justice and Moral Purpose." *Harper Lee's* To Kill a Mockingbird: *New Essays.* Ed. Michael J. Myer. Plymouth: Scarecrow, 2010: 81–97. Print.

Wood, Robin. *Personal Views: Explorations in Film.* 1976. Rev. ed. Detroit: Wayne State UP, 2006. Print.

Young, Elizabeth. *Disarming the Nation: Women's Writing and the American Civil War.* Chicago: U of Chicago P, 1999. Print.

Žižek, Slavoj. *Violence: Six Sideways Reflections.* New York: Picador, 2008. Print.

INDEX